KAUFFMAN FOUNDATION SERIES ON
Innovation and Entrepreneurship

Boulevard of Broken Dreams: Why Public Efforts to Boost Entrepreneurship and Venture Capital Have Failed— and What to Do about It, by Josh Lerner

The Invention of Enterprise: Entrepreneurship from Ancient Mesopotamia to Modern Times, edited by David S. Landes, Joel Mokyr, and William J. Baumol

The Venturesome Economy: How Innovation Sustains Prosperity in a More Connected World, by Amar Bhidé

The Microtheory of Innovative Entrepreneurship, by William J. Baumol

The Entrepreneurial Group: Social Identities, Relations, and Collective Action, by Martin Ruef

Solomon's Knot: How Law Can End the Poverty of Nations, by Robert D. Cooter and Hans-Bernd Schäfer

The Founder's Dilemmas: Anticipating and Avoiding the Pitfalls That Can Sink a Startup by Noam Wasserman

How the Internet Became Commercial: Innovation, Privatization, and the Birth of a New Network, by Shane Greenstein

EXPERIMENTAL CAPITALISM

EXPERIMENTAL CAPITALISM

THE NANOECONOMICS OF AMERICAN HIGH-TECH INDUSTRIES

STEVEN KLEPPER

PRINCETON UNIVERSITY PRESS   PRINCETON AND OXFORD

press.princeton.edu

Library of Congress Cataloging-in-Publication Data

Klepper, Steven, author.
  Experimental capitalism : the nanoeconomics of American high-tech industries / Steven
Klepper.
    pages cm. — (Kauffman Foundation series on innovation and entrepreneurship)
  Includes bibliographical references and index.
    ISBN 978-0-691-16962-0 (hardcover : alk. paper)   1. High-technology industries—
United States.   2. Entrepreneurship—United States.   I. Title.
  HC110.H53K565 2016
  338.50973—dc23
                                                        2015031273

British Library Cataloging-in-Publication Data is available

Published in collaboration with the Ewing Marion Kauffman Foundation and the
Berkley Center for Entrepreneurial Studies, New York University.

This book has been composed in Sabon and Trade Gothic

Printed on acid-free paper. ∞

Printed in the United States of America

10 9 8 7 6 5 4 3 2 1

TO FLORENCE, ARIELLE, JULIAN, AND BETTY

CONTENTS

EDITORS' PREFACE

THE CIRCUMSTANCES OF THIS BOOK ARE CAPTURED BY THE TITLE of the last chapter: "The Best of Times, the Worst of Times." Steven Klepper (January 24, 1949–May 27, 2013) formally started this book at the end of 2009, though its content reflects his decades-long research agenda on the foundations of entrepreneurship and the creation and evolution of industry. The book synthesizes and extends his research that established a new frontier in the analysis of industrial economics. The writing of the book proceeded in Steven's usual style, with the generation of long and carefully constructed outlines that underwent seemingly countless iterations. Each chapter that arose from those outlines was meticulously composed to be easily accessible, intellectually honest, and deeply thoughtful and prescient. Throughout the writing of the book, Steven had endless enthusiasm for the project and often engaged his colleagues in long, enjoyable conversations ranging from the finer points of his theoretical and empirical work to how best to communicate the ideas to others. Unfortunately, Steven was diagnosed with cancer a few years into the project. While undergoing the abject physical assaults embodied in his treatments, he continued to work on the book with the same enthusiasm and clarity of purpose that characterized the prior years. Indeed, it was the best of times, the worst of times . . .

Before his death, Steven completed and refined multiple drafts of all but the final chapter. For these completed chapters, we did a final proofreading to ensure that the information they contain meets the high standards that Steven's research always embraced. We updated to 2015 values any historical dollar figures for which Steven had also given "today's dollar" figures. For the final chapter, Steven had a well-iterated outline and developed, with the assistance of Joseph Plummer, some key sets of notes and an initial draft of the start of the chapter. As mentioned, Steven's writing process always involved the development of extensive outlines refined over multiple iterations prior to the commencement of any formal writing. Thus, his outlines always reflected very deep thinking about a problem and its proper presentation to others. Given the circumstances, we felt that the final chapter should follow the existing outline, supplemented by the initial draft and any associated notes in their original form where possible. Such a presentation provides an insightful window into Steven's thinking about the ultimate synthesis and policy implications of his life's work. Even in its raw form, the last chapter abounds with novel concepts and policy ideas about how to maintain, and enhance, high-tech entrepreneurship in a rapidly changing world. Steven always enjoyed the thoughtful academic challenge to his ideas, and our hope is that this last chapter will catalyze new lines of theoretical, empirical, and policy discussions.

The focus of the book is high-tech entrepreneurship in the United States. While entrepreneurship is not exclusive to the United States, and indeed many of the stories told herein have key international elements, the experience of the United States provides a convenient natural laboratory for such a study given the large range of policies and technologies that have arisen in the United States over the last century. The nanoeconomic approach pursued in the book involves, as Steven once wrote, "digging beneath the surface of markets to understand the forces that derive their formation and functioning." Not surprisingly, this research strategy requires a Herculean effort in data collection, and focusing on six key industries in the United States makes this feasible. However, the lessons learned from this approach, both theoretical and practical, go far beyond these six industries and any national borders. The nanoeconomic examination of, say, clustering in Silicon Valley, Akron, and Detroit, provides a transcendent explanation of why such clusters emerge (and, at least for the latter two areas, decline) regardless of time or space. Steven's carefully constructed account of the ebbs and flows of "experimental capitalism" is useful for anyone interested in understanding not only the dynamics of industries, but also the long-run dynamics of the national and world economies they induce.

One of the hallmarks of Steven Klepper's scholarly oeuvre in empirical economics was his absolutely consistent commitment to employing Occam's razor. After spending months—and sometimes years—gathering, cleaning, and analyzing nanoeconomic data related to the origin and evolution of an industry, Steven always sought to develop the most parsimonious theory that could account for the phenomena he observed. For example, Steven's theory about spinoffs as the fundamental reason behind the clustering of Akron, Detroit, and Silicon Valley has gained wide currency and opened many paths for future research. But his theory has also bumped up against long-held assumptions and theories about the general phenomenon of clustering, about these clusters in particular, their respective industries, and the firms that comprise them. His theory challenges the work of illustrious scholars in regional economics, business history, economic geography, and entrepreneurship. Readers of *Experimental Capitalism* will encounter Steven's parsimonious accounts of six industries, but they will also see that Steven was fully versed in—and had great respect for—the work of scholars whose views he challenged. Nowhere is this clearer than in Steven's story of the rise of Detroit and the American automobile industry. As Steven hastens to argue, his theory about the role of Ransom E. Olds and the Olds Motor Works in seeding the nascent automobile industry—and Detroit—simply provides a leaner account of this industry rather than contradicting the work of such scholars as the late Alfred D. Chandler, whose study of General Motors emphasized the managerial genius of Pierre du Pont and Alfred Sloan, or of scholars who underscored the role of Henry Ford and mass production methods that had originated in the Antebellum small arms industry. In short, for Steven "experimental capitalism" satisfied his criterion of theoretical parsimony in explaining the origin and evolution of high-tech industries far better than Chandler's "Managerial Capitalism," traditional economists' "agglomeration economies," and still others' more technologically deterministic interpretations.

The nanoeconomic approach requires intensive data collection, and this was often done in collaboration with Steven's PhD students. In particular (in alphabetical order): Ajay Bhaskarabhatla, Cristobal A. Cheyre Forestier, Elizabeth A. Graddy, Jonathan D. Kowalski, Romel Mostafa, Jeffrey Sherer, Kenneth L. Simons, and Sally D. Sleeper all collaborated with Steven on collecting and analyzing the data used here. Also, Guido Buenstorf played a key role in collecting and analyzing the data on Akron tire producers when he was a visiting scholar at Carnegie Mellon. Eileen Simeone, Steven's administrative assistant, also contributed to the research efforts.

We are grateful to Princeton University Press for embracing this project given the unusual circumstances. Steven's main academic home throughout his career was the Department of Social and Decision Sciences at Carnegie Mellon University, along with the campus-wide group in Strategy, Entrepreneurship, and Technological Change that Steven catalyzed, and on his behalf, we thank these institutions. We also acknowledge the key role of his family, friends, collaborators, and colleagues throughout his career.

Having great colleagues is one of the often ignored pleasures of the academy. Steven certainly embodied the best of what one would want in a colleague, and being able to assist in the publication of this book is a great honor and a fitting tribute to an academic life well lived.

Serguey Braguinsky
David A. Hounshell
John H. Miller
Social and Decision Sciences, Carnegie Mellon University

EXPERIMENTAL CAPITALISM

CHAPTER 1

INNOVATION AND THE MARKET

HOWARD FLOREY ARRIVED IN NEW YORK ON JULY 2, 1941 along with a member of his research team, Norman Heatley. Florey was the chair of the pathology department at Oxford University in Britain. For the previous few years he had been conducting research on penicillin with Heatley and Ernst Chain, a Jewish refugee from Germany. Alexander Fleming, a British doctor, had discovered penicillin in 1928. As was his custom, Fleming left out petri dishes in his laboratory that were inoculated with bacteria. A mold, later identified from the *Penicillium* family, contaminated one of the dishes, inhibiting the growth of the bacteria. Fleming dubbed the active substance secreted by the mold "penicillin" but was unable to separate it from the broth in which the mold grew to assess its therapeutic potential. Florey's lab picked up on Fleming's research roughly ten years later. Using a sample of Fleming's mold, they managed to isolate minute amounts of impure penicillin and test it in mice. Encouraged by the results, they next tried it out on a few dying patients.

Times were different, and human trials were much easier to arrange. They found an Oxford policeman who was near death. A simple prick from a rose thorn had caused him to contract an infection that led to the loss of an eye and abscesses that had spread all over his body. After getting an injection of penicillin, a miracle seemed in the offing as his condition greatly improved. But sufficient supplies of penicillin were lacking to continue his treatment. The situation got so desperate that they collected his urine and transported it by bicycle to the laboratory to extract unmetabolized penicillin in an effort known as the P-Patrol. Supplies ran out, however, and he died. But penicillin's potential was clear, which was reinforced by the next patients they treated.*

* See Sheehan [1982, pp. 31–34] for the early experiments of Florey's lab with penicillin.

These experiments established that penicillin could be a powerful weapon to treat infection, but it would have to be produced on a much greater scale to be useful. Florey tried to get British firms involved in the effort, but they were preoccupied with World War II and were unreceptive. So he turned to the Rockefeller Foundation in the United States, which earlier had supported his research. He was given a grant of $6,000 to come to the United States to interest U.S. firms and the U.S. government in the mass production of penicillin (Neushul [1993, p. 167]). Thus, on the eve of Florey's trip to America in 1941, penicillin showed promise of being helpful in the fight against infection but could only be produced in minute amounts.

Within three years all was about to change. Dramatic clinical developments would prove that penicillin was a wonder drug, effective against an extraordinary range of conditions, including childhood killers rheumatic fever and pneumonia, venereal diseases syphilis and gonorrhea, and deadly infections incurred by burn victims and wounded soldiers. By D-day in June 1944, enough penicillin would be produced to meet all of the military's needs. A year later, penicillin would be widely supplied to civilians. All these developments would usher in a new era of medicine and with it a whole new industry. But when Florey embarked for the United States in July 1941, these possibilities could hardly be imagined.

Soon after they arrived, Florey and Heatley were directed to a government laboratory in Peoria, Illinois, that was exploring the use of deep fermentation techniques to develop new uses for surplus farm products. The lab conventionally used corn steep liquor, which is a by-product of the corn starch manufacturing process, in all of its fermentation efforts. It was discovered that corn steep liquor was an ideal medium in which to grow the *Penicillium* mold, increasing the output of penicillin twelvefold (Sheehan [1982, p. 67]). And it could be grown in a submerged medium rather than in shallow layers in flasks, bottles, or pans, which it was estimated would have had to stretch from New York to San Francisco to meet the U.S. military's needs during the War (Brockman and Elder [1970, p. v]).

The findings regarding corn steep liquor were conveyed in a meeting in December 1941 with research and corporate heads from pharmaceutical companies Merck, Squibb, Pfizer, and Lederle. The meeting was organized by a committee appointed by the Office of Scientific Research and Development (OSRD), which was set up to coordinate scientific research for military purposes during World War II. Prior to the meeting, Merck, Squibb, and Pfizer had been experimenting in a desultory way with producing penicillin using the shallow culture approach (Sheehan [1982, p. 69]). Hearing about progress at the lab from the head of its fermentation division, Robert Coghill, galvanized their work on penicillin. Coghill later remarked that as a result of the lab's discoveries a new pharmaceutical industry was born.*

The OSRD sponsored an ambitious program involving several hundred scientists to synthesize penicillin in the laboratory, which at the time seemed like the more promising route toward the large-scale manufacture of penicillin. A sister federal agency sponsored research at a number of universities on various challenges associated with producing penicillin by growing the *Penicillium* mold, and it continued to support efforts at the government's Peoria lab to improve the natural production of penicillin.

The War Production Board, which was set up in 1942 to regulate production and allocation of materials during World War II, was also enlisted to help increase penicillin production. A program was set up to finance new production plants for qualifying firms and to allow for accelerated depreciation for private investments in penicillin production. More than 175 companies were considered for support. Twenty-one were selected based on their ability to contribute to the wartime effort. A total of $7.5 million ($108 million in 2015 dollars)[1] was spent by the Board on the construction of new plants and $22.6 million ($324 million in 2015 dollars) was invested by firms, much of which qualified for accelerated depreciation (Federal Trade Commission [1958, p. 52]). Firms were given regular reports on progress at the Peoria lab and other efforts supported by the OSRD and agreed to exchange information about their findings.

By 1943 penicillin's therapeutic properties had been established and the military recognized the benefits of using it on the battlefield to treat soldiers. By the second half of 1944, U.S. firms were widely producing penicillin using the submerged—or deep vat—method. Enough penicillin was produced to treat almost 250,000 patients per month, which was adequate to meet the military's demands on D-day and thereafter. Production tripled from the second half of 1944 to 1945, and by March 1945, producers and distributors were allowed to sell penicillin through normal channels. In contrast, in 1944 British firms were able to produce less than 2.5% of American production. They did not adopt submerged production until 1946, and only with U.S. help (Bud [2007, p. 49]). After

---

*Neushal [1993, Chapter 6] recounts the early developments in the United States regarding penicillin and the federal government, and Neushal [pp. 183–184] notes the effect of these efforts on private firms.

the War, U.S. firms vaulted into the forefront of the antibiotics revolution that penicillin had wrought.

How did this happen, and happen so quickly? Technological advances were made on numerous fronts. The *Penicillium* mold was adapted to grow in a submerged medium. Ways of sterilizing fermentation tanks from the outset and maintaining them free of foreign microorganisms for many days were developed. Better strains of molds were discovered. Precursors were added to the fermentation broth that increased yields and targeted new types of penicillin. Improved methods of isolating and purifying penicillin from the fermented broth were devised. The list goes on (Greene and Schmitz, Jr. [1970]).

Key to all these advances was the penicillin program sponsored and coordinated by the U.S. government. John Sheehan was working on penicillin at Merck during the War and later went on to successfully synthesize penicillin in the laboratory after everyone else had given up the effort. Reflecting on the developments that occurred during the War, he wrote:

> Only the federal government could have organized such a massive cooperative effort involving thirty-nine laboratories and at least a thousand chemists. Only the federal government could have eased the restrictions of anti-trust regulations that might have prevented the collaboration of otherwise competitive industries in their efforts to investigate penicillin and, eventually, produce and sell the wonder drug. Merck, Squibb, and Pfizer—the Big Three of the pharmaceutical industry—were the largest and most influential companies in this effort. They were not alone, however. Once the basic research was under way, another twenty or so pharmaceutical and chemical companies entered the field to produce penicillin and the chemicals needed for its production. Without a carefully defined working relationship among all these companies, the penicillin production program simply would not have taken place. (Sheehan [1982, p. 201])

Penicillin was the first of the antibiotics that unleashed a revolution in medicine and propelled U.S. firms to the forefront of the pharmaceutical industry. It is one of many triumphs in the United States in innovative industries. The term high-tech will be used to refer to the sector of the economy where technological progress is at the heart of competition among for-profit firms. This book is about the high-tech sector and how it operates in the United States.

The penicillin story that opens this book raises deep questions about how high-tech industries get started. Surely one of the great strengths of the United States in the high-tech sector is its reliance on the market. Government has to perform some basic functions such as providing for the common defense, educating the populace, funding basic research, and investing in infrastructure like roads and the Internet. But when it comes to high-tech products, where does the government's role begin and its responsibility end? Fleming and Florey's work was funded publicly in Britain. Without the wartime penicillin program sponsored and coordinated by the federal government, it seems doubtful that U.S. firms would have been in the vanguard of the antibiotics revolution unleashed by penicillin. But if private firms in the United States were making little progress on their own in penicillin and in just three years this was all transformed by a government effort, what does it say about the efficacy of the market in high-tech industries?

Questions like these abound about the high-tech sector in the United States. To answer them, six products that I have studied over the last two decades will be used as a laboratory to explore the high-tech sector: automobiles, pneumatic tires, TV receivers, semiconductors, lasers, and penicillin. Using a methodology that in many ways is a throwback to Darwin and evolutionary biologists, all the firms that ever produced these products are traced, including where they came from and how they performed. Marshaling evidence from many sources, I demonstrate that these six industries exemplify the highs and lows of American high-tech capitalism and buried in them are deep and important lessons about competition and technological progress. Indeed, I hope to convince readers by the end of the book that understanding these lessons can not only make us better workers and entrepreneurs but also show us how to shape and use public policies to make the high-tech sector perform better, to take it to new heights.

What is it about these products that drew my attention and on which I will base my claims? In their time, all of them were quintessentially high-tech and to a large extent still are. When each of the products was first produced, they were extraordinarily primitive yet sold for such high prices that few wanted or were able to afford them. But through continual innovations over many years in the products and the processes used to produce them, they became widely purchased. For example, consider the automobile industry. In 1908 Henry Ford introduced the Model T at a price of $850 (about $20,000 in 2015 dollars) when comparable cars sold for $2,000 to $3,000 (roughly $50,000 to $70,000 in 2015 dollars). Six years later the price of the Model T had been reduced by over half, to $360 ($8,400 in 2015 dollars), driven by a stream of production innovations culminating in the moving assembly line that reduced the time required to build auto chassis from twelve-and-a-half hours to less than two hours and more than doubled the number of automobiles produced per worker. But the industry was much more than Ford and the Model T. Just nine years later, in 1923, the number of automobiles produced per worker had more than doubled again through widespread innovations in equipment, machinery, body construction, and painting, among other factors. These advances took an industry that sold 23,000 cars in 1904 to one that sold 1.7 million cars in 1919 and 5.3 million in 1929, more than any other country or comparable region in the world (Klepper and Simons [1997]).

The industries that arose to produce the other five products went through similar transformations, providing a window into understanding the forces governing technological progress and economic growth in the United States. But it is the way that these forces played out in the six industries that makes them so compelling. For example, in the automobile, tire, TV receiver, and penicillin industries, a small number of firms came to dominate them for many years. Capitalism is built on the idea of competition among the many, but these industries gravitated away from this model. Why did this occur? Did it have something to do with innovation and technological change? Did it affect technological progress—did it eventually diminish the incentives of firms to innovate? Did it alter the character of innovations—did firms become more conservative and less aggressive about generating breakthrough innovations? Fortunately, the industries that were most dominated by a few firms did not start out that way, which provides an opportunity to analyze the forces that led to their domination. Some surprising conclusions emerge about how innovative competition shaped the structure of these industries and in turn promoted technological progress.

A majority of the industries also experienced great turnover in their leading firms, with famous firms like General Motors, Firestone, and Intel emerging out of the turnover. Indeed, the United States is famous for its entrepreneurial zeal that has led to the creation of so many successful firms in the high-tech sector. To understand this phenomenon, the origins of the leading firms in each of the six industries and the impetus for their formation are investigated. This reveals a process akin to biological evolution in which new firms are born (involuntarily) out of existing firms and inherit traits that influence their performance. As successful as the United States has been in generating great new high-tech firms, questions are raised about how policies adopted by states might be inhibiting the formation of such spinoff enterprises and the technological progress they generate.

Today, the most celebrated high-tech sector in the world is Silicon Valley in Northern California, which got its name from the semiconductor producers that concentrated there. Every region would like to be "the next Silicon Valley," and every country in the world would like to grow its own Silicon Valley. But how did Silicon Valley become the center of the semiconductor industry? It is hard to point to any feature of the region that made it advantageous for semiconductor producers to locate there. Two of the other six industries also heavily concentrated in one region early on—autos around Detroit, Michigan, and tires around Akron, Ohio. Neither of these regions also had any compelling natural advantages for auto and tire producers to locate there. Indeed, between Silicon Valley, Detroit, and Akron we have three of the most famous industrial clusters without an obvious geographic rationale. This fact provides a unique opportunity to study whether similar forces were at work in the evolution of all three clusters and what if anything governments might do to replicate these forces.

While Silicon Valley is the envy of the world today, Detroit is the opposite—a once great region that has fallen on hard times and is the scene of great economic devastation. Its decline has paralleled the decline of the U.S. automobile industry and its three great firms, General Motors, Ford, and Chrysler. These firms were on the top of the world for over 40 years but have all declined precipitously in recent years, with the government recently stepping in to manage the bankruptcies of General Motors and Chrysler to avert an apocalyptic collapse. Remarkably, two of the other industries—TV receivers and tires—went through similar if not more extreme declines, providing an unusual opportunity to study industrial extinction.

The specter of government policy looms throughout the six industries. We tend to think of the high-tech sector operating independently of government, which is how many Americans prefer it. The wartime penicillin program clearly breaks this mold, but it turns out that the government, in the form of the military, was also influential in the early years of the semiconductor, laser, and to some degree TV receiver industries. The question that is analyzed in all four industries is whether society's interests were promoted by the involvement of the government and how government policy might beneficially shape other high-tech industries when they are young.

Economics is conventionally divided into macroeconomics, which is the study of aggregate phenomena like inflation and unemployment, and microeconomics, which is the study of individual markets. One of my colleagues calls the methodology I use to study the evolution of new industries *nanoeconomics* to signify digging beneath the surface of markets to understand the forces that drive their formation and functioning. Every firm that entered an industry and the years they produced are tracked down, usually through annual rosters of producers compiled in buyers' guides and marketing volumes. The geographic and intellectual backgrounds of the firms are traced through searches of firm directories, announcements of new firms in trade journals, and sometimes even obituaries of firm founders. The history of innovation and the leading innovators are reconstructed by sifting through hundreds or even thousands of patents. The best performers are identified by searching for data on the periodic market shares of the leading producers. Inevitably, this kind of reconstruction is imperfect, reflecting limitations of the sources available to track any given industry. Seemingly arbitrary rules and judgments are required to make headway, and these will be spelled out carefully, mostly in footnotes to avoid interrupting the text.

Only six industries are featured in the book because the nanoeconomic reconstruction of an industry's evolution can be quite challenging. Finding the requisite sources typically requires being immersed in an industry's history. Understanding innovation requires studying an industry's scientific and technological heritage. Making sense of all the information collected requires developing a theory of the main forces governing an industry's evolution. This can be an arduous effort for even one industry, which is why evidence from only six industries is featured in this work.

Each chapter explores a different question about how the industries evolved using a mix of nanoeconomic evidence, theorizing, and case studies. Chapter 2 begins by focusing on what is called the industry life cycle. Innovative industries pass through various stages of development, like humans. At first, firms flood into an industry, but after a certain point the number of firms begins to decline despite continued growth in the output of the industry. When this process is particularly severe, only a few dominant firms are left standing at the end.

The automobile industry is a quintessential example. The longtime leaders of the industry—General Motors, Ford, and Chrysler—became three of the largest firms in the world and were household names to Americans. They dominated the U.S. industry by 1930, accounting for over 80% of its output, and maintained their dominance for many years afterward. But at its outset the industry had hundreds of competitors—at its peak in 1909 more than 270 firms in the U.S. industry produced automobiles on a regular basis. The next twenty years were an extraordinary period of prosperity in the industry. Americans clamored to buy autos, causing production to rise by an average of over 18% per year, but the number of producers declined steadily. The decline picked up steam in the 1920s, and by the start of the Great Depression in 1929 only 28 firms were still producing autos. By the time the United States entered World War II at the end of 1941, the number of U.S. automobile producers had dwindled to nine.

While the shakeout of producers in autos was particularly severe, shakeouts were also common in the other industries studied. The key questions studied in Chapter 2 are why shakeouts occur in innovative industries and how shakeouts affect technological progress and the welfare of society. Competition is generally viewed as key to the functioning of markets, and the job of antitrust policy is to maintain competition. But at first, and for quite a long time, the emergence of dominant firms in high-tech industries is potentially a great spur to technological progress. Vigorously enforcing competition can undermine technological progress and jeopardize breakthrough innovations. Three great advances of the twentieth century will be considered to illustrate the potential benefits to society of allowing a market to be dominated by a single firm, especially a market as large as the United States: mass production of automobiles, color TVs, and microprocessors.

Chapter 3 focuses on where the firms come from that ultimately dominate high-tech industries. Every country, every region, wants to develop these firms. How has the United States generated so many of them? In penicillin production, the early leaders—Pfizer, Merck, and Squibb—emerged from related industries. This is common in high-tech industries. So if a region does not have distinguished firms in related industries, it is not likely to prosper in a new high-tech industry if it sits back and leaves things to the market.

But that is only the first step. In many high-tech industries, the early leaders get displaced by new firms. Remarkably, most of these new firms are spinoffs that emerge from the leaders of the industry, founded by employees of the better incumbents. Chapter 3 explores the spinoff process in the six industries, the kinds of firms that spawn the most spinoffs, and the circumstances that spur the formation of spinoffs.

Delving into the process that generates spinoffs conjures up a biological metaphor in which spinoffs are involuntarily born out of their parents and inherit knowledge—the industrial counterpart of genes—from their unwitting parents. Detailed case studies of the formation of some of the leading spinoffs in the automobile and semiconductor industries are featured to help understand the impetus for spinoffs. The basic story is repeated over and over again. Innovative employees are thwarted and leave in frustration to pursue their agendas in their own firms. Surprisingly, it is not uncommon for leading firms to become controlled by managers with limited decision-making skills. This can create a volatile environment for employees to break off and form their own spinoff firms.

At one level, spinoffs can harm their parents by competing with them for customers and employees. At another level, spinoffs are often pioneers of major innovations their parents decline to pursue. Chapter 3 demonstrates that spinoffs can be tremendous assets that propel industries to new technological heights. Yet many states give incumbent firms the power to suppress spinoffs by enabling them to limit the mobility of their employees under the guise of protecting their intellectual property. Not only do employees become captives—modern indentured servants—but spinoffs can be stifled, destroying the golden eggs laid by the proverbial goose.

Chapter 4 considers industry clusters, in which firms in an industry congregate in one or a few regions. Clusters are commonly thought of as great national assets that help a country compete internationally. The conventional view of clusters is that they emerge because of the benefits enjoyed by their denizens—firms in clusters have a richer pool of labor to choose from, employees in clusters move more often between firms and in the process spread new ideas, and specialized suppliers and buyers are attracted to clusters, facilitating transactions. When new firms locate in a cluster the other firms located there benefit, but the new firms do not consider these effects when they choose where to locate. Therefore, private benefits fall short of the total social benefit of clustering (there is a "positive externality," to use an economist's jargon, operating in a cluster) and, consequently, many economists believe that governments need to undertake proactive policies to build up local industry clusters.

As already noted, automobiles, tires, and semiconductors were famously clustered geographically. The semiconductor industry is the prototype for what happened in all three industries. Following the commercialization of the transistor in 1949, the industry was initially concentrated in Boston, New York, and Los Angeles. The first semiconductor firm in Silicon Valley was founded in 1956 by William Shockley, who along with two other employees of Bell Labs shared the Nobel Prize that same year for the invention of the transistor nine years earlier. Shockley was a great recruiter and brought together a group of talented young employees to work in his new firm. They soon broke away to form their own firm, Fairchild Semiconductor, in frustration over his management policies. At first Fairchild was immensely successful, reflecting the innovative prowess of its founders. But like Shockley, the founders were scientists and engineers with little management experience. Combined with a few other key developments, this led to an explosive situation in which Fairchild ended up seeding Silicon Valley with an army of talented companies—sometimes called "the Fairchildren"—that caused the semiconductor industry to concentrate in Silicon Valley. Surprisingly, the rise of the automobile industry in Detroit 50 years earlier closely paralleled the development of the semiconductor industry in Silicon Valley, and the concentration of the tire industry in Akron was similar as well.

Focusing on the nano-origins of the leading firms in the Silicon Valley, Detroit, and Akron clusters suggests that the clusters were not driven by the benefits of firms locating close to each other. Rather, key to the formation of all three clusters were spinoffs. Spinoffs do not venture far geographically when they start up, so once the spinoff process gets going in a region, a cluster builds up organically. Spinoffs are all about experimentation, so clusters tend to be engines of economic growth, solidifying the United States's high-tech preeminence. But it is not clear whether any benefits accrue to firms simply from locating in clusters, an observation that would help explain the success of Texas Instruments and Motorola, two of the longtime leaders of the semiconductor industry that were located far from Silicon Valley. It is also not clear whether government efforts to engineer clusters by bringing like kinds of firms together in a narrow region will be productive.

Chapter 5 considers how high-tech industries get started, focusing on the potential role of government at their outset. Penicillin provides a role model. It was entirely a British invention, but the wartime penicillin program initiated by the U.S. government and the military was instrumental in the commercialization of penicillin and subsequent antibiotics by U.S. firms. World War II was an unusual era in which firms were no doubt more cooperative than usual, questioning whether government programs could be equally effective during peace time. But it turns out that the federal government and the military were also instrumental after the war in catalyzing the semiconductor and laser industries. They also engineered the formation of RCA after World War I and later influenced its patent licensing policies, which established a foundation for the radio and TV receiver industries.

The "market" is rife with limitations when it comes to high-tech products, particularly when they are young. U.S. capitalism is predicated on channeling individual initiative for the greater good, and much good it has generated, particularly in the high-tech sector. But without the government often getting new high-tech industries going, we might not be celebrating individual initiative today but rather lamenting its limitations.

Chapter 6 examines the opposite end of the spectrum when high-tech industries are mature and are dominated by a small number of firms. In many ways this is the dark side of U.S. high-tech capitalism, exemplified by the automobile, tire, and television receiver industries in modern times. The conventional, market-oriented view is that eventually all good things must come to an end, but the analysis of these three industries suggests that the market actually strangled itself. Prolonged shakeouts and dominance left just a few firms as the technological gatekeepers of their industry. Left to their own devices, they became conservative, slow to make or pick up on major technological developments. Yet they had accumulated such large profits and assets that they were able to survive for many years even as they sustained large losses. In effect, they were insulated from the discipline of the market. How such firms might be governed to avoid becoming ossified after many years of dominance will be considered.

The final chapter, chapter 7, synthesizes the findings of the substantive chapters regarding how high-tech industries evolve in the United States. The evidence for the six industries is supplemented with similar patterns in other U.S. industries and at times industry experiences in other parts of the world to buttress the findings for the six industries. Lessons abound for individuals, firms, regions, and nations. The last chapter is devoted to extracting these lessons so that societies can harness the talents and imagination of their members for the greatest good.

Two deep lessons emerge from the six industries about how the competitive process operates in high-tech products. The first is that technological progress requires experimentation at all levels. The wartime penicillin program was about experimentation on numerous fronts, some of it planned and some fortuitously conducted in government labs before the advent of penicillin. High-tech capitalism is all about experimentation. It is not a planned onslaught. Firms do not have grand visions about how to experiment and innovate, but decentralize such decisions to managers and employees. Yet people are extraordinarily limited in their ability to foresee the technological future. So, to make progress, a country needs many firms experimenting and competing.

In order for this to happen, talented individuals need to be able to leave established firms and set up competing firms in the same industry. Inevitably such firms end up exploiting knowledge their founders acquired at their previous employers. This knowledge is part of their employer's intellectual property. To make capitalism work in innovative industries, government must accept this reality and not go too far in enforcing intellectual property rights. Otherwise they will squelch the formation of the new firms required to advance new technologies. Intellectual property is different from other forms of private property in that it can be simultaneously used by multiple actors. And at times, government needs to stand by and let that happen, even at the expense of the firms that created the property in the first place.

The other major lesson that arises from the study of the six industries militates in the opposite direction. Too many firms in an industry can undermine each firm's incentive to innovate. Surprisingly, patents often provide little protection against innovations being copied. Innovators need to be able to embody their innovations in a large output to earn a sufficient return on their innovations. But when innovative industries are young, by definition no firm is very big. This is when government can be really helpful, as with penicillin. It can play a role as a buyer of innovative products, as a sponsor of technological experiments, and as a coordinator of firm efforts.

As new innovative industries evolve, some firms will get out ahead. They will be able to apply their innovations to a larger level of output than their competitors. This will provide them with a greater incentive to innovate than their rivals, causing new innovative industries to become dominated by a small number of firms. At first, this can be a tremendous boon to technological progress. Government needs to stand by and let it happen even if it means competition is compromised, as inevitably occurs. But protracted dominance can cause the leading firms to ossify and become impediments to technological progress. Left to its own devices, the market will eventually strangle itself. The challenge is whether public policies can be implemented to revitalize the powers of the market.

This creates quite a bit of tension when it comes to policy making in innovative industries. On the one hand, government cannot get too strict about enforcing either intellectual property or competition, especially when innovative industries are young. Moreover, it may need to step in and actively shape the evolution of innovative industries at their outset, including priming the pump for spinoffs to occur. If these steps are undertaken, no further involvement by government will be required when industries are young. But as new industries evolve, protracted dominance can lead to stagnation. If the market is left alone, once great firms and the industries they pioneered can be lost forever.

Hence, experimental capitalism requires a pragmatic approach to policy making. Historically the United States often struck the right balance between a doctrinaire attachment to the strengths of market decision making and an almost instinctive awareness of the limits of markets. It may not always have understood what it was doing, but for the most part it was successful. A major purpose of this book is to develop an intellectual foundation to interpret the successes of the United States in the high-tech sector. The collapse of once-great high-tech industries like automobiles when they became mature has also not been well understood, and another role of the book is to explain how such collapses have come about in order to figure out how they might be avoided in the future. Lessons abound not just for the United States, but for the rest of the world too.

There is always a question of what can be learned from the past that will help in the future. The world is no doubt changing fast. Throughout most of the twentieth century, the United States was by far the largest national market in the world, and this was certainly a key element in its historical success. But this advantage is beginning to wane. The world is far more interconnected through trade, reducing the importance of the size of any country's national market. Moreover, a number of areas are beginning to rival the United States in terms of the size of their markets. The European Union is roughly the same size as the United States. China is growing fast, and although poor by international standards, it is so large that it recently became the second biggest national market in the world. If its growth continues it seems only a matter time before it eclipses the United States in size, and India can't be too far behind. A number of countries, such as Japan, South Korea, and Taiwan, have figured out at times how to use government initiatives to stimulate the development of their high-tech industries to compete with the United States. And the United States is steadily falling behind the rest of the world in terms of its primary and secondary education systems.

All these developments, though, make it even more imperative for the United States to understand its past successes and failures in the high-tech sector. It is widely agreed that innovation is the key to economic growth. The United States's preeminence in innovation is being challenged from many quarters. If we don't figure out how we did it, we will soon be talking in past tense about why America's corporations (once) led the world.

CHAPTER 2

ONCE UPON A TIME

WHEN I WAS A BOY GROWING UP IN BROOKLYN IN THE 1950S, we occupied ourselves for hours with a simple game. When a car passed on the street we competed to see who could first identify the make, model, and year of the car. You could challenge someone if you thought they were wrong; the other players were the arbiters. Apart from a few stray British imports, nearly all the cars were American and there were less than ten major American car manufacturers to sort through.

Had we been born in 1900, the game would not have been practical. Between 1900 and 1910 hundreds of firms produced automobiles. By 1909 there were over 270 firms in the industry. In the next 20 years the industry lost nearly 90% of its producers, even though its production increased by leaps and bounds. The continued decline in the number of producers that followed made our game feasible.

Like autos, most innovative industries at some point go through a pronounced shakeout during which the number of firms drops sharply despite continued growth in the industry's output. This chapter is about why this occurs and its consequences for technological progress.

The first part of the chapter presents the evolution of the six products that constitute the core of the book, five of which experienced shakeouts of differing timing and severity. Three questions are raised: Why do innovative products commonly experience shakeouts, why do shakeouts differ in severity and timing across products, and how do shakeouts and associated patterns affect society's welfare?

The second part of the chapter begins by discussing alternative theories of shakeouts and features, one of which I developed. My theory is based on a self-reinforcing mechanism operating through innovation that enables the rich to get richer, eventually forcing weaker firms to exit in a new industry, giving rise to a shakeout. The power of this self-reinforcing mechanism is illustrated through extended case studies of three of the great technological advances of the twentieth century: Ford Motor Company's development of mass production, RCA's development of an all-electronic color TV receiver, and Intel's development of the microprocessor. Each of these developments is part of an evolution characterized by an extreme shakeout, and the case studies illuminate how this came about. They also represent great technological breakthroughs and so speak to the issue of how shakeouts and firm dominance affect the welfare of society.

The last part of the chapter digs into the evolution of the six products. Four experienced extreme shakeouts, and two key implications of my theory are evaluated using these four products. The other two products are also considered, and a novel theory is proposed to explain why their evolution was different.

•   •   •

New products often have champions. For example, RCA was the champion for commercial TV in the United States. If champions are successful, it is not long before they are imitated. In TVs, once the Federal Communications Commission established broadcast standards and RCA started marketing black and white TV receivers, many other firms jumped into the market and sales of TV receivers took off.

None of this is surprising. Successful new products naturally attract a lot of producers. What is surprising is what often comes next. Even though the market continues to grow for many years, new entry slows down and nearly comes to a halt. Subsequently, the number of producers starts to fall and just keeps on falling. This process can go on for many years in extreme cases. When such shakeouts are severe, it is common for a small number of producers to eventually dominate the market.

Among the six core products, four of them—automobiles, tires, TV receivers, and penicillin—experienced extreme shakeouts and came to be dominated by just a few producers. Indeed, they were originally chosen for study precisely because they experienced extreme shakeouts. If there is a common cause of industry shakeouts, it should be easiest to spot among products that experienced extreme versions of shakeouts.

The other two products, lasers and semiconductors, had a different evolution. Lasers were chosen for study because the industry did not experience a shakeout during its first 35 years. Semiconductors were studied to better understand geographic clustering, but it turns out that the industry also did not experience a shakeout during its first 35 years.

Sometimes the absence of a phenomenon is as revealing as the phenomenon itself; thus the evolution of these two industries is also considered.

The four products that experienced extreme shakeouts, autos, tires, TV receivers, and penicillin, are considered first. Figures 2.1–2.4 plot the annual number of entrants and producers (the black line is the number of producers) for each of the four products. Each graph begins at or near when the product was first sold commercially and continues for many years.

The annual number of entrants and producers in all four products (and for lasers and semiconductors as well) was laboriously reconstructed mainly from periodic rosters of producers.* To be an entrant, a firm had to start its own business; if it acquired an already existing producer, it was treated as a continuation of the existing producer, albeit possibly under a new name and/or location. For example, two of the most notable firms in the automobile industry, General Motors and Chrysler, both emerged from preexisting automobile firms. Consequently, both were treated as part of a lineage dating back to well before they were formed.† A firm was deemed to have exited either when it closed down or sold out to another firm in the industry.

There was a great deal of entry at first of auto, tire, TV receiver, and penicillin producers, initially causing the number of producers of each product to rise. Eventually the number of firms peaked in each product

---

*The main sources for the data used to construct the figures were Smith [1968] for autos, *Thomas' Register of American Manufacturers* for tires, the *Television Factbook* for TV receivers, and *Thomas' Register of American Manufacturers* and *Synthetic Organic Chemicals* for penicillin. See Klepper [2002] for a detailed discussion of data sources and procedures. Inevitably, reconstructions like figures 2.1–2.4 are imperfect. What constitutes a producer of a product has to be defined, and inevitably there is an arbitrariness to this task. Regardless of the source, it is difficult to spot small firms, especially when they are short-lived. It is also challenging to identify producers on a timely basis, causing delays in the dating of their entry and exit. Inexplicably, occasionally there are gaps in the listings of well-known firms. While some of these limitations can be overcome (e.g., gaps can be filled in for well-known producers), the others are inherent features of trying to identify and date the years of production of every firm that ever produced a product.

†General Motors was formed in 1908 as an amalgamation of a number of automobile and parts producers, including Buick Motor Co., which was its largest constituent. As such, Buick/General Motors was treated as one firm that entered in 1903 based on Buick's date of entry. Chrysler had a more convoluted history but also did not emerge from scratch. In his book on the pre-history of Chrysler, Yanik [2009, p. ix] notes how Chrysler emerged in 1925 out of the reorganization of the Maxwell Motor Co. In turn, Maxwell Motor was organized in 1913 as the successor to an early successful entrant, Maxwell Briscoe, after a merger involving Maxwell Briscoe failed. Accordingly, Maxwell Briscoe/Maxwell/Chrysler was treated as one firm that entered in 1904 based on the entry date of Maxwell Briscoe.

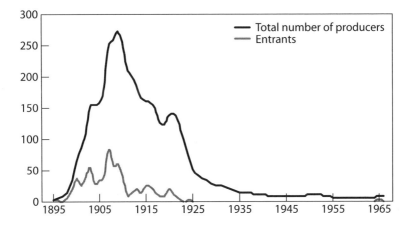

Figure 2.1: Annual Number of U.S. Automobile Entrants and Producers, 1895–1966. The gray line represents entrants; the black line, total number of producers.

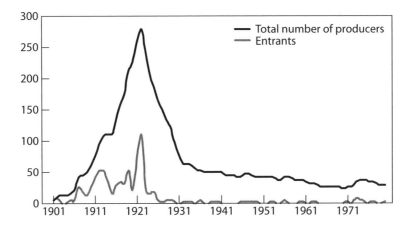

Figure 2.2: Annual Number of U.S. Tire Entrants and Producers, 1901–1980. The gray line represents entrants; the black line, total number of producers.

and then fell sharply for many years, even though the output of the product continued to grow. For example, in automobiles the number of firms rose through 1909 when it peaked at 272, after which it declined sharply even though the total output of the industry grew by an average of over 15% per year through the start of the Great Depression in 1929. By 1941 the number of firms reached a trough of 9, which represents a decline of 97% in the number of producers from its peak in 1909. The analogous

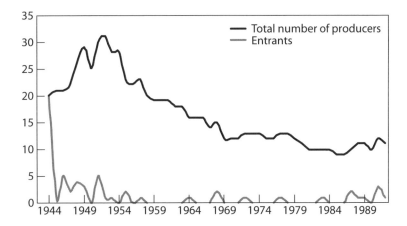

Figure 2.3: Annual Number of U.S. Penicillin Entrants and Producers, 1944–1992. The gray line represents entrants; the black line, total number of producers.

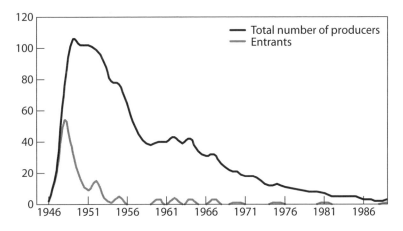

Figure 2.4: Annual Number of U.S. TV Receiver Entrants and Producers, 1946–1989. The gray line represents entrants; the black line, total number of producers.

declines for the other three products were 91% in tires (278 in 1922 to 21 in 1970), 97% in TVs (105 in 1949 to 3 in 1989), and 71% in penicillin (32 in 1952 to 9 in 1985). In each product, entry dropped sharply around the start of its shakeout and was soon negligible.

The time it took for the shakeout to begin varied considerably across the four products. In automobiles and tires entry initially increased over time, and it took 15 or more years for the number of firms to reach their peaks. In contrast, in penicillin and TV receivers, entry was heavy at the start and the number of firms peaked quickly.

To some extent these differences are related to World War II. Entry in penicillin was galvanized by the government program, and most of the subsequent entrants appear to have been largely dosage re-packagers rather than bulk manufacturers. In TVs, entry was ready to begin in 1941, but production of TV receivers was banned during the war. When the ban was lifted in 1946, the industry was ready to take off, and entry was facilitated by RCA's policy of licensing its TV technology to all comers. But it will be argued that World War II was only part of the story behind the earlier shakeouts in penicillin and TV receivers, as other, fundamental factors were at work that are revealing about the causes of shakeouts.

Given the extreme shakeouts experienced by the four products, each industry became dominated for many years by a small group of firms. Industries in which the four largest firms account for 50% or more of the total output of the industry are generally considered to be "oligopolies." Each of these four industries evolved to be an oligopoly.

In automobiles, three firms, General Motors, Ford, and Chrysler, accounted for over 80% of the production of automobiles as of the 1930s, which they maintained for many years (Bailey [1971]). In tires, four firms, Goodrich, Goodyear, Firestone, and U.S. Rubber (Uniroyal), accounted for over 70% of the production of tires by the 1930s, which they too maintained for many years (French [1991, pp. 47, 111]). In penicillin, the top four firms—initially Pfizer, Merck, Squibb, and Lilly, later joined by Wyeth and Bristol—accounted for between 70% and 80% of total output in 1956 and 1973, respectively (FTC [1958, p. 83], Schwartzman [1976, p. 131]). In TV receivers, two firms, RCA and Zenith, accounted for 40% to 50% of the market for monochrome (black and white) and then color TV receivers, and the next cadre of firms, which included GE in both monochrome and color TVs, each accounted for 5% to 10% of the market (less in the color era due to the invasion of the market by foreign firms) (Levy [1981, pp. 8–87]).

The evolution of the other two products, lasers and semiconductors, was quite different. Consider first lasers, which were first produced commercially in 1961. Figure 2.5 presents the annual number of laser entrants and producers from 1961 to 2007.* The laser industry was studied because

---

*The main source of data for laser producers was the buyers' guide compiled by the trade magazine *Laser Focus*, which annually listed the producers of many different types of lasers. See Klepper and Sleeper [2005] and Bhaskarabhatla and Klepper [2014] for a detailed discussion of the data and procedures.

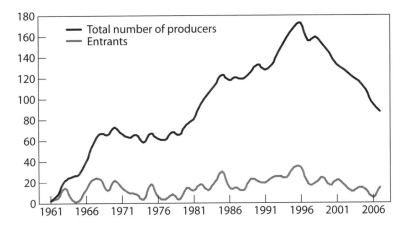

Figure 2.5: Annual Number of U.S. Laser Entrants and Producers, 1961–2007. The gray line represents entrants; the black line, total number of producers.

it did not experience a shakeout through 1994, when the original data collection ended. But when the data were extended through 2007, it became apparent that eventually a shakeout in the industry did materialize. The number of producers peaked in 1996 at 172 and then fell steadily to 87 by 2007, even though the output of lasers grew by record rates after 1996.

Clearly, a shakeout took much longer to begin in lasers than in the other four products. Perhaps not surprisingly, the industry has also not been nearly as dominated by its leading producers as in autos, tires, TV receivers, and penicillin. No systematic market share data are available for laser producers, but only two firms, Spectra Physics and Coherent, grew to be large, and neither appears to have captured nearly as large a share of the market as the two largest firms in the other four industries.

The semiconductor industry evolved much like lasers at first, and even after nearly 40 years did not show any signs of a shakeout. The industry began with the transistor, which was first produced commercially in 1949. Its main product since the early 1960s has been the integrated circuit (IC), which integrates many transistors and other devices on a single piece of silicon. The annual number of transistor entrants and producers from 1949 to 1987 is presented in figure 2.6, and the annual number of IC entrants and producers from 1965 to 1987 is presented in figure 2.7 (1987 is the last year of the data source for both products).*

---

*The main source for data for semiconductor producers was the *Electronics Buyers Guide*, which annually listed producers of many different types of integrated circuits. See Klepper [2010] for a discussion of the data and procedures.

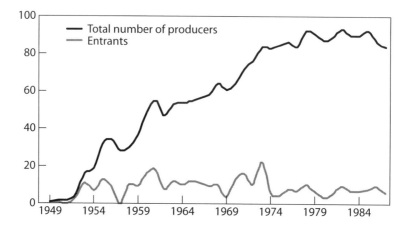

Figure 2.6: Annual Number of Transistor Entrants and Producers, 1949–1987. The gray line represents entrants; the black line, total number of producers.

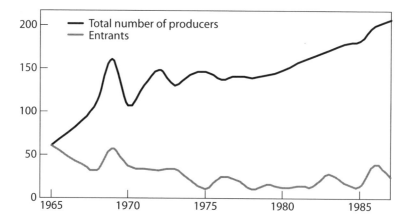

Figure 2.7: Annual Number of Integrated Circuit Entrants and Producers, 1965–1987. The gray line represents entrants; the black line, total number of producers.

The annual number of transistor producers peaked at around 100 and IC producers at around 200, but neither product experienced a shakeout through 1987. Within the industry, certain niche markets experienced shakeouts. For example, Intel introduced the first, primitive microprocessor in 1971, and by the mid-1970s over 20 firms produced microprocessors (FTC [1977]). By 2000, however, only a few firms were left producing microprocessors, and Intel had captured over 70% of the market (IC Insights [2000]). Nevertheless, the semiconductor industry as a whole contains many different types of products, and there was no sign of a shakeout in the overall industry through 1987. There has also been considerable turnover in the leading U.S. semiconductor firms, which has limited the extent to which the industry was dominated by its largest firms. The only constants over the evolution of the industry were Texas Instruments and Motorola, which consistently accounted for around 18% and 10%, respectively, of the sales of U.S. producers. (See table 3.3 in chapter 3.) In more recent years, Intel has acquired a large market share by dint of its success with the microprocessor, but otherwise there has been considerable churning in the leaders over time.

A number of questions are raised by how the six products evolved:

- Why do many innovative products experience extreme shakeouts and end up dominated by a small cadre of producers?
- Why do other innovative products not experience shakeouts at all or less severe shakeouts, and why does the timing of shakeouts differ among products that do experience shakeouts?
- What effect do shakeouts and firm dominance have on the welfare of society—in particular, what happens to the rate of technological progress as dominant firms emerge and shakeouts proceed?

The last question is the key one. One of the central concerns of economic analysis is how to set up the rules of the economic system to best service society's interests. So the ultimate question is whether society's interests are well served when a product experiences a shakeout and becomes dominated by a small cadre of firms. Proponents of competition would surely argue that this is inimical to society's interests and will cause technological progress to slow down. But without a theory of why shakeouts occur and vary in timing and intensity across products, it is difficult to address the question of society's welfare.

Accordingly, the next section begins with a discussion of shakeout theories. This is followed by extended case studies of three great technological advances, Ford's development of mass production, RCA's development of an all-electronic color TV receiver, and Intel's development of the microprocessor. Each involves a dominant firm in a product that experienced an extreme shakeout. As such, the cases provide important clues about why shakeouts and dominance occur. Each of the cases also involves a tremendous technological advance that bestowed great benefits on society, suggesting that shakeouts and dominance can actually be in society's interests.

• • •

Shakeouts have attracted a lot of attention from economists, and many theories have been proposed about them. Some have garnered a greater following, including one that I developed. My theory is featured in this chapter, but first I describe two other popular theories.

Both of these theories depict shakeouts as being triggered by particular developments. In one theory, the trigger is a technological change that increases the minimum efficient scale at which firms need to operate to achieve the lowest possible cost of production (Jovanovic and MacDonald [1994]). Once this milestone occurs, the market can accommodate fewer firms, giving rise to a shakeout. In the other popular theory, the trigger is the emergence of a de facto product standard called a "dominant design" (Utterback and Suárez [1993]). It emerges after consumers and producers experiment with different versions of a product and converge on a dominant choice. Once the dominant design emerges, the nature of competition changes, and firms may be more willing to make investments that also increase the minimum efficient scale of production. Firms that have difficulty keeping up with these developments exit, contributing to a shakeout.

My theory does not depict shakeouts as being triggered by particular product or process developments but as part of a broader evolutionary process. No one theory captures all the developments in any industry, and by featuring my theory I don't mean to rule out scale economies or dominant designs as important influences on how industries evolve. But I have argued that my theory does a better job than the scale economies and dominant design theories in explaining the extreme shakeouts that occurred in autos, tires, TV receivers, and penicillin (Klepper and Simons [1997]). Moreover, it provides a useful way to understand how great technological breakthroughs can occur in industries that experience extreme shakeouts, as the case studies exemplify.

The essence of my theory is a self-reinforcing process involving technological change. Firms innovate principally to improve their product and production process. Both typically increase the profits firms earn per unit of output sold—product innovations increase the amount buyers will pay for their product and process innovations lower the cost per unit of output. Many innovations cannot be patented or can be invented around even if patented, and consequently innovations tend to be copied quickly by rivals. Before they are copied, though, firms have a monopoly over their innovations and profit from them mainly by incorporating them in their own output. With innovations increasing the profit per unit of output that firms earn from the sale of their product, the total profits from innovation are scaled by the size of a firm's output. Consequently, as firms grow large, their incentives to innovate rise and they devote more effort to innovation. This in turn enables them to grow larger, creating a self-reinforcing mechanism.

Within the context of a new industry, this can contribute to a shakeout. Firms are assumed to enter new industries on a small scale, reflecting the difficulty of initially interesting buyers in their product. They enter when they acquire the capabilities needed to compete in the industry; for example, firms that are already producing products in related industries tend to enter early whereas others that are founded by employees of incumbent firms enter later. All firms can engage in innovation, and those that are more successful grow larger than their competition. As they grow larger, they can embody their innovations in a larger level of output, which increases their profits from innovation and hence the effort they devote to innovation. This leads to further growth, enhancing their advantage over their competitors. As the most successful firms expand, the price at which firms can sell their output falls to balance supply and demand. Eventually the price falls far enough that entry is no longer profitable and hence ceases. Subsequent price decreases undermine the profitability of smaller incumbents, causing them to exit, giving rise to a shakeout. Ultimately, the new industry becomes dominated by firms that get ahead early on and exploit the self-reinforcing economics of innovation. This implies that the leaders of a new industry will be more likely to come from the ranks of earlier entrants and will achieve their leading positions through innovation.

If the theory has merit, these last implications of the theory should hold generally in shakeout industries. Assessing whether they hold thus provides a way of evaluating the theory. Before turning to that task, the three case studies of Ford, RCA, and Intel are presented. The case studies illustrate the key mechanism in my theory in which an early entrant gets out ahead and then ratchets up its innovative efforts. Curiously, in each case the leader did not have an overarching plan regarding innovation but experimented, conditioned by its growing incentives to innovate. Tremendous technological advances resulted, illustrating how shakeouts and firm dominance can actually be in society's interests, at least when an industry is young and vibrant.

FORD MOTOR CO. AND MASS PRODUCTION

When Henry Ford sequestered himself with a small team of colleagues in early 1907 to begin work on the Model T, the American automobile market was divided into at least three camps (Casey [2008, pp. 1–12]). Urbanites who wanted to escape the city for a pleasurable drive favored large, powerful cars with the engine in the front like the German Mercedes. These cars could cruise at 50 miles per hour on good roads and cost between $2,000 and $7,500. At the other end of the spectrum were the high-wheelers made predominantly in the Midwest. These cars resembled horseless carriages and appealed especially to farmers. They typically had a buggy frame, wooden wheels at least 36 inches in diameter, solid rubber tires, a rear-mounted engine, and were priced between $250 and $950. Their light weight and high ground clearance were well suited for poor rural Midwestern roads, but they shook and vibrated fiercely, leading to broken frames and suspensions. In between these extremes were the runabouts, which looked like smaller versions of the Mercedes car. They had one- or two-cylinder engines in the front, generally accommodated two or at most three people, and sold for between $600 and $1,000. The most popular of the runabouts was Ford's Model N, which sold for $600 in 1907.

What the U.S. market needed was a lightweight automobile that could accommodate four passengers, cruise at reasonable speed, navigate inferior roads, and sell for $1,000 or less. Henry Ford's genius was in the design of cars, and the Model T fit the bill. It was not a thing of beauty but of great utility, and at a price of $850 was a bargain. Through the use of a new metal alloy, vanadium steel, it was lightweight but powerful, with a 20 horsepower engine capable of a top speed of 45 miles per hour. Drawing on experience with the Model N, its suspension and engine mounting were based on a series of triangles, which enabled the chassis to twist with ruts, holes, and bumps in the road without breaking. It employed a strengthened planetary transmission with three pedals for two forward speeds and reverse that was much easier to operate than the widely used sliding-gear transmissions. Perhaps its most novel feature was the use of a magneto integrated into the flywheel to ignite the gasoline/air mixture in the cylinders.

In early advertisements, it was claimed that: "No car under $2000 offers more, and no car over $2000 offers more except in trimmings" (Nevins [1954, p. 390]). While no doubt hyperbole, this was not too far off the mark, and the Model T took the country by storm. Deliveries began toward the end of 1908. A total of 5,986 Model Ts were sold in

TABLE 2.1:
Prices and Quantities of the Model T, 1908–1916

Year	Price	Number Sold
1908	$850	5,986
1909	950	12,292
1910	780	19,293
1911	690	40,402
1912	600	78,611
1913	550	182,809
1914	490	260,720
1915	440	355,276
1916	360	577,036

Source: Hounshell [1984, p. 224].

1908 and 12,292 in 1909, when it was the best-selling car in the United States. But that was just the beginning. In the next five years Ford Motor Co. developed a series of innovations in the production of the Model T that gave rise to what became known as "mass production." By greatly lowering the cost of producing the Model T, these advances enabled Ford Motor Co. to cut the price of the Model T by 1916 by over half, to $360. As reflected in table 2.1, this led to tremendous increases in the number of Model Ts sold. By 1916 Ford Motor Co. was selling over a half million Model Ts, accounting for nearly 50% of U.S. sales of automobiles. Henry Ford had realized his dream of creating a car for the masses.

The development of the Model T and the subsequent sharp reduction in its price is one of the most extraordinary one-two technological punches in history. To put it in perspective, imagine that Honda Motor Co. came out next year with a sedan that got 100 miles per gallon of gasoline at a price of $25,000. One can only guess how such a development would be received by the world. Then suppose that six years later the price of the car was reduced to $10,000 through the development of a new, revolutionary way of producing automobiles. Honda would undoubtedly be the most celebrated company in the world and its CEO the most heralded. Such was Ford Motor Co. and Henry Ford with the Model T and the mass production of automobiles.

Yet Henry Ford was certainly an unlikely candidate to become known as the father of mass production. He had an instinctive genius when it came to designing cars, but his production skills were sorely lacking. Indeed, he was pushed out of his second startup, the Henry Ford Company, because of his inability or unwillingness to get cars out the door. So how was Ford Motor Co. able to innovate the new system of mass production following its breakthrough with the Model T?

Hounshell [1984, p. 219] attributed it to an "alchemy of circumstances" rooted in "Henry Ford's business philosophy and its application by Ford company's financial wizard, James Couzens." To this will be added the realities of high-tech economics. Henry Ford had no master plan or even vision about mass production. But as Ford Motor Co. grew bigger, it could apply its production innovations to an ever larger output, increasing its profits from innovation. This created a self-reinforcing process in which one round of innovations made the next round even more profitable. No one, least of all Henry Ford, could have anticipated what would happen. But by articulating a philosophy of creating an inexpensive car for the masses and then getting out of the way, Henry Ford unleashed a talented group of managers to experiment under the watchful financial eye of James Couzens. The result was an astounding breakthrough in manufacturing to which Henry Ford's name was forever attached, even though Ford was hardly involved. As is recounted below, sadly this went to Ford's head, and he and his company were never the same.

Ford Motor Co. might never have gotten off the ground were it not for Couzens. Ford Motor Co. was founded in 1903 with funding primarily from Alexander Malcomson, a local Detroit coal dealer. Malcomson assigned Couzens, a 30-year-old Canadian from across the Detroit border, to look after his investment. One of Ford's top employees, "Cast-Iron" Charlie Sorensen, described Couzens as "Malcomson's peppery-tempered bookkeeper," although it is fairer to describe Couzens as the de facto manager of Malcomson's coal business. He was methodical to a fault and demanding of everyone, including himself, regularly working long hours. When Henry Ford held up the shipment of the first cars produced by Ford Motor Co. because they were not good enough, Couzens put his foot down and insisted that the cars be shipped so money would come in. To ensure that his directive was followed, he helped Ford crate the cars and nail shut the doors of the freight train that was to carry them to their destination (Barnard [1958, pp. 46–47]).

Ford Motor Co. was successful from the outset and was soon paying large dividends to its stockholders. Nevertheless, it was not long before

Henry Ford got into a dispute with Malcomson over the size of cars Ford Motor Co. should produce. Couzens sided with Ford and helped him oust Malcomson. By the autumn of 1907, Henry Ford controlled a majority of Ford Motor Co.'s stock, with Couzens the number two shareholder and the general manager in charge of the company's entire business operations. Sorensen [1962, p. 85] said there were three great men at Ford's side during the early days of Ford Motor Co.: C. Harold Wills, Walter Flanders, and James Couzens. Indeed, he declared the period from 1903 to 1913 the Couzens's era at Ford Motor Co. (p. 146). "Without the bulldog driving energy of Couzens in handling the purse strings and in constant nagging of dealers and branch agencies, the Ford company would have fallen apart almost before it had been put together" (Sorensen [1962, p. 85]).

Wills was at Ford's side during much of the development of the Model T and was instrumental in how steel was used to produce it. Flanders was the one responsible for introducing Ford Motor Co. to modern production methods. He was hired in August 1906 to oversee production at Ford Motor Co. and its manufacturing company, which had been formed as part of the effort to oust Malcomson. According to Hounshell [1984, p. 220], at that point Ford's main factory at Piquette Ave. resembled more a poorly equipped job shop than a sophisticated factory. While Flanders remained at Ford only until April 1908, he introduced a series of changes at Ford that laid the groundwork for the moving assembly line and other production innovations. Sorensen described Flanders, who was a machine tool salesman par excellence, as a "roistering genius." He schooled the company in the need for interchangeable parts and the use of single-purpose machine tools and special jigs and fixtures. He rearranged the machine tools in the order they were used in operations, which improved productivity. He implemented sales planning and the orderly delivery of parts in anticipation of the just-in-time production system pioneered much later in the Japanese automobile industry.

The next key ingredient along the way to mass production involved the construction of a new plant at Highland Park that the company began to move into on New Year's Day of 1910. The plant was designed by the famous industrial architect Alfred Kahn. It was nicknamed the Crystal Palace for its sawtooth glass roof and extensive use of windows that bathed the factory in light. Not only was the plant needed to accommodate the popularity of the Model T, but it incorporated a number of novelties that were essential elements of mass production. It had a gigantic craneway, 860 x 57 feet, that connected the buildings at the Highland Park plant, and a monorail line equipped with its own electric locomotives that facilitated movement of materials throughout the plant. Following up on Flanders's introduction of sophisticated machine tools into production, a separate department in the plant was created to design and sometimes develop prototypes of new specialized machine tools before searching for machine tool companies to build them (Nevins [1954, p. 456]). The array of specialized machine tools employed at Highland Park, such as one that could drill 45 holes in four sides of the engine bloc at one time, and the savings in labor they afforded was dazzling. Savings were so great that machine tools were ruthlessly scrapped in favor of better ones even if only a month old (ibid.).

Ford Motor Co. was constantly experimenting with how to produce its parts and was always ready to replace old processes with superior ones. Its experience with the John R. Keim plant of Buffalo was representative. The plant was one of the foremost makers of pressed steel parts for the automotive industry and supplied Ford Motor Co. with rear axle housings, among other stamped steel parts. Ford employees made frequent trips to the plant and the company invested large sums in the plant's machinery as orders increased. At the recommendation of Charlie Sorensen, the plant was eventually bought. A little over a year later a wildcat strike was called at the plant over piecework rates on some outside contracts. When warnings issued to the workers to end the strike were ignored, within three days the presses and other machinery were torn down and reassembled at Highland Park and were turning out their familiar parts (Nevins [1954, p. 460]). The top mechanics at Keim moved to Detroit, and they found numerous other applications for metal punching, pressing, and stamping that improved Ford's operations (Hounshell [1984, p. 234]).

The other outstanding development at Ford that was instrumental in the moving assembly line was the use of overhead carriers, conveyor belts, gravity slides, and rollways to aid in the transportation of materials in the plant. These apparently dated back to 1912 and early 1913 before the advent of the moving assembly line (Nevins [1954, pp. 469–471]), although their use was greatly increased as the moving assembly line was implemented. In their classic work on production at Ford, Arnold and Faurote [1919, pp. 272–273] noted that these devices greatly economized on the need for factory space for work in process, which increased the capacity of the factory. They also "produced unbelievable labor-cost reductions, so that, at the date of this writing, October 6, 1914 [when moving assembly lines were widely used at Ford], these means of transporting components in process of finishing through the air instead of on the floor, are the most surprising feature of the Ford shops interior" (Arnold and Faurotte [1919, p. 273]).

The granddaddy of all the developments at Ford and the final step in the Fordist system of mass production was the moving assembly line. Charlie Sorensen claimed that experiments with a moving assembly line had been conducted back in 1908 at the Piquette Ave. plant but nothing further was pursued at Highland Park until 1913. Reflecting the organic nature of developments at Ford Motor Co., the impetus for the moving assembly line is unclear. Indeed, even where it was first employed in the plant is not clear (Hounshell [1984, pp. 244–246]).

Hounshell's reconstruction of the evidence suggests the first moving assembly line involved the flywheel magneto. On April 1, 1913, workers in the flywheel magneto assembly department no longer stood at workbenches where they assembled an entire flywheel from parts. Instead, the flywheels rested on smooth, sliding surfaces on a pipe frame, and the workers were instructed to put on one part or just do a few simple tasks like tighten a nut and then push the flywheel to the next worker. They repeated the same process over and over for nine hours. Soon it was found that if a chain was used to move the magnetos at a set rate, the slow workers could be sped up and everyone would move at the same pace. Through various experiments and adjustments in the moving line over the course of the next year, the amount of labor time required to assemble the magnetos into the flywheel was reduced by 75%.

As Hounshell [1984, p. 248] remarked, one can only wonder how excited Ford's production engineers must have been about the possibilities opened up by the moving assembly line. Not surprisingly, it became the object of study by a number of top men at Ford, including the heads of other assembly departments. Eventually it spread to engine assembly, transmission assembly, and then the assembly of the chassis, which was "the most spectacular one" according to Sorensen and "a spectacle to beholders of every class" according to Arnold (Hounshell [1984, p. 249]).

Numerous experiments were conducted concerning the length of the chassis assembly line, the number of workers, the tasks of workers, the mechanization and pace of the line, and the flow of parts, among other factors. After seven months of experimentation, assembly time was reduced from the original 12.5 hours to 93 man-minutes, which led to further experimentation and refinement of sub-assemblies throughout the plant that led to comparable productivity gains. According to Nevins [1954, p. 475], "Soon the scientifically-timed rivers were all being fed by scientifically-timed tributaries. The whole factory became kinetic." The fundamental tenet of the moving assembly line was to bring work to the men, which according to Hounshell [1984, p. 237] brought "a regularity almost as dependable as the rising sun," and "wrought true mass production."

The moving assembly line was the result of contributions by many, but seemingly Henry Ford was not among them. Sorensen [1962, p. 126] said that Henry Ford had nothing to do with originating, planning, or carrying out the moving assembly line. He described Ford as the sponsor but not the father of mass production (ibid. [p. 114]). Indeed, according to one associate, between 1908 and 1913 Henry Ford spent little time at the plant, coming in once or twice a week and then just roaming around (Barnard [1958, p. 72]).

The only constant during this period in terms of oversight at Ford was James Couzens, who had little to do with mechanical developments but oversaw all aspects of the financial side of the company. Along with Henry Ford, he was centrally involved in the decision to build the Highland Park plant, in the purchase of the Keim factory, and in all the other major developments at Ford during this period. He was no doubt also involved in subsidiary developments along the way to the moving assembly line, as is conveyed in an incident that Sorensen [1962, p. 125] recounted. On a rare visit to the plant, Couzens discovered the use of an overhead conveyor for radiators. He demanded to know how anyone could spend money like that without him being aware of it. Apparently when Sorensen gave him figures on the labor saved by the overhead conveyor and the cost of the conveyor, Couzens quickly figured out that just a few days' operation paid for the conveyor, and he approved its use.

Sorensen went on to explain that this incident was typical of his interactions with Couzens. When Couzens was convinced that expenditures meant long-range economy and increased production, he assented to them. According to Sorensen, he never found fault with similar developments in other parts assemblies, and it was not long before Sorensen got a nice raise. Presumably the large volume of output being processed at the Highland Park plant meant that even small savings in costs per unit of output translated into such large total savings that they more than outweighed the investments required to bring them about.

This would explain how Ford Motor Co. was able to reduce the price of the Model T so much and still earn extraordinary profits. Stelzer [1928, pp. 96, 109, 126] summarizes data from Ford's financial accounts and also on the production of Model T's over Ford's fiscal year that make it possible to estimate the average cost per Model T produced from 1909 to 1916. Accounting costs depend upon arbitrary factors such as what is depreciated versus expensed and by how much, but the trends implied by Ford Motor Co.'s accounts are unmistakable. In fiscal year 1909 (ending September 30), the average cost of the Model T (computed by subtracting profits from revenues and dividing by output) was $555. This increased the next year to $639 and then fell steadily through 1916, when it reached a low of $275, which is comparable to the percentage decrease in price realized in the Model T over this period as reflected in table 2.1.

With the price decreases made possible by the great advances in production, Ford Motor Co. earned extraordinary profits (Stelzer [1928, p. 128]). In fiscal year 1908, which ended just before the delivery of the first Model Ts, Ford Motor Co.'s total profits were a little over a million dollars. In fiscal year 1916, Ford Motor Co.'s profits were $59 million, which astoundingly represented nearly a 100% rate of return on its net worth as of the beginning of the year. From 1909 to 1916, the company paid out total dividends of nearly $55 million (ibid. [p. 130]) and reinvested the rest of its profits. By the time Couzens and the other minority stockholders sold out their shares to Henry Ford in 1919 following a suit to force him to pay out greater dividends, their stock was worth several thousand times its initial par value. Couzens originally invested $2,500 ($59,000 in 2015 dollars) in Ford Motor Co. He sold his shares for over $29 million ($392 million in 2015 dollars) and went on to become a U.S. senator from Michigan.

The ultimate beneficiary of all the developments at Ford was undoubtedly the consumer of automobiles and society at large. The extraordinary reduction in the price of automobiles driven by the Model T made automobiles affordable to the masses and as such transformed American society. Henry Ford was proud of Ford Motor Co.'s accomplishments and opened his plant for technical journalists to write about its methods. The moving assembly line soon spread to the plants of the larger producers of automobiles in the industry (Spencer [1916]), although it may have taken longer for them to embrace the full range of Ford's methods. Later it spread to many other products such as vacuum sweepers and radios (Hounshell [1984, p. 261]). When World War II broke out, American mass-production industries made a quick conversion to producing war materials and out-competed the industries of its belligerents (Casey [2008, p. 122]).

As with many innovations, not all was good. The assembly line made jobs repetitive and boring, leading to extraordinary turnover of labor. To staunch the turnover, in 1914 Ford Motor Co. implemented the famous

$5 per day wage, which more than doubled the minimum wage paid to Ford workers. Workers submitted to the discipline of the assembly line in exchange for higher wages (Casey [2008, pp. 123–124]), which is a legacy the U.S. automobile industry has struggled with ever since.

The Model T and mass production forever changed Henry Ford. With his name attached to the company, he was perceived as the father of mass production and all the good emanating from it, which went to his head. Couzens could not deal with Ford's newfound assertiveness and left the company in 1915. Ford Motor Co. was never the same. Henry Ford refused to incorporate the latest technological developments into the Model T, which eventually forced him to abandon its production in May 1927 and close his plant for most of the rest of the year while he developed a replacement, the Model A. While the Model A was successful, it only slowed the decline of Ford Motor Co., which eventually ceded its gigantic lead in the industry to General Motors.

These developments will be revisited in subsequent chapters. None of them should obscure, though, the great bounty bestowed on society by the development of the Fordist system of mass production.

THE DAY THE EARTH STOOD STILL IN THE TV INDUSTRY: RCA AND THE COLOR WARS

RCA was the pioneer of commercial television in the United States. Nevertheless, after investing $50 million (well over half a billion dollars in 2015 dollars) in monochrome TV, its whole investment was put at risk by its arch-broadcasting rival, CBS. Ultimately, it was saved by high-tech economics.

By the time CBS mounted its challenge, RCA was the leading manufacturer of monochrome TV receivers and had a stake in much of the rest of the output of the TV receiver industry. Its large size gave it a tremendous incentive to develop an innovation that no one thought possible at the time: an all-electronic color TV receiver. Similar to Ford, RCA pulled off a great 1-2 technological punch. First it pioneered monochrome TV and then in less than ten years introduced a color TV receiver that was widely thought to be light years away.

The story of how RCA engineered such a breakthrough so rapidly is a testimony to the old adage that where there is a will, there is a way. The will in this instance stemmed from RCA's size, and the way arose from the power of technological experimentation. The story is filled with blind ambition, intrigue, and avarice. It nearly set the TV industry back on its heels to a bygone era. Indeed, there was a day when the earth stood still in the TV industry as it was forced to adopt retrogressive standards. This is a story of how this all came about and how high-tech economics ultimately saved the day.

The first TV systems to achieve some popularity in the 1920s used spinning discs with small holes or prisms to scan images and reproduce them at the receiver. RCA's president, David Sarnoff, recognized early on that such mechanical systems would never become popular because spinning discs limited the quality of the image that could be scanned. RCA was formed in 1919 at the behest of the U.S. Navy and the federal government under the aegis of GE, Westinghouse, and AT&T. When RCA achieved its independence in 1932, it inherited the fledgling TV efforts of GE and Westinghouse. Sarnoff had actually been supporting since 1928 the work of Vladimir Zworykin at Westinghouse on an all-electronic TV system that transcended the limitations of scanning discs, and he immediately increased support for Zworykin's system.

Zworykin's camera was especially novel. It used an optical lens to channel light from an image onto a mosaic plate composed of hundreds of thousands of tiny photocells that converted light into electricity. An electron beam scanned the plate line by line to induce a flow of electrons in proportion to the intensity of light that was stored at each point on the plate. This flow was amplified and transmitted to the receiver, where the image was reconstructed using a comparable beam of electrons, which scanned the face plate of a cathode ray tube coated with phosphors that would light up when bombarded with electrons.

By the time RCA unveiled its all-electronic system at the 1939 New York World's Fair, it had spent over $9 million (about $151 million in 2015 dollars) on TV research and testing. No other firm or individual[1] had spent anything close; RCA's total expenditures were nearly four times as great as the rest of the industry combined (MacLaurin [1949, pp. 200–220]). It petitioned the Federal Communications Commission to allow it to begin commercial TV broadcasting on its NBC network.

The newly appointed chair of the FCC, James Fly, had been the chief counsel of the Tennessee Valley Authority, where he defended the TVA from lawsuits filed by privately owned utilities that were local monopolies, and he was not going to be pushed around by RCA. The FCC authorized "limited" commercial broadcasting to begin in 1940, and Sarnoff immediately mounted an aggressive program to sell TV receivers. Fly responded by rescinding the FCC's authorization, claiming RCA was violating the spirit of its ruling. A lengthy battle ensued that drew Congress and President

Roosevelt into the fray. To solve it, an industry committee was set up to determine broadcast standards. The FCC adopted its recommendations, authorizing unlimited commercial broadcasting to begin on July 1941. Soon after, however, the United States entered World War II, and the production of TVs was banned for the war's duration. When RCA emerged from the war, its TV system was much improved, and the market for TV receivers was ready to explode. RCA licensed its TV patents to all comers at a royalty rate of 2% of sales and provided its licensees with blueprints of its initial receiver, the 630TS model, and tours of the plant where it was produced. James Fly had resigned and had been succeeded by a new chairman who was much more balanced regarding RCA's interests. But a new fly in the ointment surfaced, in the form of CBS. CBS was the number two radio broadcasting network behind RCA's NBC network. It was headed by William Paley, who was a younger alter ego of David Sarnoff and a formidable adversary of RCA. "From the earliest days of radio," remembered Paley [1979, p. 213], "when he [Sarnoff] was the 'grand old man' and I was that 'bright young kid' we were friends, confidants, and fierce competitors all at the same time."

CBS was a reluctant participant in the TV industry. It had started TV broadcasting in 1941 and began each broadcast with the following cryptic message:

> Good evening. We hope you will enjoy our programs. The Columbia Broadcasting System, however, is not engaged in the manufacture of television receiving sets and does not want to consider these broadcasts as inducements to purchase television sets at this time. Because of a number of conditions which are not within our control, we cannot foresee how long this television broadcasting schedule will continue. (Lyons [1966, p. 275] and quoted elsewhere)

CBS was not interested in seeing the TV industry begin; it was profiting from radio broadcasting and projected seven lean years during which TV broadcasting would generate sizable losses (Lyons [1966, p. 277]). It had only been doing research on TV since 1936 when it hired Peter Goldmark, a young Hungarian who had recently received his doctorate in physics at the University of Vienna, as its chief TV engineer. It allowed Goldmark to hire four other researchers, and its fledgling research group, which expanded from the fifth to the tenth floors of the CBS building, became known as the five-and-ten department (Goldmark [1973, p. 47]).

Goldmark was ambitious and would later remark how he got caught up in the competition between CBS and RCA. In 1940 he announced to the industry committee deliberating on commercial broadcasting standards that he had invented a new system for color TV that could make monochrome TV obsolete. His system was a throwback to the mechanical era of TV and some of the early mechanical color TV systems. Color TV exploits the fact that any color can be produced by a suitable combination of three primary colors, red, green, and blue. In Goldmark's system, the scene was broken down into red, green, and blue components through the use of red, green, and blue filters mounted on a revolving disc in the TV camera. By inserting similar filters in the receiver and spinning them in synchronization with the filters in the camera, the colors were reproduced.

The use of rotating discs limited the quality of the image that could be produced in the same way that earlier mechanical monochrome systems were limited. Furthermore, each color was scanned and transmitted separately in sequence, which necessitated using the UHF part of the electromagnetic spectrum, which was largely unexplored (monochrome TV used the VHF part of the spectrum). Ultimately what proved to be the most limiting factor about Goldmark's system was that it was incompatible with conventional monochrome receivers based on the FCC-approved standards. Its color signal could not be received by conventional monochrome receivers unless they were equipped with an expensive converter, nor could it receive conventional monochrome signals and display pictures in black and white without such a converter.

In its 1941 decision to authorize commercial TV broadcasting, the FCC took note of CBS's color system but indicated that it needed more field testing. Goldmark resurfaced again after the war with an improved color system and in 1946 asked the FCC to authorize it for immediate commercialization. David Sarnoff misjudged the reception to CBS's proposal. As Kenneth Bilby, Sarnoff's biographer, recounted: "[T]he suggestion of such a technological leapfrogging, which would make years of black and white development work obsolete, bordered on the ridiculous." "Horse-and-buggy stuff," Sarnoff called it, which he communicated to Bill Paley (Bilby [1986, p. 175]).

Color improves the detail perceived by the human eye, and CBS's system worked well in controlled settings that limited the size of the picture and the amount of light in the viewing room. Otherwise, its performance was questionable, and it was still incompatible with monochrome receivers. Sarnoff countered by telling the FCC that in time, say five years or so, RCA would be able to develop an all-electronic color system superior to CBS's that would also be compatible with monochrome receivers

(Bannister [2001, p. 176]). But Sarnoff underestimated the antipathy toward RCA and how it looked for a dominant firm to be appealing for more time in the face of a seemingly superior system. Moreover, few monochrome receivers had yet been sold, so compatibility was not a major issue.

CBS began running color demonstrations at its Madison Avenue headquarters in New York for special clients, including advertisers and leaders from business and government. "I found myself in show business, giving performances at two o'clock and four o'clock," Goldmark wrote in his autobiography. "I must admit I loved it. We handed out questionnaires to collect peoples' [*sic*] reactions and found nothing but enthusiasm" (Goldmark [1973, p. 88]). CBS asked the FCC to give its system a chance in the marketplace. As Bilby [1986, p. 181] observed, "This had the ring of traditional free enterprise about it, and for the first time Sarnoff professed concern. To associates, he described CBS as the industry's succubus, seeking to seduce the public with an outmoded technology. But in the press and in government circles, a groundswell of support for the CBS position began to emerge, and Sarnoff realized he could no longer temporize."

CBS was so sure that its proposal was going to be accepted that it declined an offer for VHF stations in four cities, which would later prove to be a costly decision. The FCC said it needed more time to field-test CBS's system and declined its petition. CBS suspected some kind of foul play, which was reinforced when the chairman of the FCC was hired six months later as a VP at NBC. Besides compatibility, the weak link in CBS's system was the need for UHF transmission. Subsequently, Goldmark figured out how to compress the color signal into the VHF range, even at the expense of the picture quality (Brown [1979, p. 148]). In May 1949, CBS used its modified system to televise for the first time a surgical operation and conducted an impressive demonstration of the system for the American Medical Association at its convention in the summer of 1949.

The new chairman of the FCC, Wayne Coy, was much more favorable to CBS. According to Bilby [1986, p. 183], "From the moment he first witnessed a CBS color demonstration to the commission in Washington, Coy became almost as zealous a supporter of the rotating disc system as the inventor himself. . . . Casting aside all semblance of impartiality, the traditional stance of heads of federal regulatory agencies, Coy began lobbying within the commission and among influential legislators for CBS color." Sarnoff was not surprised when the FCC voted to hold an immediate demonstration of rival color systems, with hearings set to begin in September 1949.

RCA was in a precarious position. If CBS prevailed, it could discourage consumers from buying standard monochrome sets on which it was just beginning to recoup its $50 million investment. In 1947, 179,000 monochrome TV receivers were sold, which increased to 970,000 in 1948 and would rise further to a peak of 7,738,000 in 1955 (Wooster [1986, p. 32], from *Electronic Market Data Book, 1969*, p. 8). RCA initially captured around 40% of the market (see Levy [1981, p. 98]) and also profited on much of the output of its rivals through royalties and sales of picture tubes and other components. Thus, RCA could expect to earn returns from its monochrome innovations on much of the output of the industry if it could fend off CBS. It would also preserve the potential profits that could be earned from color TV. So, like Ford Motor Co. and other dominant firms, it had a much greater incentive to innovate in color TV than any of its rivals.

RCA had only begun its research in earnest on color TV in 1946 and the same year presented an embryonic all-electronic color TV system before the FCC. It kept improving it and presented its new system, which was compatible with existing monochrome TVs, toward the beginning of the FCC hearings in October 1949. RCA knew it was going to have trouble, though, as it lacked a satisfactory color receiver. Its receiver employed three separate picture tubes for each color, which it combined into an image using mirrors. One of its top engineers described the receiver as "a steel-paneled monster six feet tall, six feet deep and thirty-one inches wide . . . accompanied by another cube two feet on a side to provide control signals" (Brown [1979, p. 155]). The quality of its pictures matched its awkwardness. At the October showing of RCA's system, "The monkeys were green, the bananas were blue, and everybody had a good laugh," Sarnoff admitted later. *Variety* (October 12, 1949) declared in a headline, "RCA Lays Off-Color Egg." When asked by the FCC about RCA's color system, Goldmark remarked that he did not think that field tests could fundamentally improve the system and suggested that RCA cease its efforts.

If RCA was going to head off approval of CBS's system, it would have to come up with a workable color receiver before the close of the FCC hearings, which continued into the spring of 1950. If it could do so, it was only a matter of time before it would have a superior system to CBS's, one that was compatible with the skyrocketing number of monochrome receivers Americans were purchasing. Sarnoff initiated a crash program in September 1949 to produce a workable receiver in six months. No expense would be spared. Any manpower in the company that could contribute to the project would be made available. Bonuses in the thousands of dollars would be paid for significant breakthroughs. Daily shifts would be increased to 16 hours, continuing through the weekends (Bilby [1986, p. 185]).

Sarnoff designated Elmer W. Engstrom, then RCA's VP in charge of research, as his "proconsul for color," and Engstrom appointed Dr. Edward W. Herold, one of the top research engineers at RCA, to direct the project. Herold later recounted the start of the project:

> I remember vividly that day in 1949—it was September 19—Elmer Engstrom called me into his office. He told me that the entire RCA case before the FCC rested on our ability to show the feasibility of a single color-picture tube. He didn't know of anyone who had a really workable idea, but it was a task that we couldn't shirk. We had to try, and we had very little time to do it in. Elmer asked me if I could coordinate a major company effort, a crash program so to speak, and show within three months that a color-picture tube was possible. . . . I don't know whether he thought I was too ignorant of the difficulty to object—after all, I wasn't a picture tube expert, and I wasn't even close to the work. In fact, however, I knew the job was just about impossible. (Dreher [1977, pp. 210–211])

The problem was no one knew how to proceed. Nineteen different approaches for developing a color receiver were identified. As Harold Law, who made key contributions to the crash program, commented later, "I must say it wasn't very encouraging. There just didn't seem to be a really workable idea" [1976, p. 753]. The 19 approaches were soon narrowed to five. The two most promising involved something called a shadow mask. Thousands of triplets of red, green, and blue phosphors would be deposited on the face plate of the picture tube. In front of the tube would be the shadow mask containing an equal number of holes corresponding to each triplet of phosphors. Three electron guns corresponding to the red, green, and blue signals coming from the camera would emit beams of electrons at different angles through each hole to reproduce the image. The angles were such that only the beam for the red color could hit a red phosphor, with the same being true for the green and blue beams.

Harold Law had learned of this idea back in 1946, and off and on over the next few years had experimented with how to deposit the phosphors on the face plate of the tube. Herold described Law as skilled as well as tenacious, and he came up with the key invention called the "Lighthouse." Law used light to simulate the electron beams. This permitted the use of photographic and lithographic processes to locate the phosphor dots in the desired positions.

The method worked so well that Law was able to construct a color picture tube of a few square inches that proved feasibility in less than the mandated three months. Soon Law's efforts were "swamped by an avalanche of others helping in many ways with the objective of making a tube with 12-in diagonal picture size" (Law [1976, p. 756]). Many challenges still had to be overcome, but as Herold recounted, "In three more months, a few hundred other people, working 7 days a week, had helped produce a dozen or so tubes with a 12-inch diagonal picture of remarkable quality" [1974, p. 142]. In total, the project consumed 70 man-years of research time condensed into six months at a cost of $2 million (nearly $20 million in 2015 dollars) (Dreher [1977, p. 212]).

Color receivers not much bigger than RCA's monochrome receiver were constructed based on two variants of the shadow mask picture tube, one with three electron guns and a second with just one gun. They were demonstrated to the press and RCA licensees by the end of March 1950 and to the FCC on April 6, 1950. The receiver was still far from satisfactory (Brown [1979, p. 199]), but viewers were dazzled. Herold [1974, p. 142] recounted a typical comment from the April 1, 1950 *TV Digest*. "Tri-color tube has what it takes: RCA shot the works with its tri-color demonstration this week, got full reaction it was looking for . . . not only from . . . FCC . . . and newsmen, but from some 50 patent licensees." The writer continued: "So impressed was just about everybody by [the RCA tube's] remarkable performance, that it looks . . . as if RCA deliberately restrained its pre-demonstration enthusiasm to gain full impact."

The FCC scheduled further comparative tests. RCA now had a color receiver that was compatible with all the monochrome receivers on the market, and it was only a matter of time before it produced a better image than CBS's color system. But that time had not quite arrived, and the FCC was not willing to wait any longer despite pleas from RCA and the rest of the industry.

On September 1, 1950 the FCC issued its first report. Unanimously, it found that the CBS color system was at least as well developed as monochrome TV had been in 1941. It was ready to adopt the CBS system as long as set manufacturers gave their assurance that in the future they would build sets with circuitry to receive color broadcasts based on CBS's system but that were also capable of receiving existing black-and-white TV signals. When these assurances were not forthcoming, the FCC issued a second report on October 10, 1950 adopting the CBS system and authorizing commercial broadcasting in color to begin November 20, 1950. In adopting the CBS color system as the nation's color TV standard, however, the

FCC left in place its black-and-white TV standards. The new color standard said nothing about backward compatibility with the nation's existing black-and-white television system. RCA challenged the FCC's decision all the way up to the Supreme Court but lost.

On June 25, 1951, CBS began one hour per day of color broadcasting in the afternoon (Smith [1970, p. 17]). This was the day the earth stood still in the TV industry—the industry was frozen into a regressive standard. Virtually no one could receive CBS's color broadcasts. CBS also lost its audience and sponsors for the next hour of broadcasting because viewers were slow to switch back to CBS's non-compatible monochrome programs (Brown [1979, p. 214]).

CBS had to make a go of it on its own, which Sarnoff predicted would be a challenge even for an experienced manufacturer. CBS purchased Hytron Radio and Electronics Corporation, the fourth largest manufacturer of tubes, and its wholly owned subsidiary, Air King, one of the top 15 set manufacturers, for $18 million ($162 million in 2015 dollars) in CBS stock. According to the chief engineer at Air King, it proved impractical to produce CBS's receiver (Jacobson [2001]). In fact, CBS never produced more than a token number of receivers and eventually wrote off Hytron's facilities. Sarnoff later said at a staff luncheon, "They [CBS] were seduced by a spurious technology. Mechanical parts and electronics won't mix. They're like oil and water. I warned Bill, but he wouldn't listen" (Bilby [1986, p. 197]).

CBS saved face owing to a government-imposed ban on the manufacture of color TVs during the Korean War (a ban that it or one of its affiliates may have helped engineer). The future of color TV was left to an industry committee set up under the direction of W.R.G. Baker, who had headed the industry monochrome committee whose recommendations were adopted by the FCC when it authorized commercial broadcasting back in 1941. RCA kept experimenting and improving its color system, and along with significant contributions by a few other firms, including ironically Hytron/CBS, RCA's color system was soon superior to CBS's. Even CBS recognized this and endorsed the July 1953 recommendation of the industry committee, which was based largely on RCA's system. The FCC, which was now headed by a new, more balanced chairman, reversed itself and adopted the industry's recommendation, with color broadcasting authorized to begin on January 22, 1954. RCA declared victory and in full-page ads in various newspapers took full credit for the new standards, which infuriated its rivals.

It was estimated that by mid-1953, RCA had spent $21.5 million (more than $188 million in 2015 dollars) on research and development related to color TV. From the standpoint of the return it earned on monochrome TV, this turned out to be well worth the investment. In the period 1949 to 1955, the royalties alone that RCA earned from its monochrome patents were nearly enough to cover its entire investment in monochrome TV. It earned much more from the sale of its own monochrome TVs and also the sale of picture tubes and other components to its rivals (Biting [1963]).

Color TV, however, was another story. No one bought its color TV receivers when they were put on the market in 1954. They were too expensive and their picture quality was limited. RCA's rivals had always resented paying royalties for RCA's patents, and it was not long before they left the color market and began jeering RCA. Zenith, which never paid RCA TV royalties and hounded RCA in court over its patent policies, called the RCA color system "a Rube Goldberg contraption." Ralph Cordiner, head of GE, said that if you have a color TV receiver, "you've almost got to have an engineer living in the house" (Dreher [1977, p. 214], cited many places).

Once again incentives related to size kicked in at RCA. Motivated by the large market it projected for color TV receivers and prospective licensing revenue from its color patents and component sales to its rivals, RCA continued improving its color TV system and reducing the cost and price of its color receiver. Ultimately, consumers became saturated with monochrome TV, and the market for color TV receivers turned out to be enormous.

RCA was estimated to have invested $130 million (more than $1 billion in 2015 dollars) in color TV, including losses from NBC color broadcasts and subsidized receiver sales, before it earned any return from color TV. But by all accounts its profits on color TV generated a handsome return on this investment as well. In just the 1960s, U.S. sales of color TV receivers were $8.6 billion ($55–65 billion in 2015 dollars), and RCA's market share was around 40%. It also earned substantial profits on the sale of color picture tubes and other components to its rivals.

Yet one component of RCA's anticipated profits never materialized— royalties from its rivals on its color TV patents. The Justice Department had long been after RCA. As far back as 1930 it initiated an antitrust suit that led to RCA becoming an independent company. In 1954 it lodged a new antitrust suit against RCA, which it followed up with another suit in 1958 involving criminal charges. To settle these suits, RCA agreed to make all of its color TV patents available to its domestic rivals free of charge. This turned out to be the beginning of the end for RCA and the rest of the U.S. industry, a story that will be picked up again in chapter 6.

INTEL AND THE MICROPROCESSOR: THE INVENTION THAT NEVER WAS

In the summer of 1990, the U.S. Patent and Trademark Office issued patent number 4,942,516 to Gilbert Hyatt for a single-chip microprocessor. That was 19 years after the first microprocessor was marketed by Intel and billions of microprocessors had been purchased and incorporated into every kind of device imaginable.

How could a patent be issued in 1990 on a device that was nearly 20 years old with such a large market, and to an obscure inventor who had apparently played no role in its development? *Byte Magazine* [1991] crystallized the question in an article in January 1991 entitled, "Micro, Micro: Who Made the Micro?" Hyatt was issued his patent for work done in 1968, but thanks to a protracted battle over his patent he was in store for quite a payday. At a customary royalty rate of 3% of sales, in just 1989 alone Hyatt would have been due royalties of $210 million.

The most remarkable aspect of the patent ruling was that Hyatt outlined his ideas on a single-chip central processing unit (CPU) but never reduced them to practice or showed they could be reduced to practice based on the technology of the day. Indeed, the idea of a "computer on a chip," as it was often called, had long been discussed and was viewed as inevitable. Stanley Mazor, who worked at Intel on the first chips later given the name "microprocessor," noted that at the dawn of the integrated circuit era in 1962, the CPU of a minicomputer was composed of about 16,000 transistors (Mazor [2009]). Since then, advances in semiconductor technology had caused the number of transistors on an integrated circuit or "chip" to double every year. At that pace, the number of transistors on a chip after 14 years would be $2^{14} = 16,384$, making it possible to put the entire CPU of a minicomputer on a chip. Thus, it was only a matter of time—until 1976 according to Mazor's calculations—before a microprocessor was developed. Outlining ideas about a microprocessor simply did not cut it—talk was cheap. Later Hyatt's patent would be overturned on these grounds.

According to Mazor's reasoning, Intel was actually five years ahead of schedule when it announced its first microprocessor in 1971. The irony is that Intel never set out to invent the microprocessor nor did it see itself as inventing anything worthy of a patent (Schaller [2004, p. 302], Berlin [2005, p. 183]). Its first two microprocessors (they were not called that back then) resulted from orders initiated by two customers, who supplied some of the core ideas that guided Intel's efforts. Indeed, Intel would not have owned the rights to either device had it not fumbled both orders. One customer asked for a big price concession, and the other declined to pay anything, depriving Intel of the raison d'être for the contracts—quick cash. Intel's booby prize was that it ended up owning all the intellectual property on the jobs. Such was the invention of the microprocessor at Intel.

While Intel did not initiate the idea for the microprocessor, it was certainly ingenious in how it went about executing its initial customers' orders. At the time, no one really knew how to make a CPU on a single chip and sell it as such, including Hyatt. In retrospect one can look back and see devices that preceded Intel's that might deserve the moniker of a microprocessor. However, either they were not really confined to a single chip or were not sold as such. Right from its conception, Intel was focused on producing semiconductor devices with large potential markets, recognizing the need for a large output over which to amortize R&D costs (Moore [1994, p. 27]). This shaped how Intel approached the customer orders that led to the microprocessor.

Once it realized what it had, though, Intel escalated its investments in R&D as its market grew. A little luck was required along the way in the form of IBM and its famous personal computer. But Intel capitalized on its luck, ratcheting up its investment in R&D until all its competitors fell by the wayside. Its prize turned out to be what many consider the most important innovation of the twentieth century. Like mass production and all-electronic color television, the microprocessor was not the result of a grand vision but grew out of initiatives undertaken by employees. Once the microprocessor emerged, though, Intel exploited high-tech economics to become the dominant microprocessor producer. It prospered enormously, but in the end, the true beneficiary has been society at large, which has used the microprocessor to control countless applications and drive the world's information systems.

The story of the microprocessor began with a senior manager at Sharp Corporation in Japan, Tadashi Sasaki, and a small Japanese calculator company, Busicom (see Aspray [1997] for the full story). Robert Noyce visited Sasaki in Japan in 1968 to drum up business for the newly formed Intel. Noyce was an icon in the semiconductor industry who Sasaki admired. He was a co-founder and past general manager of Fairchild Semiconductor, the first of the great Silicon Valley semiconductor firms, and was one of the co-inventors (with Jack Kilby of Texas Instruments) of the integrated circuit. He had left Fairchild in frustration along with Gordon Moore, the head of R&D at Fairchild and himself a leading light in the industry, to form Intel in 1968. Noyce was so respected that in his high-tech exposé, *Inside Intel*, Tim Jackson [1997, p. 18] quipped that the two most important words of [Intel's] business plan were *Robert Noyce*.

Sasaki had become intrigued with an idea suggested by one of his employees for a calculator on a chip. He wanted to steer some business Intel's way but was thwarted by an exclusive agreement Sharp had with another U.S. semiconductor producer. Instead, he secretly lent 40 million yen to Busicom, which was headed by a graduate of his university department (university ties are strong in Japan), to develop a calculator on a chip with the proviso that it would secure its chips from Intel.

Intel's initial success came in 1970 with semiconductor memories, which was the first product Intel worked on after its formation. Although Busicom's business did not centrally involve memories, Intel welcomed the business, in part to ease its cash-flow problems. In June 1969 Busicom sent three engineers to work out a contract with Intel to produce a set of 12 chips to power a new line of high-performance programmable calculators. The Japanese team had worked out 80% to 90% of the logic schematics for their chip sets and anticipated that it would not take Intel long to produce them (Aspray [1997, pp. 8–9]). Their plan was to stay in California and work with Intel on the order. Marcian E. "Ted" Hoff, Jr. was assigned to be their liaison at Intel.

Hoff was hired from Stanford, where he was a post doc working on adaptive systems (neural networks), to be manager of Intel's Application Research Department. Hoff had no design responsibilities on the project, which was not expected to take up much of his time. "[B]ut soon I was sticking my nose where it didn't belong," recalled Hoff. "Normally you wouldn't do that, but [Intel] was a start-up company, and a lot of us had hopes for its financial success, so I didn't want to let major effort go into something disastrous" (Berlin [2005, p. 185]).

Hoff thought the Busicom design was too complicated and expensive to implement and would not have a sufficient market to justify its cost. Drawing an analogy to DEC's PDP-8, a popular minicomputer at the time, he thought it preferable to keep the instructions to run the calculator simple, offload them as much as possible to memory chips, and have a single processing chip run the instructions to perform all the functions of the calculator (Aspray [1997, p. 9], Berlin [2005, p. 185]). Not only could the processor act like a calculator, but it could be programmed to perform other applications as well.

The Japanese team, whose primary spokesman was its junior member, Masatoshi Shima, was not crazy about Hoff's proposal (Aspray [1997, pp. 8–9]). They felt it suffered from a number of problems, including not understanding how calculators really functioned. Hoff went to Noyce with his ideas. Noyce asked question after question using his characteristic Socratic approach that had worked so well in the laboratory. Although Hoff did not report to Noyce and Intel could ill afford a technical employee to get distracted by something the customer did not want, Noyce told Hoff to go ahead and develop his ideas in his spare time (Berlin [2005, pp. 185–186]).

With Stanley Mazor aiding him, in two weeks Hoff completed a block drawing of the architecture for three chips, two of which were memory chips and the third was the key processor that would control the calculator (Berlin [2005, p. 187]). In the meantime, Shima stayed at Intel to work on improving and completing his ideas (Aspray [1997, p. 10]). In October, Busicom management visited Intel and considered Hoff's and Shima's proposals. To Hoff's surprise, they chose his. Shima stayed on to work with Mazor on what he perceived as shortcomings in Hoff's design, and in December he returned to Japan. Then a second customer entered the picture, Computer Terminal Corporation (CTC).

CTC was already a customer of Intel (Schaller [2004, p. 324]) and wanted to shrink the number of logic chips it was using in its intelligent terminals. Hoff was redeployed to the CTC project, which made sense as he was not skilled in chip layout and fabrication, the steps that remained on the Busicom project (Aspray [1997, p. 10]). CTC had already worked out a detailed set of instructions for its chips and needed Intel to design and produce them. Hoff saw the potential to use one processor chip to accommodate CTC's needs, which not only could make the project economical but also produce a chip with broader potential, similar to his proposal for Busicom (Faggin [1992]). A contract was soon agreed to with CTC to develop Hoff's ideas.

While Hoff was working on the CTC project, the design of the chips for Busicom was handed off to Les Vadasz. He headed Intel's design team for the MOS (metal oxide on silicon) semiconductors that were slated to be used on the Busicom project. However, Vadasz and his team were preoccupied with Intel's main business, memory chips, and had little time to work on the Busicom project (Aspray [1997, p. 10]). Shima returned to Intel in April 1970 and was furious when he found out how little progress had been made. Intel had just hired Federico Faggin from Fairchild to work on the project. He was the object of Shima's wrath until Shima realized Faggin had only been on the job for a week (Aspray [1997, p. 10]).

Faggin was an expert on the silicon-gate technology that Intel was using on its MOS devices and that would prove to be the foundation of Intel's overall success (Bassett [2002, p. 181]). Previously, MOS transistors used metal, mainly aluminum, as their gate electrodes (a "gate" controls the flow of current in the transistor). Silicon-gate MOS was a process innovation that had the potential to allow more transistors to be packed onto a chip. Fairchild began working on it in late 1967. Sustained work began in February 1968 after the arrival of Faggin from Fairchild's Italian affiliate for what was anticipated to be a six-month stay. By the time Moore and Noyce left Fairchild to form Intel in 1968, Faggin had developed silicon-gate technology to the point where the remaining challenges to make it manufacturable could be evaluated.

Intel picked up where Fairchild left off, hiring many of the key employees from Fairchild (Bassett [2002, pp. 177–180]). Faggin came later after his visa status was sorted out. He turned out to be the perfect person for the Busicom project. Not only was more work still to be done on the architecture and logic design devised by Hoff and Mazor, but turning their plans into silicon required a number of innovations in circuit design and layout (Faggin [1992], Bassett [2002, p. 269]). Faggin was not only up to the task, but worked tirelessly, 12 to 16 hours a day, for nine months to complete the Busicom project. Shima stayed at Intel from April to November 1970 and worked with Faggin and Mazor, who had been assigned to help Faggin. Shima worked out a logic schematic that he felt was instrumental in the layout of the chips and also worked on logic simulation and a test program (Aspray [1997, p. 11]).

By March 1971 full chip sets were sent to Busicom for testing. By this point, competition had heated up in the calculator industry. Prices had fallen to the point where the overdue contract with Intel was wildly overpriced. Both Faggin and Hoff lobbied Intel to make price concessions to secure rights to the chip set, which otherwise would have been Busicom's property. An agreement was reached in two steps whereby Intel gave up $60,000 of the original $100,000 advance from Busicom in exchange for all rights to the chip set (Jackson [1997, p. 72]). Later Intel named the microprocessor chip the 4004; the number 4 reflected the 4-bit words the chip processed (a bit is short for Binary digIT and takes on a value of either 0 or 1). In April, Busicom began producing calculators using the new chip set.

Like the 4004 (and supporting chips), the CTC order was interrupted by other, pressing priorities, especially memories. At one point it appeared it would be finished before the 4004. However, Hal Feeney, who had been hired away from General Instruments to work on the project, was reassigned to work on a new memory product. Faggin was assigned to both projects, but was devoting most of his attention to the 4004. Hoff and Mazor worked briefly on the CTC project and then Feeley returned as the chip's primary developer under Faggin's direction (Schaller [2004, p. 320]). They worked together to translate what Faggin had learned on the 4004 to the new chip (Faggin [1992]).

According to CTC, in July 1971 Intel finally delivered its chip, later named the 8008 (2 x 4004) to reflect the use of 8-bit words needed to service CTC's terminals. The chip worked but was inferior to the approach CTC was using on its terminals. CTC declined to pay Intel, saying the chip was "a year late and a dollar short" (Schaller [2004, p. 329]). However, Seiko, the Japanese watchmaker, was interested in the chip and Intel let CTC out of the deal (originally for $100,000) in exchange for full rights to the chip (Malone [1995, p. 13]).

Intel continued its work on the 8008 and eventually put it on the market in April 1972 (Schaller [2004, p. 329]), at which point Intel had two processors with the potential to be used in a wide range of applications. But exactly what applications? Computers were one possibility, but back then only 20,000 or so computers were being produced. Even if Intel could capture 10% of this market it would not generate that much revenue (Malone [1995, p. 15]). In part it would be up to Intel to dream up applications and sell them to customers.

Before it marketed either the 4004 or 8008, Intel debated internally whether it would be worth the effort to develop applications for its new chips. Noyce was a big booster for the microprocessor. According to everyone interviewed by Leslie Berlin, Noyce's biographer:

> In the midst of all this confusion and uncertainty, one fact emerges with surprising clarity—Bob Noyce was absolutely essential to the microprocessor's development and success at Intel. He encouraged its development; he lobbied for its introduction; he dreamed of its future importance; he promoted it tirelessly within the company and to customers. (Berlin [2005, p. 183])

Ultimately the go-ahead was given by Arthur Rock, the chairman of the board who had arranged the financing for Intel (and before that Fairchild) and was a leader in the new venture capital industry that had sprung up in Silicon Valley (Noyce and Hoff [1981, p. 13], Aspray [1997, p. 12]).

In the summer of 1971, Hoff and Mazor were sent out on the road in the United States to give technical seminars on the 4004 and 8008. Faggin did the same in Europe (Faggin [1992]). On November 15, 1971, a month after its successful IPO, Intel announced its 4004 chip set with a bold ad: "A new era of integrated electronics—a micro-programmable computer on a chip!" More than 5,000 people wrote to the address at the bottom of the ad asking for more information (Berlin [2005, p. 203]).

Faggin heard a fair amount of criticism—some valid—about the architecture and performance of the microprocessors in the course of his travels (Faggin [1992]). In early 1972 he started pitching ideas to management for a new, improved version of the 8008, employing the latest developments in the industry (Bassett [2002, pp. 275–276]). He was put off until the market for the new microprocessors could be gauged and then received the go-ahead that summer. Shima was hired by Intel to work with Faggin. Hoff and Mazor also worked on the new chip (Malone [1995, p. 18], Jackson [1997, p. 109]), which was christened the 8080 when it was brought out in April 1974. "The 8080 really created the microprocessor market," Faggin said. "The 4004 and 8008 suggested it, but the 8080 made it real" (Faggin [1992]).

The extraordinary nature of the 8080 was quickly recognized by engineers. It was designed into hundreds of products in just its first year (Malone [1995, p. 19]). Microprocessors began to be used in scientific instruments, appliances, cars, and a host of other devices, reflecting that it was often more efficient to write software to move electrons than to design and fabricate mechanical parts to do the same tasks (Bylinsky [1975]). Subsequently Intel invested a great deal of effort to develop the market for microprocessors. It commissioned software to program its devices, developed hardware to simulate applications and debug programs, hired application specialists and technical salesmen to promote its products, and tirelessly ran seminars on the microprocessor throughout the world.

Intel had the head start it craved in a new market. In Gordon Moore's view, the first company in the market always finds the bull's-eye—"it shoots at a blank wall, finds the bullet hole, and then paints the target around it" (Berlin [2005, p. 172]). In this case, the bull's-eye turned out to be gigantic once microprocessors were used to create personal computers, which began in the latter part of the 1970s.

Intel had a head start, but it was not long before competitors caught on to the size of the new market. Its two most formidable challengers were Motorola, which had long been a leader of the semiconductor industry, and Zilog, which was formed in 1974 by Faggin and Shima, after Faggin became disenchanted with his treatment at Intel (Jackson [1997, pp. 115–120]). Each developed a popular 8-bit microprocessor to compete with the 8080. All the firms soon set their sights on the next generation of microprocessors, which would crunch 16-bit words, improving their performance.

It would be the 16-bit processors that would really stimulate the personal computer market. At first, Intel stumbled, taking much too long to develop a 16-bit processor that ultimately was stillborn (Malone [1995, p. 153]). Realizing that it was in danger, in 1978 Intel came out with a stop-gap 16-bit processor, the 8086. To coax customers into the 16-bit world, it also developed a cheaper variant of the 8086, dubbed the 8088, that externally used 8-bit words but internally processed 16-bit words for greater speed (Jackson [1997, p. 203]).

In 1979 Motorola came out with a 16-bit processor, the 68000, that was widely acknowledged to be superior to the 8086 (Malone [1995, p. 147]). But Intel mounted a legendary marketing campaign known as Operation Crush to publicize its other advantages, including the full suite of microprocessor and complementary products it had developed, its excellent customer service and support, and a futures catalog to indicate what could be expected from Intel in the near term. The campaign was enormously successful as Intel racked up one design win after another, in part reflecting some of the difficulties customers were having in using Motorola's 68000 microprocessor (Jackson [1997, pp. 194–196]). Meanwhile Zilog also developed a 16-bit processor but was much too small to compete with all the complementary products and services supplied by Intel; soon it faded (Malone [1995, p. 161]).

The coup de grace of Operation Crush came when IBM chose the 8088 for its new personal computer in 1981, impressed by Intel's commitment to its 8086 microprocessor line and its heavy investment in support chips (Malone [1995, pp. 159–160]). The rest is history. The market for the IBM PC exploded. It was not long before other personal computer makers joined in with IBM clones that also used Intel's microprocessors. Intel ramped up its R&D in microprocessors, and just one year after IBM chose the 8088, Intel came out with four new microprocessors (Jackson [1997, p. 221]). Intel never looked back. It committed to devoting at least 10% of its sales to R&D, which is high even by high-tech standards (Malone [1995, p. 171]). It developed a succession of microprocessors under the x86 designation, including the 80186, 80286, 80386, and 80486, all of which were descendants of the 8080. As its sales grew along with the personal computer market, Intel's R&D expenditures grew in tandem, and the firm began to pull away from the pack (Jackson [1997, p. 335]).

As of 1987, Intel was the market leader in microprocessors and related devices (Integrated Circuit Engineering [1988]). Its share of the personal computer market was especially large, reaching 85% in 1993 (Malone 1995, p. 231]). *IC Insights* (2000) estimated that in 1999, Intel accounted for 78% of the sales of all 32- and 64-bit microprocessors (the ones primarily used in computers), which in turn accounted for 98% of all microprocessor sales (and 77% of all units shipped).

Intel's main competition has been at the high end of the computer market from so-called RISC (Reduced Instruction Set Computer) processors and in more recent years at the low end of the PC market from cheap processors. But its R&D is so large that it has developed processors to service all the different niches. Perhaps the most potent challenge to Intel's dominance has come from copycats. In the semiconductor industry copycats are called second sources, reflecting the fact that customers commonly require vendors to come up with a second source for their products to make sure they are not fleeced once they become wedded to one firm's products. IBM asked Intel for a second source for the 8086, and Intel chose AMD, another spinoff from Fairchild (Jackson [1997, p. 207]). Intel revealed its secrets to AMD, which naturally kept down the prices it could charge for its microprocessors. Later it tried to rein in AMD, which set off a firestorm of legal battles lasting many years.

Like Ford and RCA, Intel has become a powerhouse, employing over 80,000 people worldwide by 2000 (Intel annual report 2000, p. 17). Except for a few recessionary and industry down years, its profits have regularly provided its shareholders with a 25% or greater return on equity (Intel annual reports). Just as Ford's initial investors got wealthy from their stock holdings, Intel was the source of many millionaires. An investment of $2,350 in 100 shares of Intel at its founding in 1968 was worth $438,554 in 1992 ([Malone 1995, p. 197]) and continued climbing subsequently.

The real beneficiary of the microprocessor, though, has been society at large. Apart from Gilbert Hyatt's attempt to get a patent on the microprocessor, nothing has stopped competitors from trying to copy Intel, which has kept down prices and insured that the benefits of innovation were passed on to consumers. Michael Malone, in his book, *The Micro-*

processor: A Biography [1995, p. 252], compared the development of the microprocessor with the Manhattan Project:

> The Manhattan Project is often pointed to as the quintessential example in our century of using a combination of genius and teamwork to overcome a seemingly impossible task. But the hundreds of scientists and engineers of the microprocessor industry, as well as their thousands of counterparts in the semiconductor equipment business, have performed a comparable task—and then repeated it a half dozen times.

Perhaps the last word should be left to Frederico Faggin, who along with Ted Hoff is today recognized as one of the fathers of the microprocessor: "The microprocessor is one of the most empowering technologies that mankind has ever produced, and it belongs to mankind; thus it is mankind's progress that should be celebrated. The microprocessor is a remarkable creation of the human spirit" (Malone [1995, p. 251]).

•   •   •

In each of the case studies, the featured innovator was an early entrant—RCA and Intel were the pioneers of their products and Ford Motor Co. was among the first quarter of the firms that entered the automobile industry. This is consistent with my theory of shakeouts, which predicts that the leaders of new industries will disproportionately come from the ranks of the earliest entrants and will achieve their leading position through innovation. If the theory provides a useful way to understand shakeouts, then these predictions should hold generally for all the leaders of shakeout industries, not just the very top firm. In this section, this prediction is put to the test for the four extreme shakeout products: autos, tires, TV receivers, and penicillin.

First, the leaders of each industry have to be identified. What constitutes a leader of an industry? In my theory, leaders are firms that grow large and stay in the industry longer than their rivals. This implies two criteria to be deemed a leader—a firm must produce for some minimum number of years and, at some point after the industry has been established, it must have achieved a substantial market share. This is operationalized by requiring leaders to have produced in an industry for at least 30 years and to have been among the largest firms in the industry at some point after the industry was ten years old. For each of the four shakeout products, the data collected for each firm reflect how long it produced, so the former criterion could be readily implemented. The latter criterion requires periodic information about the leading producers, which is more difficult to come by, but in one way or another could be implemented for each of the four shakeout products.*

To assess whether the leading firms in each industry disproportionately came from the ranks of the earliest entrants, entrants in the four industries were divided into cohorts of roughly equal size according to when they entered. More firms entered in autos (725) and tires (603) than TV receivers (177) and penicillin (59). Accordingly, four entry cohorts were distinguished in autos and tires, three in TV receivers, and two in penicillin. For each cohort, table 2.2 reports the percentage of entrants that produced for at least 30 years and at some point after their industry was ten years old were among the largest firms in the industry.

The patterns are striking. Apart from the ordering of the second and third entry cohorts in automobiles, the later the entry cohort, the lower the percentage of firms that became leaders. Indeed, in all four products the percentage of entrants that became leaders is more than twice as high in the first entry cohort than in all the others. Furthermore, no firm that entered in the last entry cohort ever became a leader in any of the industries.

The patterns are even more pronounced among the firms that dominated each industry. In automobiles, Ford, General Motors, and Chrysler were the dominant producers. Ford entered in 1903. As noted earlier, both General Motors and Chrysler emerged out of preexisting firms and were treated as part of a lineage that predated their formation. General Motors was a merger of many constituents, the largest and most important of which was Buick, which entered in 1903. As such, Buick/General Motors was also dated as entering in 1903. Chrysler emerged in 1925

---

*The sources used to identify periodically the largest firms were: Bailey [1971] for autos; Buenstorf and Klepper's [2009] list of leading tire firms circa 1922 and three other firms, Armstrong, Lee, and Norwalk, that were successful later tire firms, as reflected in French [1991]; the lists of periodic leaders in TV receivers in Datta [1971] and Levy [1981]; and the periodic leading penicillin producers listed in FTC [1958] and Schwartzman [1976]. The leading firms by industry, with each firm's entry date in parentheses, are: autos—Packard (1900), H.H. Franklin (1901), Studebaker (1902), Jeffery/Nash (1902), Buick/GM (1903), Ford (1903), Standard Wheel/Willys (1903), Reo (1904), Maxwell-Briscoe/Chrysler (1904), Hudson (1909), Hupp (1909), and Paige-Detroit (1909); tires—Fisk (1901), Goodrich (1901), Pennsylvania (1901), U.S. Rubber (1901), Buckeye Rubber/Kelly-Springfield (1902), Goodyear (1902), Firestone (1906), Dayton Rubber (1911), Lee (1911), Mansfield Tire & Rubber (1913), Mohawk (1913), Pharis (1913), Giant/Cooper (1916), General (1916), Norwalk (1916), Armstrong (1917), Gates (1918), Dunlop (1920), and Seiberling (1922); TV receivers—RCA (1946), Admiral (1947), GE (1947), Zenith (1948), and Colonial/Sylvania (1949); and penicillin—Abbott (1943), Bristol (1943), Lilly (1943), Merck (1943), Pfizer (1943), Squibb (1943), and Wyeth/American Home Products (1943).

TABLE 2.2:
Percentage of Leading Firms by Entry Cohort

Automobiles

1895–1903	1904–1907	1908–1912	1913–1966
3.7%	1.1%	1.6%	0.0%

Tires

1901–1913	1915–1919	1920–1922	1923–1980
7.6%	3.1%	1.5%	0.0%

TV Receivers

1946–1948	1949–1950	1951–1989
5.3%	2.0%	0.0%

Penicillin

1944–1947	1948–1989
25.0%	0.0%

from the reorganization of Maxwell Motors, which itself was a reorganization of Maxwell-Briscoe, one of the early leaders of the industry that entered in 1904 (in the second cohort). As such, Maxell-Briscoe/Maxwell/Chrysler was dated as entering in 1904. The leaders of the other industries were more straightforward. In tires, Goodrich, Goodyear, U.S. Rubber, and Firestone were the dominant producers. All entered by 1906 in the first entry cohort. The top three TV receiver firms were RCA, Zenith, and GE. All entered by 1948 in the first cohort, as did all the other leading TV receiver producers except one, Sylvania (that entered in 1949 in the second cohort). Last, in penicillin every firm that made it into the ranks of the leaders at some point entered in the first cohort during the wartime penicillin program.

Did the leading firms also dominate innovation in each of the four extreme shakeout industries as my theory of shakeouts predicts? Evaluating this prediction requires a way of measuring each firm's contribution to innovation in its industry. A laborious but straightforward way of doing this is through patents. The U.S. Patent and Trademark Office (USPTO) maintains records of every patent ever issued. Patents are issued to inventors and not firms, but inventors who work for firms typically assign their patents to their employers when they are issued, which is recorded in the USPTO's database. For each product, the USPTO's records were used to compile a list of relevant patents assigned to each producer of the product. The total number of these patents was used as the measure of the firm's contribution to innovation in its product line.

As is widely recognized, counting patents is a crude way to measure innovation, but it has the virtue of being objective. Many innovations are not patented, either because they are not inherently patentable (this is particularly true of innovations improving a firm's production process) or because patenting would reveal too much and facilitate inventing around, without infringing, the patent. Patents can also differ greatly in value. More practically, the USPTO classifies patents into technological classes, and these classes correspond imperfectly to products. This can make it challenging to restrict a firm's patents to a particular product category. No doubt all these limitations are serious, but it turns out that the patterns are so extreme that it seems unlikely that patent counts are seriously wanting as a measure of innovation for our purposes.

Table 2.3 reports the number of patents assigned to the top five patenters and to all firms in each of the four products for 30-year periods spanning each product's formative era, including the early part of its shakeout.* Firms that were leaders of their industries are designated by asterisks. The

*The firm patent counts were based on lists of patents assigned to each of the producers of the four products. These lists were laboriously assembled as follows. For tires, the monthly trade journal *India Rubber World* listed patents in tires and rubber issued in the prior month, the inventors of the patents, and their assignees. All of the monthly patents from 1901 to 1930 whose main USPTO patent class was 152, Resilient Tires and Wheels, were used to compile a list of tire patents assigned to each tire producer. For automobiles, the list of patents assigned to each producer was based on *Google Patents*, which scanned the front pages of all patents issued by the USPTO. The patents were searched by firm assignee and date of application. For each automobile producer, a list of patents applied for in the period 1901–1930 and assigned to it was compiled. Some of the firms produced other products before autos (they and their prior products were identified using sources discussed in the next chapter), and patents related to these prior products were excluded when formulating the counts of patents assigned to each auto producer. Unlike autos, the leading TV receiver and penicillin patenting firms were diversified firms that operated in many product areas and so were assigned many patents other than in TV receivers and penicillin respectively. To restrict their patent counts to the desired product, only patents in appropriate classes were considered. For TV receiver producers, only patents whose main USPTO class was 348, Televisions, were considered. Among these patents, a list was compiled for each TV receiver producer of the patents applied for in the period 1946–1975 and assigned to it. For penicillin, patents whose main class was either: 435, Chemistry: Molecular Biology and Microbiology; 514, Drug, Bio-affecting and Body Treating Compositions; or 540, Organic Compounds, were considered. Within each main class the search was further restricted to sub-classes pertinent to penicillin, which included subclass 43 in main class 435, subclasses 190–199 in main class 514, and subclasses 300–349 in main class 540. Within these areas, a list was compiled for each penicillin producer of the patents applied for in the period 1946–1975 and assigned to it.

TABLE 2.3:
Number of Assigned Patents to Top Five Patenting Firms in Automobiles, Tires,
TV Receivers, and Penicillin

Automobiles, 1901–1930	Tires, 1901–1930	TV Receivers, 1946–1975	Penicillin, 1946–1975
General Motors* (783)	Goodrich* (457)	RCA* (949)	Wyeth* (97)
Packard* (743)	Fisk* (404)	GE* (224)	Bristol* (95)
Chrysler* (196)	Goodyear* (384)	Zenith* (186)	Pfizer* (52)
Willys-Overland* (187)	Firestone* (304)	Motorola (185)	Lilly* (49)
Studebaker* (115)	U.S. Rubber* (214)	Philco (127)	Squibb* (42)
All firms (2903)	All firms (2264)	All firms (2116)	All firms (462)
% top five: 70%	% top five: 78%	% top five: 79%	% top five: 73%

*Industry leader.

patterns are quite similar in the four products despite large differences in the number of firms that ever produced them. The top five patenters accounted for between 70% and 79% of all the patents assigned to producers of each product. Among the 20 collective top patenters, all but two were leading firms, and these two were leading TV receiver producers that exited just short of the 30 years required to be a leader (only two other TV receiver firms qualified as leaders, and they were among the next five highest patenters). Including the next five highest patenters in each product, the top ten patenters accounted for between 83% and 93% of the patents assigned to producers of each product. The vast majority of the rest of the firms either did not patent at all or were assigned very few patents over their lifetimes.

It is hard to escape the conclusion that in each of the four products becoming a leader involved entering early, growing big, and investing heavily in innovation, as my theory predicts. This hardly proves the theory; indeed, nothing can prove a theory, but it lends support to the theory's main ideas. It also does not mean that other theories don't have something to contribute to our understanding of shakeouts. For example, in automobiles, scale economies in production have always been prominent and surely played a role in the industry's prolonged shakeout (Katz [1977]). But between the case studies and the patterns reported above, it appears that the imperatives of innovation profoundly influenced the evolution of the four products.

Lasers and semiconductors were also innovative industries. Yet it took 35 years for the laser industry to experience a shakeout, and after 38 years the semiconductor industry still had not experienced a shakeout. Why were these industries different if indeed shakeouts are the result of a self-reinforcing process involving innovation?

This is quite challenging to answer. It is often far more difficult to explain the absence of a phenomenon than the phenomenon itself. Here I advance a novel theory to try to explain what made these two industries different. The laser industry did ultimately undergo a shakeout, which provides an opportunity to probe the theory.

The data sources used to compile the lists of laser and semiconductor producers provide a clue about what may have made these products different. Rather than report a single list of producers, both data sources separately listed the producers of many different variants of its product. For example, many different types of materials have been used to generate laser light, including gases, solid-state crystals, semiconductors, and chemical dyes. These lasers operate on different technological principles and generate different wavelengths of light, which dictates what they can be used for. Consequently, they tend to define separate market segments, and the data source reports the producers of each type of laser separately—in later years many types of lasers are distinguished. Similarly, the semiconductor data source separately reported producers of different types of transistors and a myriad of different types of integrated circuits.

Over time, more types of lasers and semiconductors were distinguished in the data sources, reflecting that many new variants of each product with its own market were developed. If the capabilities required to compete in each market segment were different, the introduction of new product variants could provide continued opportunities for new firms to enter, fueling a prolonged rise in the number of producers.

If this is what drove the rise in the number of laser producers for the first 35 years of the industry, something had to change in terms of market segmentation for the industry subsequently to go through a shakeout. Indeed, an important technological development occurred in the late 1980s that appears to have fundamentally altered the segmentation of the industry. Materials in lasers must be stimulated to a higher energy state in order to lase. Lasers based on solid-state crystals, for example, can only be stimulated by another light source. Historically this source was a flash or arc lamp of the kind used in photography, but such lamps generate many wavelengths of light, most of which do not stimulate solid-state crystals. This limited the efficiency of solid-state lasers and the market for them. It was always known, however, that in principle solid-state lasers could be more efficiently stimulated by light from semiconductor lasers, but only with advances made at Stanford in the 1980s was this principle turned into reality. This innovation of diode-pumped solid-state (DPSS) lasers opened up a rich vein of further innovations in solid-state lasers that generated increased demand for them.

At first, the Stanford innovation created opportunities for new firms to enter the solid-state segment, but then the solid-state segment experienced its own, mini-shakeout (Bhaskarabhatla and Klepper [2014]). This can be seen in the top panel of figure 2.8, which presents the annual number of producers and output (since 1985) of all types of solid-state lasers. Since 1997 the number of solid-state producers (the black line) has been steadily declining even though the output of solid-state lasers (the gray line) has been increasing sharply. One explanation for this pattern is that the opportunities to improve solid-state lasers and the enlarged market for them encouraged solid-state producers to invest in innovation, which ultimately fueled a shakeout among solid-state producers akin to the shakeouts in autos, tires, TV receivers, and penicillin.

The use of semiconductor lasers to stimulate solid-state lasers had another effect on segmentation in the laser industry. It has always been possible to use optical devices to alter the wavelength of light produced by a laser. But this was not generally cost effective until the advent of solid-state lasers stimulated by semiconductor lasers. By altering the wavelengths of these lasers, solid-state lasers could be used in applications previously serviced by gas and chemical-dye lasers. Consequently, producers of these types of lasers began to exit the industry, as can also be seen from figure 2.8. Beginning with the second panel, the annual number of producers and output (since 1985) are presented for chemical-dye and the main types of gas lasers. Apart from carbon dioxide (CO_2) lasers in the bottom panel, the number of producers and the output of each of these laser types fell in tandem in recent years as solid-state producers encroached on the markets for these lasers. The market for helium-neon gas lasers was also adversely affected by the development of new semiconductor lasers that generated visible red light, which previously was the exclusive domain of helium-neon lasers. Coupled with the shakeout in the solid-state laser sub-market, these developments contributed to a shakeout in the overall laser industry.

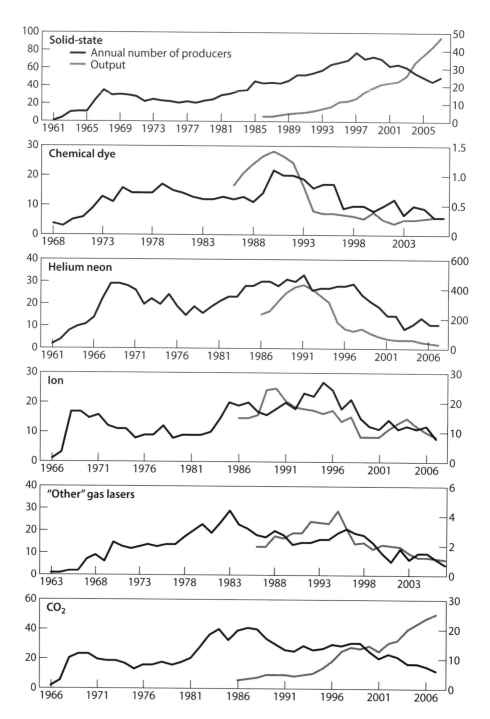

Figure 2.8: Annual Number of Producers (black line) and Output (gray line in thousands) of Solid-State Lasers (top) followed by Chemical Dye, Helium Neon, Ion, "Other" Gas Lasers, and CO$_2$.

There is a useful lesson here for how innovative industries evolve. Expressed succinctly, segmentation is the enemy of shakeouts. As long as an industry is segmented, firms in different segments can coexist. Even if some segments experience shakeouts, if innovation is rich enough to keep creating new segments then an innovative industry need not experience a shakeout. But if developments occur that cause producers in different segments to compete, a shakeout can ensue. Alternatively, if an industry is never very segmented, then competition will be more intense from the outset and a shakeout will occur sooner.

This kind of reasoning can help explain differences in the timing of the shakeouts in autos, tires, TVs, and penicillin. Both TVs and penicillin were not very segmented when they began, so their shakeouts started quickly. Autos and tires were not as segmented as lasers and semiconductors, but initially did have some distinct segments. In autos, different kinds of cars serviced rural and urban consumers until the Model T was introduced in 1908. Once these two broad sub-markets were fused, competition intensified and the advantages of size in innovation took over, causing the number of firms to start declining in 1909. In the tire industry in the 1910s, two different types of tires competed. The traditional tire used cotton fabric meshed with rubber to construct the plies of the tire, which form the body of the tire below the tread. The threads in the cotton fabric rubbed against each other, causing heat and premature failure of the tire. These were removed in one direction in the cord tire, which increased the lifetime of the tire but sold at a higher price. In 1923, Firestone introduced an innovation in the cord tire that led to the so-called balloon tire with greater lifetime and comfort, which took over the entire industry. This was just at the beginning of the shakeout in tires, and by creating one broad market it may have played a similar role to the Model T in fueling the shakeout.

Thus, conditions have to be ripe for shakeouts to occur. Sometimes they are ripe from the outset of an industry, whereas in other cases the conditions do not materialize until later, if at all. Firms have an incentive to develop innovations with broad appeal, so it is not surprising that most innovative industries eventually experience shakeouts. How long it takes for this to occur appears to be fundamentally related to how segmented the industry is at its outset and the extent to which new segments are created over time.

CHAPTER 3

THE BEST AND THE BRIGHTEST

Ford, Intel, Goodyear, Spectra Physics, Cadillac, Buick, Firestone, and AMD are just some of the famous names of U.S. firms that arose in the six core industries analyzed in this book. They exemplify the steady flow of great new firms that characterized the United States throughout the twentieth century. What makes the United States such a fertile breeding ground for new firms?

A country cannot be great over a sustained period without a steady flow of great new firms. So understanding the circumstances that lead to the creation of successful new firms is of paramount importance. To many economists, these circumstances are obvious. Have government educate the populace, finance basic research, and invest in infrastructure, then leave the rest to the market. Keep taxes low to provide incentives to invest in new firms. Minimize regulations to facilitate the formation and growth of new firms. Make sure the playing field is level so incumbents cannot prey upon new firms. In effect, let the market operate, and the reward will be a steady stream of new firms, some of which will thrive and become leaders of their industries.

This is the Field of Dreams theory of firm creation. In the movie, *Field of Dreams*, the main character played by Kevin Costner builds a baseball field in the middle of nowhere after hearing a voice whisper: If you build it, he will come. Eventually the great player Shoeless Joe Jackson comes along with seven of his ex-teammates to save the day. Translated into economic terms, if you let the market operate, great new firms will come. As technological advances open up new opportunities for innovation, new firms will arise to exploit the opportunities.

A cursory examination of the most prominent firms today suggests that new firms in the United States come from many different quarters. There does not appear to be any single formula to their success, supporting the idea that if the right incentives are provided, new firms will somehow get created. Look at Microsoft and Apple, two of the great U.S. firms in computing. Both were started by college dropouts without any work experience to speak of. Look at Genentech and Google. Both had founders that came from universities—Genentech was co-founded by a professor at UC San Francisco and Google was founded by two Stanford graduate students. Throw in firms like Intel that were started by individuals who worked in their industry for many years, and you have quite a mix of origins. Just let the market operate and they will come.

A close examination of the six industries, however, reveals much more rhyme and reason to the creation of great new firms than this cursory examination suggests. A defining characteristic of the nanoeconomic approach is reconstructing the evolution of a new industry, including the evolution of its leaders, by tracking down the origins of its firms to figure out where its leaders came from. This is not easy. Sometimes you get lucky and find someone who has done a lot of the heavy lifting for you. Other times you have to tap into many diverse sources, some of which can only be found by mucking around in dusty records. Along the way, lots of judgment calls and interpretations are required to make order out of the disparate information.

What emerges from all this effort does not support the Field of Dreams theory of new firms. Sure, new firms can and do come from diverse backgrounds. You occasionally see this in the six industries. But, generally, this is confined to the early evolution of industries, if it happens at all. Subsequently, the creation of great new firms resembles something akin to a biological process of reproduction and heredity. Over and over again, the best new firms are spinoffs of incumbent firms in their industry—and not just spinoffs of any firms in their industry, but typically the best ones. Top employees of some of the leading firms leave to establish the next generation of leaders in the industry. Not surprisingly, spinoffs start out looking like their erstwhile parents but soon enough veer in a different direction. Often they displace the early leaders of their industry, including in some cases their prominent parents.

Indeed, judging from the six industries, it seems that spinoffs were often needed to take their industry to new heights. If a country cannot generate these firms, its growth in a new industry can be stunted. The biological process underlying the creation of new firms thus can be essential to the health of an economy over the long run. But this is not your ordinary biological process. Typically there is no mating going on—spinoffs usually have only one parent. And the parent typically does not voluntarily play its role. If anything, it resists producing offspring.

It is certainly strange for an economy to rely so centrally on unwitting, and at times unwilling, parents to breed its leaders. This is why many economies fail to generate the steady stream of firms they need to sustain their economic well-being. Even the United States does not operate on all cylinders when it comes to spinoffs. Tapping into the potential of an economy to create great new firms requires a deep understanding of how new industries evolve and the origins of their leaders. This chapter focuses on the process giving rise to the best and brightest firms in our six core industries.

To lay the groundwork, two polar extremes are considered at first: the TV receiver and automobile industries. Both are industries where it has been possible to reconstruct the leaders of the industry over time and to trace their origins. They illustrate the typical way new industries begin, pioneered by firms that were successful producers of related products. The TV receiver industry is the exemplar of this evolution.

As discussed in the previous chapter, RCA pioneered TV in the United States. It was ready to start selling TV receivers when it unveiled its new electronic TV system at the New York World's Fair in 1939, but between the FCC and World War II, the launch of the TV receiver industry was delayed until 1946. RCA's chief, David Sarnoff, was TV's greatest proponent. For many years, he had been exhorting manufacturers of radio receivers to follow RCA into the brave new world of television. As far back as July 7, 1936, RCA's licensees, which included pretty much the entire radio receiver industry, were invited to a TV progress demonstration where Sarnoff declared there was room for everyone in this new industry with "unfathomable potential" (Bilby [1986, p. 126]).

TV receivers were a natural extension of radio receivers, and who better to begin producing TVs than the radio set manufacturers? At the start of the TV receiver industry, *Thomas' Register of American Manufacturers* listed 266 firms as producing radio receivers in its directories for 1945 to 1948. While RCA was the largest radio producer with an estimated 15% of the market, not far behind were Philco, Zenith, Emerson, and Galvin (later renamed Motorola) (MacLaurin [1949, p. 146]). These major firms had pioneered battery-operated radio receivers for farms without electricity, portable radios, car radios, and small sets that sold for as little as $6.95. Close behind these five firms was Sears Roebuck, the national retailer that sold radios manufactured by Colonial. Also among the leaders was GE, which along with Westinghouse had agreed to wait two and a half years to reenter the radio receiver market after a consent decree in 1932 to settle an antitrust suit against RCA and its owners.

A total of 177 U.S.-based firms entered the TV receiver industry between 1946 and 1989, most by 1953. Of these, 56 (31.6%) were firms that were also producers of radio receivers in 1945–1948 as reflected in *Thomas' Register of American Manufacturers*. Table 3.1 reports the market shares of U.S. TV receiver producers with at least 3% of the market in 1951–1953 or at later points through 1980. Also listed is the estimated radio market share in 1940 of each firm as reported in MacLaurin [1949, p. 146]. The ten largest TV producers in 1951–1953 were all radio producers (or, in Sears's case, marketed the radios of other manufacturers). Seven of the ten were among the top ten radio producers in 1940. Not surprisingly, given their well-developed distribution networks for radios that they used to market TVs and their overall experience, the radio producers got the jump on the other early entrants into the industry.

What could not have been anticipated is that this early lead would become permanent. Notwithstanding shifts in their relative positions, table 3.1 indicates that the leading radio producers continued to dominate the U.S. TV receiver industry throughout its entire history, even as the U.S. industry wilted in the face of foreign competition initially from Japanese producers. RCA was the leading radio producer in 1940 and was pioneer of both monochrome and color TVs. Zenith, which was the third largest radio producer in 1940, was its greatest challenger. Motorola, which was the fifth largest radio producer in 1940, sold its television business to the Japanese producer Matsushita (parent of Panasonic) in 1974, but through 1980 the Motorola product maintained its market share under the Quasar brand. GE, the sixth largest radio producer in 1940, was not far behind. While Admiral, Philco, and Emerson continued a descent that had begun with black and white sets, no non-radio U.S. firm broke into the ranks of the leaders. Eventually Japanese and other Asian firms took over the entire U.S. market, but it was business as usual in the United States regarding its indigenous leaders.

The automobile industry began much like the TV receiver industry. The automobile was pioneered in Europe, and the first commercial producers in the United States emerged around 1895. In a comprehensive report on the U.S. automobile industry, the editors of *Automobile Quarterly* compiled figures on the production of the leading makes of automobiles annually from 1896 to 1970 (Bailey [1971]). The producers and the market shares of the makes are reported in table 3.2 for every five years from 1900 to 1925, after which there was little change among the leaders of the industry. The producers are divided into two groups of early and later entrants. The early entrants all entered by 1902 and produced a

TABLE 3.1:
Periodic Market Shares of Leading U.S. TV Producers

Firm	Estimated 1940 Radio Share (Rank)	1951–1953 TV Share	1959–1960 B&W TV Share	1968 Color TV Share	1980 Color TV Share
RCA	14.4% (1)	14.7%	14.4%	30.0%	21.0%
Philco	14.2 (2)	12.7	9.4	4.0	1.2
Zenith	8.9 (3)	6.2	16.3	20.0	20.5
Emerson	8.9 (4)	4.5	4.6	—	—
Motorola	8.0 (5)	9.5	7.9	7.0	5.0 (Quasar)
GE	3.0 (9)	7.8	7.5	5.3	7.5
Sears*	5.5 (6)	3.6	6.7	6.0	7.5
Magnavox	—	—	2.7	9.0	7.0
Admiral	—	11.1	9.5	6.5	0.5
Sylvania	—†	2.9	3.1	—	4.0
Westinghouse	—	2.0	3.1	—	—

Sources: MacLaurin [1949, p. 146] for the estimated 1940 radio shares, Datta [1971, p. 295] for 1951–1953 and 1959–1960 B&W TV shares, and Levy [1981, pp. 84–85] for 1968 and 1980 color TV shares.

*Sears marketed TVs that were produced by firms that also produced radios.

†Sylvania entered by acquiring Colonial, which ranked sixth in the radio industry based on its production for Sears.

leading make in 1900 or 1905. The later entrants include all other firms that produced a leading make in 1905 or later.

The backgrounds of auto producers can be traced primarily through a massive 1,612-page compendium called the *Standard Catalog of American Cars, 1805–1942* (Kimes [1996]).* The *Standard Catalog* compiles a dossier on the cars that each automobile firm produced and provides information about how each firm started. If a firm that appears in the *Standard Catalog* produced other products before automobiles, I classified it as a diversifier. I divided new firms into two groups. If a firm's

---

* Smith [1968], which recorded whether a firm produced other products before automobiles, was also employed.

founder worked previously for another automobile firm, I classified the firm as a spinoff, and the last employer of the main founder was classified as the spinoff's parent firm.* I grouped all remaining new firms appearing in the catalog into a residual category of (other) startups.

Among the ten early entrant leaders, five were diversifiers. The leading producer in 1900, Pope, was the leading bicycle producer in the United States. The leading producer in 1905, Olds Motor Works, was a leading engine producer. White, Packard, and H.H. Franklin produced sewing machines, electrical equipment, and castings, respectively. A sixth firm, Thomas B. Jeffery, was a refugee from the bicycle industry. It was formed by its namesake after the sudden death of his partner in the second largest bicycle firm in the United States, Gormully and Jeffery. Stanley, Locomobile, and Cadillac were startups headed by men who had operated successful businesses in other industries. The diverse business heritage of the early leaders reflects that the automobile was not a simple extension of any one product but shared elements of bicycles, engines, and carriages and wagons, among other products.

Thus, similar to TV receivers, the early leaders of the automobile industry tended to come from related industries. But unlike TV receivers, table 3.2 indicates that it was not long before most of the early leaders were displaced by a new set of firms. Among the ten leaders listed as early entrants, only Cadillac consistently produced a leading make in subsequent years, and it did so as a division of General Motors, which acquired it in 1909. Twenty firms listed as later entrants in table 3.2 introduced leading makes of automobiles beginning in 1905, and one other, C. H. Metz, made the list in one year, 1914. Eighteen of these 21 firms were new firms created to produce automobiles. Fourteen were spinoffs, mostly of leading automobile firms. In effect, an insurrection toppled the leaders of the industry. Not just any insurrection, though, but a veritable civil war among the leading firms.

Spinoffs played a fundamental role in the long-term leadership of the industry. Ford Motor Co., which was the leader of the industry for many years until displaced by General Motors, was itself a spinoff. Ford Motor

---

* Numerous rules and judgments are required to handle cases that are not clear-cut. For example, firms that started out producing automobile engines and then a few years later full cars were considered to be new firms and not diversifiers. If a firm had at least one founder that previously worked at another automobile firm then it was classified as a spinoff. In cases where a long-term employee of an automobile firm founded two spinoffs in succession, the long-term employer was designated as the parent of both spinoffs. See Klepper [2007] for details about the firm classification procedure.

TABLE 3.2:
Market Shares of Leading U.S. Automobile Firms, 1900–1925

Early Entrants	Entry Year	Origin	Entry Location	1900	1905	1910	1915	1920	1925
Pope	1895	Diversifier	Hartford, CT	36					1
Stanley	1896/1901	Startup	Watertown, MA		2				
Locomobile	1899	Startup	Bridgeport, CT	18					
Knox	1900	Spinoff	Springfield, MA	0.3					
Packard	1900	Diversifier	Warren, OH/Detroit, MI		2	2			
H.H. Franklin	1901	Diversifier	Syracuse, NY		4				
White Sewing M.	1901	Diversifier	Cleveland, OH	0.02	4				
Olds/GM	1901	Diversifier	Detroit/Lansing, MI		26		1	2	1
Cadillac/GM	1902	Startup	Detroit, MI		16	6	2	1	1
Thomas B. Jeffery	1902	Startup	Kenosha, WI		16		2	2	3
Later Entrants									
Studebaker	1902	Diversifier	South Bend, IN			8	5	3	4
Union/Buckeye	1902	Diversifier	Anderson, IN			2			
Ford	1903	Spinoff	Detroit, MI		7	18	56	22	44
Buick/GM	1903	Startup	Flint, MI		3	17	5	6	5
Standard Wheel/Willys	1903	Startup	Terre Haute, IN			9	10	6	6

				3	6	5	2	4
Maxwell Briscoe/ Maxwell/ Chrysler	1904	Spinoff	Tarrytown, NY/Detroit, MI	3	6	5	2	4
Reo	1904	Spinoff	Lansing, MI	4	4	2		
Stoddard	1904	Diversifier	Dayton, OH	1				
E.R. Thomas-Det./Chalmers/ Chrysler	1906	Spinoff	Detroit, MI		4	1		
Brush	1907	Spinoff	Detroit, MI		6			
Oakland/GM	1907	Spinoff	Pontiac, MI		2	1	2	1
Hupp	1909	Spinoff	Detroit, MI		3	1	1	3
Hudson	1909	Spinoff	Detroit, MI		3	1	2	7
Paige-Detroit	1909	Spinoff	Detroit, MI					1
Chevrolet/GM	1911	Spinoff	Flint, MI			1	6	12
Saxon	1913	Spinoff	Detroit, MI			2		
Chandler	1913	Spinoff	Cleveland, OH				2	
Dodge Brothers/Chrysler	1914	Spinoff	Detroit, MI			5	7	5
Dort	1915	Startup	Flint, MI				1	
Durant	1921	Spinoff	New York, NY				3	

Source: Kimes [1996]. Production data by make from the *Automobile Quarterly* and for the industry from the Federal Trade Commission [1939] were used to compute market shares of each make.

Co. was founded by Henry Ford after he was ousted from his second startup, Henry Ford Motor Co., which went on to success after it was reconstituted as Cadillac following Ford's ouster. General Motors was formed in 1908 as an amalgamation of 22 car and parts companies, but its most important constituent turned out to be Chevrolet, which it acquired in 1916. Chevrolet was a spinoff founded by William Durant, the organizer of GM, after he was ousted from GM in 1910 due to his failure to integrate his many acquisitions. Chrysler evolved out of the efforts of Walter Chrysler, the ex-president of Buick Motor Co., to reorganize two prominent companies that also began as spinoffs, Maxwell and Chalmers, and it solidified its position through the later acquisition of another prominent spinoff, the Dodge Brothers.

The importance of spinoffs in the automobile industry raises two obvious questions: Where did all these spinoffs come from, and why were they formed? The contrasting experience of the TV industry raises a third question: Why were spinoffs prominent in automobiles but not TVs?

These questions will be addressed not just in the context of the automobile and TV industries but also for semiconductors, lasers, tires, and penicillin. Penicillin was much like the TV industry in terms of the evolution of its leading firms, but the other three industries closely resembled autos, particularly semiconductors and lasers. The next section focuses on where all the new firms came from that became leaders of the automobile, semiconductor, laser, and tire industries. The story will always be the same. After laying out the story, we will return to consider why TVs and penicillin did not afford the same opportunities for spinoffs and, most importantly, what is learned from the experiences of the other four industries about what it takes for a country to renew its vigor through the creation of new firms.

• • •

Focusing first on the automobile industry, where did all the spinoffs come from that produced leading makes of automobiles beginning in 1905? And how distinctive were these firms? Were their origins different from the mass of other entrants that never reached the top ranks of the industry?

The second question is easier to answer. Among the 725 total entrants between 1895 and 1966, 120 (17%) were classified as diversifiers, 145 (20%) as spinoffs, and 460 (64%) as startups (Klepper [2007]). Spinoffs accounted for 67% (14 of 21) of the later leaders of the industry even though they were only 20% of the 725 entrants. Clearly, spinoffs were distinctive performers.

The first question concerning the origins of the spinoffs can be analyzed by dissecting the spinoff process statistically. Considering first the rate at which firms spawned spinoffs, the most prolific spawners were all leading firms. Through 1924 the top five parents in terms of number of spinoffs were Olds Motor Works and Buick/GM with seven each, and Cadillac, Ford, and Maxwell-Briscoe/Maxwell with four each. Standardizing by their years of production through 1924 (after which entry was negligible), firms that produced leading makes of automobiles spawned approximately 3.5 times as many spinoffs per year of production—.087 spinoffs per year (54 total spinoffs in 624 collective years of production) versus .026 spinoffs per year for the rest of the firms (88 total spinoffs in 3,443 collective years of production).

Spinoffs of the leading firms were also superior performers. One measure of a spinoff's performance is whether it ever produced a leading auto make. Among the 54 spinoffs of the firms that ever produced leading makes, 11, or 20%, also produced leading makes versus 4 out of 88, or 5%, of the spinoffs of other firms.* Another way to measure a spinoff's performance is by longevity—many firms do not make it past five years of production, and the majority do not produce for more than ten years. Excluding spinoffs acquired by other automobile firms (it is unclear how long they would have survived if not acquired), 58% of the spinoffs of the leaders that were not acquired earlier produced for over five years and 20% produced for over ten years versus 30% and 13%, respectively,

---

*The 11 spinoffs with parents that both produced leading makes include (parent in parentheses): Ford (Cadillac), Reo (Olds Motor Works), E.R. Thomas-Detroit (Olds Motor Works), Brush Runabout (Cadillac), Oakland (Cadillac), Hudson (Olds Motor Works), Hupp (Ford), Chevrolet (Buick/GM), Dodge (Ford), and Durant Motors (Buick/GM). The 4 spinoffs that produced a leading make but their parent did not include (parent in parentheses): Knox (Overman), Maxwell-Briscoe (Northern), Paige-Detroit (Reliance), and Chandler (Lozier). The first group of 11 includes one spinoff, Ford, whose parent, Cadillac, did not produce a leading make until after Henry Ford's departure, and another spinoff, Oakland, that did not produce a leading make until after its acquisition by General Motors. On the other hand, the number of spinoffs with parents that both produced leading makes is to some degree understated because it does not include either Chrysler or E-M-F/ Studebaker as spinoffs (neither was classified as an entrant). Chrysler emerged from a reorganization of two spinoffs that was engineered by Walter Chrysler, a prominent employee of Buick/GM. Studebaker achieved its leading position by collaborating with and then acquiring E-M-F, which was formed by Walter Flanders, a prominent employee at Ford Motor Co., and two other industry veterans after getting control of two other automobile firms, Wayne and Northern.

for the spinoffs of the other firms. Thus, the spinoffs of the leading firms were superior performers both in terms of producing leading makes and longevity.

Why did the leading incumbents spawn so many successful spinoffs? Did the founders of leading spinoffs abscond with good ideas before their parents had an opportunity to patent them or protect them in some other way, as suggested in some economic theories? Alternatively, did the leading spinoffs capitalize on ideas their successful parents declined to pursue? Cringley expresses a popular variant of this view:

> At the heart of every start-up is an argument. A splinter group inside a successful company wants to abandon the current product line and bet the company on some radical technology. The boss, usually the guy who invented the current technology, thinks this idea is crazy and says so, wishing the splinter group well on their new adventure. [1993, p. 37]

These are just two of many views of what motivates spinoffs. Surely there is no single reason spinoffs occur. But insights can be gleaned about the factors underlying the formation of the most successful spinoffs by digging into their histories. Three of the pioneers of the automobile industry, Ransom Olds, William Durant, and the Dodge brothers, were centrally involved in the formation of a number of the leading spinoffs. Through their stories we can begin to learn about the nature of the civil war that gave rise to so many successful automobile spinoffs.

BILLY DURANT: THE CONSUMMATE WHEELER-DEALER

William Crapo Durant was born on December 8, 1861, in Boston to a prosperous family on his mother's side and a wayward father.* Some years earlier at age 54 his maternal grandfather had moved to Flint, Michigan, where he amassed considerable wealth and rose to become governor of the state. Following her father's death, in 1872 his mother moved the family to Flint, where Billy Durant attended high school. Six months short of graduation, he left to follow in his grandfather's footsteps and make his fortune.

As a young man, Durant distinguished himself as a superb salesman and organizer. After numerous business successes, he stumbled across a

---

*This section is based on Gustin [1973], Pelfrey [2006], Dunham and Gustin [1992], and Kimes and Ackerman [1986].

cart with a novel suspension. Enlisting the help of his friend Dallas Dort, he formed the Durant-Dort Carriage Company to develop the cart. By age 42 Durant was a millionaire. Durant-Dort integrated backwards into component production and became one of the largest buggy producers in the United States. Durant raised capital and hawked the company's products while Dort minded the store.

Durant was approached in 1904 by the directors of the Flint Wagon Works to take over ownership of the Buick Motor Company. Buick needed additional funding to develop an automobile based on a novel "valve-in-head" engine that generated unusual power for its size. Durant put Buick's engine through rigorous testing for almost two months. Convinced that he had a first-rate product, he expanded Buick's capitalization from $75,000 to $1.5 million using his contacts, reputation, and enormous energy to sell stock in Flint and elsewhere. He built the biggest factory in the industry in Flint and developed an extensive wholesale and retail distribution network using Durant-Dort's carriage dealers. By 1908 Buick was the number two automobile manufacturer, with an annual production exceeding 8,000 cars.

With Buick at its center, Durant organized General Motors (GM) in 1908 to combine 22 separate parts and automobile companies, including Buick, Olds Motor Works, Cadillac, and Oakland. Dallas Dort was not part of GM, and without his steadying influence, GM was soon in trouble. Poor inventory control, little oversight in production, and a limited awareness of capital needs led Durant to lose financial control of GM to bankers. They quickly righted the company by closing down some subsidiaries and consolidating others.

One of the casualties of the reorganization was Buick's fast-selling Model 10, which was GM's answer to Ford's Model T. Reportedly, some of the new management did not like the comparison to a low-priced automobile and preferred to produce a larger car (Gustin [1973, pp. 142–142], Dunham and Gustin [1992, p. 85]). According to Kimes and Ackerman [1986, p. 13], Durant felt that "[b]ankers did not know automobiles. They wouldn't be convinced if he told them what a success he had made of his Durant-Dort company before the turn of the century by building low-priced buggies instead of high-priced carriages. They wouldn't be convinced either if he told them what Henry Ford was trying to do with the Model T."

Unlike Henry Ford, Durant did not hate bankers. But he felt that "it would be better to let the new group handle the business to suit themselves, and if I ever expected to regain control of General Motors, which I certainly intended to do, I should have a company of my own, run in my own way" (quoted in Kimes and Ackerman [1986, p. 13]). So in 1911, Durant organized three companies, Chevrolet Motor Car Company, Mason Motor Company, and Little Motor Company in Detroit and Flint, each headed by an ex-Buick employee.

Mason was organized to produce motors. Initially Little designed a small but not durable car and Chevrolet, an uneconomical large car. Durant combined these efforts under the Chevrolet banner and introduced several cars, including the low-priced Chevrolet Four-Ninety, that were well received. In 1916 Chevrolet sold 62,522 cars, which increased to 125,004 in 1917 (Kimes and Ackerman [1986, pp. 20–21]), vaulting it into fourth place in the industry.

In 1916 Durant realized his ambition to regain control of GM using Chevrolet, which he subsequently merged with GM. In the next four years GM expanded in a number of directions, which again proved to be Durant's undoing. He was still trying to manage GM himself, which was too much for any man, while at the same time aggressively buying GM's stock to prop up its price. Walter Chrysler, the head of the Buick division of GM, described how Durant would summon him from Detroit to meet in New York, where Durant was based, only to keep him waiting for days as he communicated with "half the continent" through eight or more telephones arrayed on his desk (Chrysler [1950, p. 156]). Eventually Chrysler quit GM in frustration, and in 1920, when the boom following World War I came to an abrupt halt and the country plunged into a sharp recession, Durant lost financial control of GM for good. GM subsequently recovered and used Chevrolet, which became the top-selling make in the industry, to displace Ford as the industry leader.

Durant went on for one last hurrah in the automobile industry, organizing Durant Motors in 1921 through a sale of $5 million in stock to personal friends. His first product, a four-cylinder car, was well received. He followed up with a low-priced car that enabled Durant Motors to attain fifth place in the industry in 1923. Durant wanted to sell a full range of cars, which led to the ill-advised purchase of Locomobile, a luxury car that was on the decline. Durant Motors remained among the leaders for the rest of the 1920s but started losing money in the latter part of the 1920s and ceased producing in 1932, hit hard by the Great Depression.

Undaunted, Durant continued to dabble in business ventures, dying penniless in New York in 1947 at age 85. His biographer described him (Gustin [1973, p. 15]) as a man who "[p]ut organizations together, and he did it with dramatic flair. He was an extremely complex and paradoxical personality, a supersalesman who spoke in a soft voice, a builder of fortunes who cared very little about money and who ultimately died without leaving any."

RANSOM OLDS, THE CURVED DASH RUNABOUT, AND THE EXODUS FROM OLDS MOTOR WORKS

Ransom Eli Olds also was a pioneer, developing the first great car in the industry, the Curved Dash Runabout.* Like Durant, he too was pushed out of the company he headed, Olds Motor Works. And like Durant, he went on to found another automobile company, Reo, which achieved great success. But unlike Durant, Olds eventually withdrew from active management of Reo to enjoy the fruits of his endeavors.

Olds was born in Geneva, Ohio, on June 3, 1864, the youngest of five children. His father moved the family to Lansing, Michigan, where he opened P.F. Olds and Son, a machine shop, in 1880. The son was Wallace, but it was not long before Ransom displaced his older brother in the family business. Later he bought out his father, and the company thrived under his leadership, developing a series of steam engines and then a gasoline engine that garnered substantial sales. Olds himself was intimately involved with product development as well as managing the business, receiving 34 patents over his lifetime (May [1977, p. 32]).

After tinkering with electric automobiles, Olds developed his first gasoline powered vehicle in 1896. To finance his growing engine business and his experimentation with automobiles, the company was reorganized in 1899 as Olds Motor Works, which required Olds to cede majority control to his principal stockholder, Samuel Smith. Smith had made his money in copper mining and brought in his son Fred to help manage the company, which ultimately proved to be Olds's undoing.

The company was moved from Lansing to Detroit, where the Smiths were based. Olds experimented with different types of automobiles in 1899 and 1900 before settling on the Curved Dash Runabout in 1901. It was a two-seater powered by a one-cylinder engine that sold for $650. Although other firms offered similar cars at comparable prices, orders flooded in for the car after a savvy marketing campaign that began in early 1901. Despite a disastrous fire that burned down its Detroit plant and ultimately led the firm to return to Lansing, Olds Motor Works was still able to sell 425 Runabouts in 1901. By 1903 the Runabout was the

---

*This section is mainly based on May [1977].

number-one seller in the industry at 4,000 units, and its sales climbed to over 5,000 units the next year (Bailey [1971, p. 139]).

Like most of the cars of its era, the Runabout was largely an assembled car. It was produced on an unprecedented scale, which required an elaborate system of subcontracting and parts assembly. Despite novelties that were forerunners of the mass production system developed by Ford, Olds soon found himself in a dispute with Fred Smith over the adequacy of the firm's production methods. Smith wanted defects in the car reduced and at the end of April 1903 established his own engineering operation when Olds did not develop the improved engine he sought. A feud between the two ensued, and Olds was replaced as general manager and vice president by Smith in early 1904. Within the year, Olds sold off all his stock and left the company for good.

Never one to look back, it was not long before Olds was involved in a new car company, the R. E. Olds Company—shortened to his initials, Reo, after objections from Fred Smith and the other stockholders of Olds Motor Works that its name infringed upon their rights. Much later the company's name would be immortalized by the rock group Reo Speedwagon, the trade name that Reo used for the trucks it profitably introduced in 1911.

Olds had apparently resisted efforts by the Smiths at Olds Motor Works to develop larger cars (May [1977, p. 212]), so it came as somewhat of a surprise that Reo initially developed a two-cylinder, 16 horsepower touring car with room for five people that sold for $1,250. It was jointly designed by Olds and his chief engineer, Horace Thomas, who was hired away from Olds Motor Works along with a number of its other top employees. Reo was immediately successful, and by 1908 it reached the number four position in the industry with sales of almost 4,000 units. It never developed a low-priced car to compete with the Model T but remained within the ranks of the leading makes until 1923, by which point Olds had long departed from active management of Reo to enjoy his wealth.

Following Olds's departure, Olds Motor Works went on to develop ever larger cars. It had an opportunity in 1905 to adopt a new four-cylinder car developed by its chief engineer, Howard Coffin, that was a compromise between the Curved Dash Runabout and the larger cars favored by the Smiths. Plans for the car advanced to the purchasing agent, Frederick Bezner, who began to negotiate contracts for the parts, only to have the Smiths withdraw their support at the last minute. It was not long before Coffin left, along with Roy Chapin, the head of sales at Olds Motor

Works, and two other employees to found a new firm, E.R. Thomas-Detroit, to develop the car. This latter company was successful immediately, shipping 500 cars by the middle of 1907 and rising ultimately to the eighth leading make.*

Under Smith's direction, Olds Motor Works had two more years of outstanding sales with the Curved Dash Runabout but drifted off into much larger, more expensive cars with limited markets. It was bailed out by William Durant, who paid $3 million for the company in the formation of General Motors in 1908. Fred Smith was not heard from again until 1928 when he wrote his memoirs, *Motoring Down a Quarter of a Century*. Although devoted almost entirely to his experiences at Olds Motor Works, Smith never mentioned the name of Ransom E. Olds (May [1977, p. 239]). Nevertheless, Olds's name lived on for more than a century in the Oldsmobile model produced by General Motors, reflecting the profound influence Olds had on the U.S. automobile industry and, as will be discussed in the next chapter, on Detroit as its capital.

THE DODGE BROTHERS

The Dodge brothers, John Francis and Horace Elgin Dodge, were also early pioneers of the automobile industry. They supplied engines and transmissions to Olds Motor Works and were instrumental in the success of Ford Motor Co. Like Durant and Olds, though, they ultimately were forced to leave the company they had helped to succeed to found their own spinoff, which rose to become the second leading producer in the industry. Neither brother ever got much of a chance to smell the roses, as both died just six years after the start of their great success.

John Dodge was born on October 25, 1864, and his brother Horace was born three and a half years later on May 17, 1868, in Niles, Michigan. From their earliest days the brothers were inseparable. Following in the footsteps of their father, they worked together as machinists for various firms, which continued after their family moved to Detroit in 1886. Capitalizing on an improved ball bearing patented by Horace, they formed a bicycle company in 1897, which they sold in 1900 to open their own machine shop. "Make everything as good as it can possibly be made, and if there is a better way of making it, make it that way, and get the right price for it" (quoted in Kollins [2002a, p. 169 of volume 1]), was their credo,

---

*See Renner [1973, pp. 20–25] for the E.R. Thomas-Detroit story.

which served them well. Soon they were making engines and transmissions on a large scale for Olds Motor Works and supplying parts to other auto manufacturers.

Different accounts exist about their initial deal with Henry Ford and Ford Motor Co. According to McPherson [1992, p. 4], Ford was so impressed with their competence that he offered them 10% ownership of Ford Motor Co. if they would produce engines for his company, and they were sufficiently impressed with Ford to risk their business future on him. McPherson claims that Horace redesigned Ford's rear axle and other parts and made important changes in the motor. Their initial contract with Ford called for them to supply 650 engines, transmissions, and axles at a price of $250 each, which necessitated a substantial investment by the Dodge brothers. According to Hyde [2005, p. 34], when Ford fell behind in payments to the brothers, they agreed to write off overdue payments and extend Ford credit in exchange for 10% of Ford's stock.

As Ford thrived, so did the Dodge brothers. They were Ford's principal supplier and Ford their only customer, making them de facto employees of Ford. When Ford's Highland Park plant was opened in 1910, the Dodge brothers also opened a new plant to provide the production capacity to meet the ever-growing demand for the Model T. However, Ford increasingly began producing its own parts. This put the Dodge brothers in a precarious position, which John Dodge likened to "being carried around in Henry Ford's vest pocket" (Kimes [1996, p. 459]). In 1912 they proposed that Ford purchase their business. When Henry Ford did not act over the next year, they decided to enter into automobile manufacturing themselves.

They earned millions in dividends from their Ford stock, which they used to finance their entry into automobiles. The car they introduced in 1914 was produced using nearly the same methods as Ford's Model T, both in terms of the plant in which it was made and the specialized machinery employed to manufacture it (Hyde [2005, p. 107]). The two cars were not direct competitors, though. The Dodge car sold for $785 versus the Model T touring version that retailed for $490. The Dodge car was more powerful and improved on a number of the Model T's features, including its planetary transmission. Dodge teamed with the body manufacturer Edward Budd in the design of the steel body of their initial car, which became popularly known as the first all-steel body automobile. In 1915 they built approximately 45,000 cars, the best first year of any firm up to that point (Kimes [1996, p. 459]), boosting Dodge into third place in the industry. In 1919 the Dodges worked with Budd to pioneer the inexpensive all-steel closed body automobile, and by the end of 1919 the Dodge make was the second leading seller in the industry.

Calamity struck in 1920. First John died on January 14 from pneumonia that he had caught from Horace. Later in the year, on December 10, Horace died at his winter home. "Inseparable in life, the brothers were now joined in death" (Kollins [2002b, p. 177]). Burdened by a cumbersome governance arrangement, the widows of the brothers sold the company on May 1, 1925, for $146 million (about $2 billion in 2015 dollars), and three years later it was resold to Chrysler for $170 million. Like Ransom Olds and the Oldsmobile, the Dodge brand long survived the brothers into the twenty-first century, reflecting the extraordinary durability of the product they created.

The picture that emerges from the spinoffs, exemplified by the three featured pioneers, is of an industry very much in flux, with power struggles occurring within the leading companies over their future direction. Buyers differed in terms of the kinds of cars they wanted, and questions abounded about what kind of cars firms should produce. Many strongheaded men were involved in the leading companies, which coupled with technological and marketing uncertainties inevitably led to numerous conflicts and spinoffs that reshaped the industry.

The conflicts were not always about new ideas. Durant was twice pushed out of GM because of his management style. The Dodge brothers left Ford Motor Co. because Henry Ford was not responsive to their concerns. Ransom Olds quarreled with the Smiths over how to manage production. Some of the other leading spinoffs had a similar impetus. For example, Alanson Brush, who was involved in founding Brush Runabout and Oakland, left Cadillac over a dispute with its head, Henry Leland, over the use of his patents (Szudarek [1996, p. 203]).

When conflicts did occur over new ideas for automobiles, they never involved employees trying to exploit their employer's intellectual property to the detriment of their employer. Invariably it was the opposite—the employee would try to convince the employer of the merits of an idea, only to form a spinoff after failing. This was the case when Coffin and Chapin left Olds Motor Works to found E. R. Thomas-Detroit. Among the other leading spinoffs, Chandler Motors was also formed when its parent, Lozier, declined to produce an inexpensive version of its luxury car that was proposed by some of its top executives (Kollins [2002b, p. 142]).

Why did better firms spawn spinoffs at higher rates and have better performing spinoffs? Perhaps two mechanisms are at work that are reminiscent of the nature-nurture debate concerning human intelligence and performance. One is that what makes a firm is the quality of its employees. If better employees are more qualified to start their own firms and to found better firms, then better firms would have more and better spinoffs. If employees are thought of as the genes of a firm, this would be tantamount to saying that better firms are more fit genetically and thus spawn more and better offspring. The other mechanism, which is analogous to the nurture argument, is that there is more for employees to learn at better firms. This would also make employees at better firms more fit to found their own firms, leading to more and better performing spinoffs.

Examples can readily be found that support both mechanisms in the automobile industry. Consider the nature mechanism and Olds Motor Works. Its head, Ransom Olds, took over his father's business, which thrived under his leadership, and he oversaw the development of the Curved Dash Runabout that took the industry by storm. Is it any wonder that when he was forced out of his company, his next firm, Reo, was so successful? Two of the key employees of Olds Motor Works were Roy Chapin and Howard Coffin. They both joined Olds Motor Works after college and within a few years rose up the ranks to become head of sales and chief engineer, respectively. Is it surprising that when they left Olds Motor Works in frustration after the Smiths reneged on the car they wanted to build, the next two firms they founded, E. R. Thomas-Detroit and Hudson, were very successful?

At the same time, the amount these men and other founders of successful spinoffs may have learned at their parent firms—the nurture mechanism—should not be underestimated. Many produced cars that borrowed consciously or unconsciously from their parents. Chandler succeeding with an inexpensive version of its parent's luxury car is one example. The Dodge Brothers succeeded with a car that had many similarities to the Model T and that was produced using virtually the same production process as the Model T. Even Henry Ford may have learned a lesson from his first parent, albeit a negative one. After his departure, his parent succeeded by bringing in to head the firm a manufacturing specialist who previously supplied engines and transmissions on a large scale to Olds Motor Works. Similarly, instead of trying to produce his own car in its entirety, Henry Ford brought in the Dodge Brothers, who were also large-scale suppliers to Olds Motor Works, to make the Ford's engine, transmission, and chassis.

The combination of talented employees learning from the experiences of their parents contributed to many successful spinoffs. These spinoffs pioneered new car designs and introduced novel production methods that were critical contributors to the tremendous growth of the automobile industry during its formative years. They also shaped the Big Three producers that dominated the U.S. industry for so long. It is difficult to imagine how the U.S. automobile industry could have been so successful without them. Remarkably, the same can be said about spinoffs in the semiconductor industry, to which we now turn.

Semiconductor diodes and rectifiers were sold before World War II, but it was the invention of the transistor at Bell Labs in 1947 that effectively launched the semiconductor industry. Before the transistor, the vacuum tube was the workhorse of electronics applications. Vacuum tubes were used to detect and amplify signals in radios, TVs, tape recorders, and other equipment and were beginning to be used in computers. But vacuum tubes were bulky and fragile, generated a great deal of heat, and did not last long. The transistor, which was a tiny solid-state device, could perform the same functions as the vacuum tube without many of its disadvantages. Ultimately it proved to be revolutionary, and the three scientists at Bell Labs credited with the invention of the transistor, John Bardeen, Walter Brattain, and William Shockley, were awarded the Nobel Prize for physics in 1956.

Bell Labs was the research arm of AT&T, the main provider of telephone service in the United States. AT&T produced transistors in its manufacturing subsidiary, Western Electric, which also produced its telephone equipment. Soon after the invention of the transistor, antitrust authorities began pressuring AT&T to divest itself of Western Electric. To avoid this, AT&T agreed to use Western Electric only for its own needs and pledged to stay out of the commercial or "merchant" market for transistors. It also licensed its transistor patents to all comers at nominal rates and produced transistors only for its own use and that of the military. As part of its licensing agreements, AT&T held various symposia in the 1950s to disseminate its latest research findings about transistors, including manufacturing know-how documented in a black notebook known as Ma Bell's Cookbook.

Numerous firms took out a transistor license from AT&T, and the merchant semiconductor market took off. The share of the sales of U.S.

TABLE 3.3:
Market Shares of Leading North American Merchant Producers, 1957–1990

Vacuum Tube Firms	Entry Year[a]	Origin	Metropolitan Location	57	60	63	66	75	80	85	90
General Electric	1951	Diversifier	Syracuse, NY	9	8	8	8	C	C	C	C
RCA	1951	Diversifier	Camden, NJ	6	7	5	7	4	3	2	
Raytheon	1951	Diversifier	Boston, MA	5	4	—	—	1	1	1	0.5
Sylvania	1953	Diversifier	New York, NY	4	3	—	—				
Westinghouse	1953	Diversifier	Elmira, NY	2	6	4	5	C	C	C	C
Philco-Ford	1954	Diversifier	Philadelphia, PA	3	6	4	3	C			
Other Early Leaders											
Texas Instruments	1953	Diversifier	Dallas, TX	20	20	18	17	20	19	18	15
Transitron	1953	Spinoff	Boston, MA	12	9	3	3	0.5			
TRW	1954	Spinoff	Los Angeles, CA	—	—	4	—	C	C	C	C
Hughes	1955	Diversifier	Los Angeles, CA	11	5	—	—	C	C	C	C
General Instrument	1955	Diversifier	Long Island, NY	—	—	—	4	3	2	1	0.5
Delco Radio (GM)	1956	Diversifier	Kokomo, IN	—	—	—	4	C	C	C	C
Fairchild	1957	Spinoff	Mountain View, CA	—	5	9	13	9	7	5	A
Motorola	1958[b]	Diversifier	Phoenix, AZ	—	5	10	12	8	11	13	17

Later Leaders				1957	1960	1963	1966	1975	1980	1985	1990
Signetics	1961	Spinoff	Sunnyvale, CA				—	—	5	6	5
Analog Devices	1965	Startup	Boston, MA					—	1	1	2
AMI	1966	Spinoff	Santa Clara, CA				—	4	2	1	1
National	1967	Spinoff	Santa Clara, CA					10	11	10	9
Harris	1967	Diversifier	Melbourne, FL					2	3	3	4
Intel	1968	Spinoff	Santa Clara, CA					7	10	10	17
AMD	1969	Spinoff	Sunnyvale, CA					2	5	7	6
Mostek	1969	Spinoff	Dallas, TX					2	6	A	
Micron Technology	1978	Spinoff	Boise, ID						—	0.5	2
VLSI Technology	1979	Spinoff	San Jose, CA						—	1	2
LSI Logic	1980	Spinoff	Milpitas, CA						—	2	3

Sources: See Tilton [1971] for sources for 1957, 1960, 1963, and 1966 market share data; the 1975, 1980, 1985, and 1990 market shares are based on annual compilations of ICE.

"—" indicates firm was producer, but no market share data reported; "C" represents Captive producer [producing just for their own use] in the listing of Integrated Circuit Engineering (ICE); "A" indicates Acquired by a semiconductor producer.

[a] Dates for receiving tube firms and early leaders based on Tilton [1971].

[b] According to Tilton [1971], Motorola used semiconductors only for its own purposes before 1958.

producers of semiconductors by the largest producers is reported periodically in table 3.3. Figures for 1966 and earlier years are based on Tilton [1971, p. 66]. Figures for later years are based on annual reports for 1974–2002 compiled by the firm Integrated Circuit Engineering (ICE) on the semiconductor sales of all U.S. firms whose sales exceeded a minimum threshold.* The leaders are divided into three groups. The first group is composed of vacuum tube producers, who were among the earliest entrants into the industry. The second group is composed of other early entrants that ascended into the ranks of the leaders by 1966. The last group is composed of later entrants that were among the ten largest firms on the ICE listings in 1975, 1980, 1985, and 1990.

Following automobiles, semiconductor firms were classified as diversifiers, spinoffs, and (other) startups. Unlike the *Standard Catalog of Automobiles*, no single source was available to trace the backgrounds of all the firms. However, for producers in Silicon Valley, the trade organization SEMI (Semiconductor Equipment and Materials International) compiled a rich genealogy of every entrant through 1986 that lists its founders (in order of importance) and their prior affiliation. For firms outside Silicon Valley, diverse sources were tapped to trace their backgrounds. Ultimately, it was possible to trace the backgrounds of all the leaders in table 3.3 and the rest of the entrants through 1986 that showed up on the annual lists of the largest producers compiled by the ICE.†

Eight firms produced most of the vacuum tubes in the United States when the transistor was developed, and as table 3.3 indicates, six of the eight became early leaders of the semiconductor industry. The second group of other early leaders in table 3.3 did not enter quite as early as the vacuum tube producers, but all ascended into the ranks of the leaders by 1966. The majority of these firms were also diversifiers. Motorola, Delco,

---

*Table 3.3 includes only merchant producers and thus excludes AT&T and also IBM. IBM produced transistors for its own computers and was reputed to be the largest producer of semiconductors in the United States.

†Web searches, various studies of the industry, and the report, *Profiles 1997*, prepared by ICE were particularly useful in tracing firm backgrounds. As for automobiles, rules were required to handle firms whose backgrounds were not clear-cut. Following common practice, spinoffs were defined broadly to encompass firms founded by employees of both merchant and captive semiconductor producers and financed by existing firms in related industries as well as by more conventional sources. Sometimes spinoffs were organized as subsidiaries of the firm that financed them. In a few cases, the most prominent being National Semiconductor, the financing firm was actually a semiconductor producer that used its new entity to transform its semiconductor operations. The parent of each spinoff was defined as the employer of the firm's primary founder.

Hughes, and General Instrument were all experienced electronics producers and Texas Instruments was a small geophysical services company. The other three early leaders were new firms that were spinoffs of incumbent semiconductor firms. The most important of these was Fairchild Semiconductor, which was a spinoff of Shockley Semiconductor Laboratory, the first semiconductor firm in Silicon Valley founded in 1956 by William Shockley following his departure from Bell Labs.

Similar to automobiles, table 3.3 indicates that most of the early semiconductor leaders were displaced by later entrants, who are listed under the third category of later leaders. All the vacuum tube firms declined over time, and most of them either exited or retreated into captive production (i.e., producing just for their own use). All of the other early leaders also declined and either exited or retreated into captive production with the exception of Texas Instruments and Motorola, which were still the top two producers as of 1990. Fairchild was quite successful at first, garnering 13% of the market as of 1966, when it displaced Motorola as the number two producer. But it subsequently declined and was acquired by National Semiconductor in 1987.

Similar to autos, the later leaders were predominantly spinoffs. Of the 11 later leaders listed in table 3.3, nine were spinoffs. One other firm, Monolithic Memories, also ascended into the ranks of the ten largest firms during the period 1975–1990 (for one year, 1986), and it too was a spinoff. Fairchild's influence on the industry was dramatic; Signetics, National, Intel, AMD, LSI Logic, and Monolithic Memories were all spinoffs of Fairchild. AMI was founded by an ex-Fairchild employee after working for a short-lived semiconductor producer, General Micro-electronics (GM-e). VLSI was founded by one of the top managers at Synertek, who had also worked at Fairchild before co-founding Synertek. The other two spinoffs were descended from Texas Instruments (TI)—Mostek was a spinoff of TI and Micron was a spinoff of Mostek.

To put the performance of these spinoffs in perspective, it is necessary to trace the origins of all semiconductor producers. As noted earlier, it was possible to trace the backgrounds of all the firms on the ICE listings, but these were the largest firms in the industry and thus not representative of semiconductor firms overall. To provide a more representative benchmark, all the firms that ever produced integrated circuits in the annual listings of the *Electronics Buyers Guide*, which was the data source used to compile the annual list of IC entrants and producers in figure 2.7, were considered. In total there were 600 such firms, and it was possible using various sources and rules for difficult cases to trace the backgrounds of 468 of them.* Among the 600, 326 (54%) were classified as diversifiers, 103 (17%) as spinoffs, 39 (7%) as startups, with the remaining 132 (22%) having unknown backgrounds. Even if the unknowns were all spinoffs, the fraction of entrants that were spinoffs would be 39%, which is still considerably less than the fraction of later leaders that were spinoffs, 83% (10 of 12). Similar to automobiles, semiconductor spinoffs were exceptional performers.

To gain further insights into the origins and performance of the spinoffs, the 99 entrants through 1986 that showed up in one or more years on the ICE listings of the largest semiconductor producers from 1974 to 2002 were exploited. Among the 99 firms, 54 were themselves spinoffs of other firms on the ICE listings. The top four spawners of these spinoffs were all leading firms in the industry at one point. Number one, not surprisingly, was Fairchild, with 15 spinoffs on the ICE listings. Intel was number two with six ICE spinoffs, and National and TI were tied for third with three ICE spinoffs. Both Intel and National were themselves spinoffs of Fairchild, which reflects the tremendous influence Fairchild had on the industry, as discussed further in the next chapter on industry clusters.

All told, 19 firms on the ICE listings were among the leaders of the industry at some point. They spawned 39 firms on the ICE listings during the 427 collective years they produced semiconductors through 1986, for a spawning rate of .091 spinoffs per year. The other 80 firms on the ICE listings spawned 15 ICE spinoffs over their collective 774 years of production through 1986 for a spawning rate of .019 spinoffs per year. These patterns are similar to automobiles, where firms that produced leading makes spawned .087 spinoffs per year versus .026 spinoffs per year for the rest of the producers.

Similar to the automobile industry, the spinoffs of the leading semiconductor firms were also more likely than the spinoffs of the other firms to become leaders of the industry. Among the 39 spinoffs of the 19 leaders

---

* A firm was classified as a diversifier if it showed up in *The Electronic Buyers Guide* as a producer of another type of electronics product, in Dun and Bradstreet's *Million Dollar Directory* of firms, or in *Thomas' Register of American Manufacturers* at least five years before producing ICs. State incorporation records were also checked, and if a firm was incorporated at least five years before producing ICs it was also classified as a diversifier. The backgrounds of new firms were traced using the Silicon Valley genealogy, *Profiles 1997*, occasional profiles of firms in weekly issues of the trade journal *Electronic News*, Web searches, and a few small firm genealogies that were previously compiled. See Klepper [2010] and Kowalski [2012] on the detailed procedures used to determine the backgrounds of semiconductor firms.

on the ICE listings, eight, or 21%, were among the leaders of the industry at some point. In contrast, among the 15 spinoffs of the other firms on the ICE listings, only one (VLSI), or 7%, attained the ranks of the leaders, and it may have owed its success to its founder's prior stint at Fairchild. Nearly all of the 54 spinoffs were very long-term survivors (the ICE firms were the top firms in the industry), so a comparison of the five- and ten-year survival rates of the spinoffs of the leaders and other ICE firms is not very useful. Although the number of spinoffs of the leaders and other ICE firms is certainly small, making it difficult to draw confident conclusions, it appears that, similar to automobiles, better semiconductor firms spawned better spinoffs.

The parallels continue when the reasons for the leading spinoffs in semiconductors are dissected. The main impetus for their formation was disagreements among high-level decision makers. Similar to automobiles, many disagreements revolved around new technologies, but a number were also spurred by managerial concerns. Curiously, some of the ideas that led to spinoffs were initiated by their parents, who got cold feet when it came time to develop them into full-fledged products. Three sets of semiconductor spinoffs are featured to convey the main types of disagreements that spurred the formation of leading spinoffs. The first of the three involved perhaps the most important innovation in the history of the industry, the integrated circuit. The second illustrates what can happen when a leading firm gets controlled by owners with little feel for a new industry, similar to the Smiths and Olds Motor Works. The last spinoff echoes an oft-repeated tale of corporate woe in which an acquiring company from another industry brings in its own, ignorant management team and the prior managers go off to greener pastures.

SPINOFFS AND THE DEVELOPMENT OF THE IC AT FAIRCHILD SEMICONDUCTOR

The "tyranny of numbers," it was called (Reid [1986, pp. 9–23]). Electronic circuits are composed of five types of discrete elements: resistors, capacitors, inductors, diodes, and transistors. Resistors restrict the flow of electricity, capacitors store energy in an electric field, inductors hold energy in a magnetic field, diodes allow electrical current to flow in one direction but not the other, and transistors switch electrical current on and off, amplify it, or cause it to oscillate. Before ICs, electrical circuits could contain thousands of these components wired together by hand. Not only were connections expensive to make, but as the number of components in a circuit grew, the chance of one failing and dooming the circuit increased exponentially. Such was the tyranny of numbers.

The search for a solution to the tyranny of numbers occupied a number of firms and inventors in the 1950s. Each branch of the U.S. military sponsored its own pet approach. The ultimate winner of the race was an idea developed almost simultaneously by Jack Kilby, a recently hired employee of Texas Instruments (TI), and Robert Noyce, one of the eight co-founders of Fairchild Semiconductor. The innovation was called the monolithic integrated circuit. All the discrete elements of a circuit would be fabricated on a single piece of silicon and connected internally.

Kilby actually reduced his idea to practice first in September 1958. But it required thin gold wires to connect the elements, which was hardly practical. Noyce's entry in the derby was conceived a few months later. Fairchild had made a breakthrough in transistor fabrication when it discovered that oxidation on the surface of the silicon protected the transistor from shorting out. It turned out that the silicon dioxide layer was also ideal for depositing thin strips of aluminum that could be used to connect the different circuit elements, thereby forming what became known as a monolithic integrated circuit (IC). Noyce exploited this idea in his design of a monolithic IC, which enabled Fairchild to beat TI to the market with the first practical IC.

A number of innovations were required, though, to make Noyce's idea workable. The challenge was to figure out how to separate all the elements on the circuit so current flowed through the aluminum strips rather than through the body of the circuit. This task was assigned to a group headed by another of Fairchild's co-founders, Jay Last. He pursued two approaches over the next year. Eventually a new technique was developed to diffuse impurities into the silicon wafer to isolate electrically regions on which the circuit elements were fabricated. Using this new process, members of Last's group and other engineers developed a family of ICs to perform different functions. All told, it took two years to transform Noyce's ideas into workable ICs, which gave Fairchild a six-month lead over its closest competitor, Texas Instruments (Lécuyer [2006, pp. 157–159]).

It took little time, however, for Fairchild to lose that lead. Fairchild prospered making silicon transistors, but ICs were initially a drain on its finances. Tom Bay, Fairchild's marketing and sales manager, accused Last of "pissing away a million dollars" on ICs and tried to curtail his program. Gordon Moore, another of Fairchild's co-founders who also headed its R&D Department, was not supportive either. He was skeptical about the market potential of ICs, which he later acknowledged was his single biggest mistake at Fairchild (Moore and Davis [2004, p. 27]). "Most of us working in the laboratory . . . did not realize at first that we had barely scratched the surface of a technology that would be so important. It was just another product completed, leaving us looking around for a new device to make, wondering, 'What's next?' " (ibid. [p. 28]).

Last saw things quite differently. Following the contentious meeting in which Bay expressed his misgivings about ICs, he "stood up, announced he was taking a leave of absence—effective immediately—and walked out" (Berlin [2005, p. 122]). Arthur Rock, a young banker who had helped arrange the initial funding of Fairchild Semiconductor, had recently left New York for California to set up a fund with a partner, Tom Davis, to back new electronics companies. Rock had become a close friend of Last and arranged a meeting between Last and Henry Singleton, a PhD engineer who had left his research job at Litton Industries in Los Angeles to start a high-tech conglomerate called Teledyne.

Singleton wanted to start a division of Teledyne to develop advanced semiconductor devices for the military, and the IC provided an ideal opportunity. Before Last accepted his offer, he made one last overture to Noyce, asking him about the future of ICs at Fairchild. Noyce was preoccupied with other problems at Fairchild and put him off, asking if Last could wait until later in the week to talk. That was all the answer Last needed. In February 1961 he resigned from Fairchild along with two other co-founders, Jean Hoerni and Sheldon Roberts, to start the Amelco division of Teledyne (Berlin [2005, pp. 122–123]).

Less than three months later, four physicists and engineers who had worked with Last and Hoerni in Fairchild's R&D laboratory took preliminary steps toward the formation of their own company to produce ICs, Signetics. They saw ICs as a revolutionary technology that Fairchild was not fully exploiting. Lehman Brothers, a financial services firm based in New York, which had made enormous profits on a deal involving Litton Industries almost a decade earlier, organized a $1 million investment syndicate to finance Signetics. Unlike Last and Hoerni's amicable departure, Noyce viewed the Signetics's group as defectors, which would color Fairchild's later dealings with Signetics (Lécuyer [2006, pp. 217–220]).

At first ICs were more expensive than conventional discrete circuits, and both Amelco and Signetics struggled. Within a couple of years their fortunes reversed, aided by a 1963 directive from the director of Research and Engineering at the Department of Defense urging the military services to embrace ICs. Signetics particularly benefited from the directive and by 1964 was the largest supplier of ICs in Silicon Valley. By this time Fairchild had recognized the error of its ways. It responded by introducing a line of ICs similar to Signetics's at half the price, which eventually enabled Fairchild to displace Signetics as the leading IC producer in the United States. Luckily for Signetics, Fairchild initially ran into severe manufacturing problems with its ICs, which enabled Signetics to maintain a significant share of the market, but it would never regain its leadership in the IC business (Lécuyer [2006, pp. 220–243]).

SPINOFFS AND REWARDING INNOVATORS AND TOP MANAGERS

When Fairchild Semiconductor was founded, its financial benefactor, Fairchild Camera and Instrument (FC&I), was given an option to buy it for $3 million after two years or $5 million after eight years. Exercising the $3 million option was a no-brainer given Fairchild Semiconductor's early success.

The two companies could not have been more different. FC&I was an old-line Eastern company that began by supplying cameras and aerial equipment to the Department of Defense, whereas Fairchild Semiconductor was part of the new breed of electronics and computer upstarts that would come to define Silicon Valley. In his article of December 1983 in *Esquire* magazine entitled, "The Tinkerings of Robert Noyce," Tom Wolfe described a visit to Fairchild Semiconductor by FC&I's chairman and CEO, John Carter, that crystallized the strains that eventually came between the two companies:

> Carter arrived at the tilt-up concrete building in Mountain View in the back of a black limousine with a driver in the front wearing the complete chauffeur's uniform—the black suit, the white shirt, the black necktie, and the black visored cap. That in itself was enough to turn heads at Fairchild Semiconductor. Nobody had ever seen a limousine and a chauffeur out there before. But that wasn't what fixed the day in everybody's memory. It was the fact that the driver stayed out there for almost eight hours, *doing nothing.* . . . People started leaving their workbenches and going to the front windows just to take a look at this phenomenon. It seemed that bizarre. Here was a serf who *did nothing all day* but wait outside a door in order to be at the services of the haunches of his master instantly, whenever those haunches and the paunch and the jowls might decide to reappear. It

wasn't merely that this little peek at the New York-style corporate high life was unusual out here in the brown hills of the Santa Clara Valley. It was that it seemed *terribly wrong.*

Fairchild Semiconductor helped make John Carter and FC&I very rich. Its success fueled a sharp increase in the stock price of FC&I, which enabled Carter to amass a fortune through the exercise of stock options. Managers and engineers at Fairchild Semiconductor, in contrast, had few or no stock options and saw little of this wealth. When they asked Carter for more options, they were turned down (Lécuyer [2006, p. 257]). Other parent companies in the East followed a similar practice. Certainly this was a formula for spinoffs if ever there was one. Indeed, in his study of the emergence of Silicon Valley as the center of the semiconductor industry, Lécuyer [2006, p. 258] remarked, "In this environment, the formation of new firms seemed to be the only way for silicon technologists to exploit the new business opportunities and reap the financial benefits of their work."

Charles Sporck certainly felt this way. Sporck, who had come to Fairchild in 1959 from General Electric, was the head of its manufacturing department. Fairchild had prospered through various efforts he had undertaken to restructure its manufacturing operations, including moving the assembly of transistors offshore to Hong Kong and later to other Asian countries. Yet he and other top managers at Fairchild were chagrined by the lack of stock options and the failure to recognize their accomplishments (Lécuyer [2006, p. 260]). By the mid-1960s, another tension arose. According to Sporck [2001, p. 139], "Whatever the actual numbers, it was felt in Mountain View that the Syosset [i.e., FC&I headquarters] folks were using large profits generated by semiconductor operations to fund acquisitions that didn't make a lot of sense." Increasingly they began to feel that the FC&I management did not appreciate what it took to be successful in the long run in the semiconductor business, which Sporck claims motivated him more than money to want to strike out on his own (Sporck [2001, p. 208]).

An initial opportunity in 1966 to start a new firm financed by the British electronics firm Plessy fell through after extensive discussions. During the prior year, two talented employees of Fairchild, Bob Widlar and Dave Talbert, had left to join Molectro, which by this time was owned by National Semiconductor. Sporck had tried to dissuade them from leaving Fairchild, but to no avail. A year later they plotted to replace their bosses at National and turned to Sporck. National was a small semiconductor firm with total sales in 1967 on the order of $7 million (Sporck [2001, p. 207]). According to Sporck [p. 210], an examination of National's balance sheet indicated the firm was essentially bankrupt. Its inventory was out of control, and it had too many employees for its level of sales. Sporck proposed a plan to National whereby he would bring competent people from Fairchild to completely turn the company around if they were given free rein to run the company and ample stock options to profit from their efforts.

And so it went. Sporck immediately slashed employment at National's Danbury, Connecticut, plant by over half and moved its headquarters to Silicon Valley. Widlar and Talbert were leading developers of "linear" ICs, which are used for amplification and other non-digital applications. At Molectro's Silicon Valley plant, National concentrated on linear ICs and launched a new line of digital ICs to compete with a popular IC configuration from Texas Instruments. National's ICs were faster and more reliable than TI's, and in subsequent years National successfully re-engineered other complex ICs in TI's product line. Its leaders were also creative in using independent salesmen and application engineers to expand National's product line. The firm acquired a significant cost advantage over its competitors by assembling all its ICs overseas, initially in Singapore where labor costs were substantially below those in Hong Kong. National's sales increased to $42 million by 1970 and employment increased from 300 to 2,800, enabling National to become one of the leading firms in the industry (Sporck [2001, pp. 211–217], Lécuyer [2006, pp. 267–273]).

National was by no means the only spinoff motivated by a failure of East Coast owners to motivate their top semiconductor employees in Silicon Valley. After Jean Hoerni was fired from Amelco, in 1963 he helped start a semiconductor division in Silicon Valley for Union Carbide. But he soon grew frustrated over dealing with an East Coast company that did not understand the semiconductor business and refused to grant him any stock options. Consequently, Hoerni left to start a new semiconductor venture, Intersil (for "international silicon"), to focus on advanced ICs for calculators and electronic watches (Lécuyer [2006, p. 263]). Philco-Ford's acquisition of Silicon Valley-based GM-e in 1966 had a similar effect. It canceled outstanding stock options and moved the company to its base in Philadelphia. Four different groups of employees left to form spinoffs, including one of the later leaders in table 3.3, AMI (Sporck [2001, p. 149], Lécuyer [2006, p. 263]).

NEW LEADERSHIP AND SPINOFFS

It wasn't just ossified leadership by out-of-touch East Coast companies that led to spinoffs. Changes in leadership that came from outside of a company, particularly involving acquisitions of semiconductor firms by industry outsiders, were also a major impetus for spinoffs. The stories of VLSI and LSI Logic, two of the later leaders that were founded in 1979 and 1980, respectively, are typical.

Jack Balletto, one of VLSI's founders, had also been one of the founders of its parent firm, Synertek. Synertek was formed in 1973 with a $1.25 million initial investment from four sponsoring firms. The two main customers for its memory chips were Atari and Apple, and it did about $20 million in sales with a pre-tax profit of 15%. Although that was a pretty good return on investment, Synertek could not go public or raise any money from venture capitalists to support a second fabrication facility at a cost of $5 million. So the whole company was sold to Honeywell for $22 million.

What happened next was recounted by Balletto to Rob Walker, one of the pioneers in the development of ASICs—application specific integrated circuits—customized for different buyers:

> I went from badge number three and a founder of a company that was taking on all the big guys like Intel and Fairchild to Honeywell employee number 649,312. Honeywell management was incredibly screwed up. We had meetings with the top five people at Honeywell who assured us they understood how small companies grow and would leave us on our own. That was fine until we had the first budget meeting. Our Synertek engineering guys had designed all their chips on Tymeshare* [sic] since we never could afford in-house design automation. With Honeywell money, we said, great, now we can get our own computer. Our engineering guys picked Prime as the most cost effective in-house computer solution and submitted a purchase order.
>
> Honeywell management then made it clear that Prime Computer was run by a bunch of Honeywell turncoats so we couldn't buy a Prime machine. Digital and IBM were also politically incorrect. In fact, the only choice given us was to buy a Honeywell machine. The appropriate Honeywell computer would not be available for another year, so our engineers had to design a 16-bit microprocessor on Tymeshare. I knew then that this merger was a mistake, and six months later I left to form VLSI. (Walker [1992, pp. 184–186])

---

* A Silicon Valley–based company that sold customers timesharing access to a mainframe computer.

Wilfred Corrigan told Walker a similar story (Walker [1992, pp. 36–37]) about his departure from FC&I to found LSI Logic. Right after his college graduation as a chemical engineer in 1960, Corrigan left London for a job in Boston at Transitron, one of the early leaders of the transistor industry. It was not long before he discovered that European engineers were underpaid at Transitron and moved to Motorola's semiconductor division in Phoenix. Success followed. He moved up to become head of Motorola's transistor department. When Lester Hogan left Motorola to become the CEO of FC&I in 1968, he took Corrigan with him. In 1970 Corrigan became the general manager of the semiconductor division, where he first got involved with ICs. He became president and CEO of FC&I in 1974, replacing Lester Hogan, who was made vice chairman. In 1977 Corrigan was elected chairman as well as CEO.

In 1979, FC&I became the target of a hostile takeover by Gould. Despite Corrigan's best efforts, he eventually gave up fighting a buyout and sought the best price for FC&I's stockholders. That came from Schlumberger, the giant French oil field services company.

It did not take long for the fireworks to start. Corrigan characterized Schlumberger as having an unusual business culture, a kind of "French-Tex" combination of sophisticated Europeans and Texas Rednecks. After the buyout, Schlumberger wanted to interview FC&I's senior staff to talk about replacing some of Fairchild's management. Corrigan's relationship with his new bosses quickly degenerated:

> "Hold on a minute," I said. "You have to understand that you just paid a half-billion dollars for Fairchild, and I think the smart thing to do is to let me spread 200,000 shares of Schlumberger stock around to the top 100 people as a gesture of your good will so that bonding will take place. All the Fairchild people are cashing in their stock options against the $66 price, and you've got to give more stock to the group."
>
> "That's not our policy," they said.
>
> To interview all our people, Schlumberger sent out their human resources director, a guy from the oil patch.
>
> "Well, I am going to want to talk to all of these guys," he demanded.
>
> I didn't want this redneck pissing off our people and so I said, "No you're not."
>
> "How are you going to stop me?"
>
> "Simple," I said. "I am going to tell the guards to throw you out."
>
> If this was going to be how Schlumberger was going to handle us Silicon Valley types, I could see that this wasn't going to work out.

FC&I withered under Schlumberger's leadership. Eventually it was acquired by National Semiconductor in 1987 for $122 million, less than

25% of the price Schlumberger paid for it (Sporck [2001, p. 168]). Corrigan left the company in February 1980 and headed a group that founded LSI Logic, which was one of the pioneers in developing ASICs. Similarly, VLSI also pioneered ASICs, whereas Synertek withered under Honeywell's stewardship; after seven years Honeywell sold Synertek and exited the semiconductor business.

Most of the featured spinoffs came out of successful firms and were themselves successful. A question raised in the context of the automobile spinoffs was to what extent better firms have more and better performing spinoffs because they provide better learning experiences for their employees. Gordon Moore co-authored a paper that provides a unique opportunity to gain some traction on this question.

Moore is one of the most celebrated figures in the history of the semiconductor industry. He co-founded Fairchild and Intel and is the author of Moore's law. Recently he reflected on the origins of Silicon Valley and what employees of successful incumbent semiconductor firms learned that enabled them to found successful semiconductor firms of their own (Moore and Davis [2004]).

His first lessons came under Fairchild's first general manager, Ewart (Ed) Baldwin. "He brought to Fairchild Semiconductor," wrote Moore, "the knowledge of the simple things that every MBA knew (in general) but within a technological context." This included setting up an organizational structure with a manufacturing department and an engineering department and a sales force, each with separate responsibilities. "All these things sound obvious," Moore recounted, "but we didn't know them, and they take a while to figure out."

The "we" in Moore's account are the technologist-managers, who Moore characterized as "the firm builders who do the hard work of making viable enterprises out of science." At Fairchild, Moore and his fellow budding technologist-managers began to learn about aligning the goals and incentives of the firm with those of its talented technical employees. They learned about how to establish a system of mass production. And they learned how to manage innovation to plot the shortest path to workable discovery. Fairchild was a key place to go to learn these skills. "Managers and entrepreneurs in Silicon Valley," Moore noted, "long spoke of the importance of 'Fairchild University' as an educational, managerial training ground."

The lessons continued after Fairchild. Technologist-managers had to learn not just how to create new technology but how to transmit that knowledge throughout their organization. Fairchild learned the hard way that as it matured and its production teams became more competent, it was more difficult to transfer something to them—they preferred to re-develop the knowledge themselves rather than accept what had already been done. Moore and Noyce remedied that problem at Intel by deliber-ately not establishing a stand-alone R&D Department but instead making R&D people perform development work right in the production plant.

They also learned about how to evaluate the future potential of a tech-nology, which they had failed to anticipate with ICs at Fairchild. But even more importantly, they learned that markets for intermediate products had to be broadened by deliberate action, which they took to heart with the microprocessor, as discussed in the prior chapter. Another lesson they learned that started at Fairchild is that markets could be developed by setting prices below current costs and then systematically lowering costs by studying and improving the production process.

The lessons that Moore recounted were general ones about structur-ing and managing semiconductor organizations. The *Electronics Buyers Guide* lists producers separately of many different types of ICs. Analyz-ing semiconductor spinoffs and their parents demonstrates that spinoffs also learned specific lessons about how to compete that were embodied in the specific ICs they chose to produce. Aggregating the various types of ICs into eight broad categories, the probability of a spinoff produc-ing an IC in any of the eight categories was twice as great if its parent also produced an IC in the category. A similar doubling of the probabil-ity also held when ICs were disaggregated into 50 different categories (Klepper, Kowalski, and Veloso [2011]). None of this is surprising, but it drives home the practical as well as general lessons that employees take with them when they form their own spinoffs. Many of the same themes emerge from the laser industry, to which we now turn.

Lasers are the culmination of a long quest to harness the light of atoms. The theory behind the laser dates back to the idea of stimulated emission postulated by Albert Einstein in 1916. Stimulated emission requires elec-trons to be excited to a higher energy state. When they drop back to their normal energy state, they give off a photon of light. If the photon is reflected back and hits an excited electron, it gives off another photon of the same energy. Charles Townes of Columbia University and Arthur Schawlow of Bell Labs worked out how these ideas could be used to de-velop a laser, which is an acronym for *Light Amplification by Stimulated Emission of Radiation*. A race ensued to produce the first workable laser, which was won by Theodore Maiman of Hughes Research Laboratory. In 1960 he used a doped synthetic ruby crystal to produce red laser light. Soon after Maiman's breakthrough, lasers based on a range of materials were developed, and many firms began selling lasers for both military and commercial purposes.

Klepper and Sleeper [2005] used various sources to trace the backgrounds of the entrants into the industry from 1961 to 1994, dividing them into diversifiers, spinoffs, and startups, as in autos and semiconductors.* All told, the backgrounds of 465 of the 486 entrants through 1994 could be identified. Two hundred and ninety-three, or 63% were classified as diversifiers, 79 or 17% as spinoffs, and the remaining 93 or 20% as startups. One of the 79 spinoffs was later reclassified as a startup based on interviews with its founders.

No data are available on the market shares of laser producers, in part because most firms sell systems embodying lasers as well as the lasers alone and don't report the production of lasers separately. To identify the leaders of the industry, five industry experts were consulted. They were given names of prominent and long-lived laser producers and asked to add and delete firms to come up with their own subjective lists of early and later leaders of the industry. Table 3.5 lists the early and later entrants that at least two of the experts nominated along with the backgrounds of those entrants.

The laser industry went through the same kind of transformation as the auto and semiconductor industries in terms of its leading firms. Among the nine early leaders, four—RCA, Raytheon, GTE/Sylvania, and Hughes—were major defense electronics producers that diversified into lasers. The other five included two startups and three spinoffs. Subsequently, only four of the early leaders, including two of the spinoffs, maintained their positions. They were joined by 13 other firms, all of which were new. Nine of the 13, or 69%, were spinoffs, whereas spinoffs only constituted 17% of the entrants into the industry. Once again, spinoffs were exceptional performers.

Similar to automobiles and semiconductors, the leading firms spawned more and better spinoffs. The three firms that spawned the most spinoffs, Spectra Physics with six and Coherent and Hughes with five each, were

---

*Business directories such as Dun and Bradstreet's *Million Dollar Directory*, U.S. Patent Office records, and listings of producers of laser components and systems producers were used to identify firms that produced other products at least four years before being listed as laser producers. These firms were classified as diversifiers. Spinoffs and their parents were identified primarily through searches of the monthly issues of the trade magazine *Laser Focus* for announcements of entrants and retrospective articles detailing the histories of firms. Publication searches for the initial officers of firms and the Web were also used to track down the origins of both spinoffs and startups. See Klepper and Sleeper [2005] for detailed procedures used to classify the backgrounds of the firms.

both early and later leaders. In total, the 22 firms listed in table 3.4 that were either early or later leaders spawned .073 spinoffs per year of production of lasers versus .021 spinoffs per year of production for the rest of the firms. Among the spinoffs of the leaders, 26.7% were also either early or later leaders of the industry versus only 10.4% of the spinoffs of the rest of the firms.* In terms of longevity, 79% of the spinoffs of the leading firms that were not acquired earlier produced for over 5 years and 68% produced for over ten years versus 60% and 39%, respectively, of the spinoffs of the other firms.†

Additional information was collected about the laser spinoffs in 2003 by a doctoral student, Jeffrey Sherer, under my guidance. Although many of the spinoffs were founded in the 1960s and 1970s and had long since exited, Sherer did a heroic job of tracking down founders of 72 of the 79 firms originally classified as spinoffs. Each founder was interviewed and asked to fill out a questionnaire. Questions focused on the work histories of the founders, why they founded their spinoffs, and the extent to which their spinoffs exploited knowledge they learned working for their parents.

Similar to the founders of semiconductor spinoffs, the laser firm founders mainly had technical backgrounds, ranging from technical managers such as the director of technology development to research scientists and engineers. Their main motivation for founding their spinoffs was, similar to autos and semiconductors, some kind of disagreement or different perception about what kinds of lasers were worth producing and developing.

To illustrate, table 3.5 reproduces a table from Klepper and Sleeper [2005] concerning the impetus for the founding of eight representative spinoffs, including four of the later leaders of the industry, Uniphase, Laakman, Lexel, and Omnichrome. Each spinoff initially produced one of the eight main types of lasers. The four later leaders, as well as Cynosure and Laser Diode Labs, pursued ideas that arose at their parent firms but were either rejected, abandoned, or not aggressively pursued by their parents.

---

*There were 30 spinoffs of parents that were leaders of the industry, and eight of these spinoffs also became leaders of the industry, including (parent in parentheses): University Laboratories (Optics Technology), Korad (Hughes), Coherent (Spectra Physics), Apollo (Korad), Lexel (Coherent), Liconix (Coherent), Laakman (Hughes), and Uniphase (Spectra Physics). There were 48 spinoffs of parents that were not leaders of the industry, and five of these spinoffs became leaders of the industry, including (parent in parentheses): Quantronix (TRG/Control Data), American Laser (Control Laser), XMR (ILC), Omnichrome (Electro Optical Systems), and Cymer (Helionetics).

†These computations exclude firms still in the industry in 1994 that were too young to have produced for five and ten years, respectively.

TABLE 3.4:
Early and Later Leading Laser Producers and Their Origins

Early Leader	Entry Year	Origin	Later Leader	Entry Year	Origin
Spectra Physics	1961	Startup	Spectra Physics	1961	Startup
Korad	1961	Spinoff	Korad	1961	Spinoff
Raytheon	1961	Diversifier			
RCA	1962	Diversifier			
Optics Technology	1962	Startup			
Hughes	1963	Diversifier	Hughes	1963	Diversifier
Sylvania/ GTE	1963	Diversifier			
Coherent	1967	Spinoff	Coherent	1967	Spinoff
University Laboratories	1967	Spinoff			
			Holobeam	1968	Startup
			Apollo	1969	Spinoff
			Quantronix	1969	Spinoff
			American Laser	1971	Spinoff
			Candela	1972	Startup
			Lexel	1974	Spinoff
			Liconix	1974	Spinoff
			Laakman	1980	Spinoff
			Uniphase	1980	Spinoff
			XMR	1981	Spinoff
			Omnichrome	1982	Spinoff
			Spectra Diode Labs	1985	Startup
			Cymer	1987	Spinoff

For example, Uniphase continued efforts abandoned by its parent, Spectra Physics, to develop a miniaturized version of Spectra's helium-neon laser, which led to hand-held scanners. Similarly, Laakman used technology its founders developed at its parent, Hughes, which Hughes did not aggressively pursue to pioneer less expensive carbon dioxide lasers that were widely adopted by commercial users. Acquisitions spurred the formation of the other two spinoffs, Questek and JEC. Questek's founders felt they were not adequately compensated in the acquisition and left to found their own firm, while the founders of JEC exploited a regional market that their parent abandoned after it was acquired.

Similar to the semiconductor spinoffs, laser spinoffs generally produced products that were similar to their parents. Among the 78 firms ultimately classified as spinoffs, 72 had parents that produced or researched their spinoff's initial laser at or before the entry of the spinoff (Klepper and Sleeper [2005]).* Consistent with this overlap, most spinoff founders indicated that their parent was an important source of knowledge for their spinoff. Responding to a question with four possible answers, 26% of the spinoff founders indicated they would not have started their spinoff without knowledge learned at their parent, 36% indicated that an important aspect of their spinoff's work originated with information learned at their parent, and 28% indicated that they exploited general knowledge they acquired at their parent. Only 10% of the spinoffs said they learned nothing of value from their parent.

Overall, the patterns regarding spinoffs in the laser industry are very similar to those in autos and semiconductors. Spinoffs disproportionately dominated the ranks of the later leaders. The main impetus for their formation was some kind of disagreement. Leading firms spawned more and better spinoffs. Similar to "Fairchild University," laser spinoffs appear to have learned a great deal from their parents about lasers generally and specific types of lasers.

Turning now to tires, it appears that the learning process may go back quite a ways.

Spinoffs were not as prominent in the tire industry as in autos, semiconductors, and lasers, but they were still a significant force in the industry. They were much more challenging to trace than in the other industries, and little information exists on why they were formed. But the concentration of the industry around Akron in Northeastern Ohio

---

*The original numbers reported in Klepper and Sleeper [2005] are 73 of 79, but these have been adjusted for the spinoff that was reclassified as a startup.

TABLE 3.5:
Strategies of Spinoffs and Parents

- Helium Neon (HeNe)—Uniphase (spinoff, 1980), Spectra Physics (parent): Employees involved in an effort to redesign Spectra's HeNe lasers left to found Uniphase after Spectra abandoned the effort due to a pessimistic outlook on the HeNe market. Uniphase developed a smaller and improved version of Spectra's HeNe laser that prompted a patent infringement suit that was amicably settled. The laser was initially sold to customers similar to Spectra's, but eventually it opened up a new market for hand-held scanners.

- Carbon Dioxide (CO_2)—Laakman (spinoff, 1980), Hughes (parent): Kathy and Peter Laakman licensed technology they had patented at Hughes to develop a sealed-off CO_2 laser that Hughes did not aggressively pursue. Laakman initially targeted Hughes's military customers but soon successfully marketed its laser for commercial and medical applications.

- Solid State (NdYag)—JEC (spinoff, 1980), Holobeam (parent): After Holobeam was acquired and moved from the northeast to Florida, JEC's founders left to form a distributor and also serviced Holobeam's northeastern customers. JEC developed an NdYag laser as a replacement for Holobeam's unit and then developed a complete NdYag laser for marking systems. Holobeam's acquirer developed a competitive system to JEC's after initially concentrating on Holobeam's main NdYag laser for resistor trimming.

- Dye—Cynosure (spinoff, 1992), Candela (parent): Founders of Candela purchased its research division to develop a smaller, cheaper dye laser they were working on at Candela after Candela declined to commercialize it. It competed with Candela in certain medical applications, which ultimately resulted in a patent infringement action by Candela.

- Ion—Lexel (spinoff, 1974), Coherent (parent): Using a technology partly from another firm, Coherent explored the use of a ceramic tube to improve its ion laser but ultimately abandoned it due to manufacturing difficulties. Employees who suggested a solution to the manufacturing problems that was not heeded left to develop a similar laser for lower-power applications than Coherent's market. Later they developed a higher-power version of the laser that competed with Coherent's ion laser.

- Semiconductor—Laser Diode Laboratories (spinoff, 1968), RCA (parent): After RCA encountered difficulties in developing semiconductor lasers for defense applications, an employee involved in the effort left to develop a semiconductor laser for battlefield imaging through smoke and fog. Laser Diode Laboratories was not successful with its initial plan.

- Excimer—Questek (spinoff, 1984), Lambda Physik (parent): When Lambda Physik was acquired, the founders of Questek left to develop a similar excimer laser to Lambda Physik with a better software interface and superior field service. Questek initially targeted similar scientific users as its parent but did not fare well in direct competition with its parent. It was modestly more successful when it focused on ophthalmic applications not serviced by its parent.

- Helium Cadmium (HeCd)—Omnichrome (spinoff, 1982), Xerox (parent): After an internal dispute, Xerox abandoned HeCd lasers. Employees with greater confidence in HeCd lasers left to continue their production using intellectual property and inventory supplied by Xerox. Omnichrome targeted reprographic applications, with Xerox its main customer.

provided a unique opportunity to study how the accumulation of industry experience by founders affected the performance of their spinoffs.

A trade journal, *India Rubber Review*, ran a regular column featuring industry news in the Akron area, which made it possible to trace the origins of many of the tire entrants in Northeastern Ohio. A total of 126 Ohio firms entered the tire industry through 1930, after which entry into the industry was negligible. This level of entry was more than in any other state. To make it feasible to track down the origins of tire entrants, attention was restricted just to the 126 Ohio entrants. Following the other industries, various sources were used to classify entrants as diversifiers, spinoffs, and startups.* Larger cities periodically compiled city directories listing for every worker his or her employer and position. These directories made it possible to trace in detail the work histories of founders of all the spinoffs.

The backgrounds of all but nine of the 126 Ohio entrants could be traced. Similar to automobiles, most of the entrants were new firms—44 were spinoffs, 56 were startups, and 17 were diversifiers. Three of the top four firms in the U.S. tire industry, Goodrich, Goodyear, and Firestone, were located in Akron. Collectively, they had 13 spinoffs, hereafter referred to as "direct spinoffs" for short.† Only one other Ohio firm, Mason, was comparably fertile, with four spinoffs. The work histories of the founders of the spinoffs revealed that nine other Ohio spinoffs were founded by individuals who at one point had worked for Goodrich, Goodyear, or Firestone but subsequently moved on to other tire firms. These spinoffs of the three leaders, hereafter referred to as "indirect spinoffs" for short, provided an opportunity to explore whether the lessons founders extracted from their previous experience might even precede their (immediate) parent.

Although lacking comprehensive market share data for the leading tire firms, table 3.6 shows the comparative performance of the different types of spinoffs based on the number of years they produced tires.‡ Consider

---

*Diversifiers were easiest to trace. They tended to come from the rubber and rubber machinery industry and were identified mainly using lists of producers in these industries compiled from *Thomas' Register of American Manufacturers*. New firms were classified as either spinoffs or startups using various sources, including the *India Rubber Review*, county histories, obituaries, and state incorporation records. As in the other industries, rules and judgments were required to classify firms into the three categories. See Buenstorf and Klepper [2010] for the specific rules employed.

†This includes one spinoff of Diamond Rubber, which was acquired by Goodrich in 1912.

‡Only two of the 44 spinoffs (one direct and one other) were acquired by other tire firms before they amassed ten years of production and so acquisitions were ignored in these computations.

TABLE 3.6:
Years of Tire Production for Different Types of Spinoffs in Ohio

Type	Number	Number (%) > 5 years	Number (%) > 10 years	Average Years
Direct	13	10 (77%)	6 (46%)	16.5
Indirect	9	5 (56%)	4 (44%)	22.3
Other	22	7 (32%)	3 (14%)	7.9

first the percentage of firms that produced tires for over 5 years. The direct spinoffs performed best, with 77% of them producing over 5 years, followed by the indirect spinoffs, with 56% producing over five years. Both did far better than the rest of the spinoffs, which only had 32% that produced for over five years. By ten years of age, the indirect spinoffs virtually caught up with the direct spinoffs, with 46% and 44% respectively of the direct and indirect spinoffs producing for over 10 years versus only 14% of the other spinoffs. In terms of the average years of production, the indirect spinoffs actually produced the longest, 22.3 years, versus 16.5 years for the direct spinoffs and 7.9 years for the other spinoffs. Once again, the spinoffs of the leading firms were exemplary performers, including not just their direct but also their indirect spinoffs.

These patterns suggest that nurturing began early at the leading tire firms. Recall that in the semiconductor industry, the only two later spinoff leaders that did not have parents that were later leaders were founded by individuals who previously worked at Fairchild Semiconductor. It seems plausible that nurturing began early in the semiconductor industry as well. Indeed, it will be argued in the next chapter that the importance of heritage also started early in the automobile industry. Heritage appears to run very deep.

The only group of firms whose heritage has not yet been considered is the penicillin producers. Their story is short and sweet. All the firms that ever made it into the ranks of the leaders were participants in the World War II effort. These firms were handpicked by the government and were all diversifiers. Similar to TV receivers, to the extent there were spinoffs of penicillin producers, they did not get far in the industry.

● ● ●

What can be learned from the various industries about spinoffs and their place in the capitalist order?

Spinoffs were clearly a force to be reckoned with in automobiles, semiconductors, lasers, and to a lesser extent tires. The early leaders of these industries tended to come from related industries. But in time, many of these firms were displaced by spinoffs, which accounted for a much higher share of the later leaders of their industry than entrants overall. The best firms were especially rich sources of these spinoffs.

A number of the best firms became controlled at some point by people who did not seem very adept at managing people or ideas, which provided the impetus for frustrated innovators to leave those firms and establish many of the leading spinoffs. Ransom Olds left Olds Motor Works because the Smiths thought they knew best how to run the company, only to run it into the ground. Charles Sporck and others left Fairchild because they felt FC&I did not know how to run a semiconductor business, which ultimately was borne out by Fairchild Semiconductor's decline. Jack Balletto and Wilfred Corrigan left their respective firms because they justifiably had little confidence in the ability of their acquirers to run their businesses. The list goes on.

In each instance, the "wrong" people got control of successful firms, and those with ideas about the best course of action for their firms left to found their own firms. Even spinoffs prompted by differences of opinion about technical ideas could be explained similarly. In many of these cases, the ideas that emerged within firms were not a good match with the abilities of key decision makers to evaluate them. For example, Gordon Moore acknowledged how little managerial experience and training he had to bring to bear in evaluating the prospects of the IC. Similarly, the Smiths had little expertise to fall back on to evaluate the kinds of cars Olds Motor Works should have developed after Ransom Olds's departure.

What is perhaps surprising is how frequently these kinds of situations arose in the evolution of the automobile, semiconductor, and laser industries. In retrospect, these industries developed in many different directions based on rich opportunities for innovation. Trying to assess where an industry is headed technologically and what innovations should be pursued is certainly challenging in such settings. As we saw in the prior chapter, even the most successful firms don't have grand strategies regarding innovation. Ideas bubble up from below, initiated by talented employees. In such an environment, it is hardly surprising that decision makers at the top might have trouble figuring out which ideas are worth pursuing.

This would seem especially the case during the early evolution of innovative industries. At this stage many technological directions can be pursued. Perhaps the greatest challenge is figuring out which ones are likely to succeed technically—i.e., what technological goals are attainable. This is very much the domain of Gordon Moore's technology managers. But by their very nature technologists have limited managerial training and experience. They may be good at making judgments about whether inventions are likely to succeed technically, but they are far more limited in their ability to judge the market potential of innovations. The situation is even worse when people not steeped in the technology get control of successful firms, such as the Smiths with Olds Motor Works and the executives of FC&I with Fairchild Semiconductor. What is perhaps surprising is how often power struggles and acquisitions result in inexperienced people grabbing the helm of successful companies.

Disagreements are hardly limited to successful firms, and many auto, semiconductor, laser, and tire spinoffs emerged from disagreements in lesser firms. Yet it is notable that with few exceptions, these spinoffs did not perform very well. Firms need certain capabilities to enter and prosper in any industry. While training within an incumbent firm is clearly desirable, it appears that unless this training is within a leading firm it is not terribly valuable. Exactly how spinoffs learn their trade from the prior experience of their founders is unclear, but it appears that in new industries the nature of that experience is of paramount importance.

Spinoffs may not have been prominent in TV receivers and penicillin because their technologies did not generate as much discord as in the other industries. Based on a survey of TV industry engineers and executives, Levy [1981, p. 36] concluded there was only one major innovation in TV receivers after the industry was launched—color TV. As discussed in chapter 2, RCA dominated the development of the color TV receiver. Pretty much the rest of the firms in the industry just stood by until the technology was commercially ready and then licensed it from RCA. In penicillin, all the participants in the war effort had access to the early technological developments. Their main task was to figure out how to produce penicillin as cheaply as possible, which did not engender a lot of disagreements.

When disagreements do arise, spinoffs are an essential component of experimental capitalism. They insure that promising opportunities for innovation are not missed or unduly delayed. One can only imagine how different the evolution of the U.S. automobile, semiconductor, laser, and tire industries might have been without spinoffs. Without Ford Motor Co. and Chevrolet, how long would it have taken U.S. automobile producers to develop economical cars with broad appeal to the masses?

Without Amelco and Signetics, what fate might have befallen the integrated circuit? Without Laakman and Uniphase, how long would it have taken to develop smaller carbon dioxide and helium-neon lasers and the many applications they opened up? Eventually these innovations would probably have been introduced. But who knows how long they would have been delayed and what impact this would have had on the success of the respective industries in the United States?

One of the great virtues of capitalism is the decentralization of decision making. If the "wrong" people get control of successful firms or are at the helm when promising new ideas arise, the "right" people within the firm have recourse to take their ideas elsewhere. On rare occasions these people may be able to finance their own spinoffs, such as when the Dodge brothers used the riches they had earned from Ford Motor Co. to finance their new firm. But most often they will have to get help from other investors outside their firm. If these outsiders are better positioned than insiders to evaluate the ideas and talents of the prospective founders, then spinoffs will be founded and new directions pursued. Incumbents may get hurt, but their industry will be propelled forward, and ultimately society will be the beneficiary.

That, at least, is the theory. Incumbents, however, are not likely to be cooperative. As Moore noted, "Large firms struggle against spin-offs. Spin-offs are often costly in terms of market share and human capital [they hire their parent's employees]. A spin-off is not always (perhaps not often) a net positive for the established firm. Most established firms, Intel and other Silicon Valley firms included, would squelch most spin-offs if they could" (Moore and Davis [2004, p. 34]). Indeed, Jackson [1997] claims that Intel was quite adept at squelching spinoffs. Moore acknowledged, though, that spinoffs can impart social benefits even as they impose private costs, and they were instrumental in the emergence of Silicon Valley as a dynamic entrepreneurial region (Moore and Davis [2004, p. 34]).

This creates quite a tension. Incumbents will want to squelch spinoffs, but society needs them. Without the efforts of incumbents to explore new ideas and train workers, though, spinoffs would not be possible. Yet if spinoffs can exploit these efforts, it will undermine the incentives of incumbents to undertake the efforts in the first place. A fine line has to be walked from a policy standpoint to make this work. Ideas and training of employees are part of a firm's intellectual property. Yet if spinoffs are to occur, they will use the intellectual property of their parents. Unlike tangible private property, ideas can be simultaneously used by multiple firms. But firms have to have enough incentive to create the ideas in the first place.

These tensions have been particularly prominent in the semiconductor industry. Intel's adoption of silicon-gate technology, discussed in the prior chapter in the context of the invention of the microprocessor, provides a useful illustration. Fairchild had begun sustained work on silicon-gate technology in February 1968 after the arrival of Frederico Faggin from its Italian affiliate. Six months later Intel, which was founded by Robert Noyce and Gordon Moore of Fairchild, was incorporated. It quickly hired Gene Flath, who was the manager of a large fraction of Fairchild's IC manufacturing (Bassett [2002, p. 178]), as its manager of manufacturing. He in turn quickly hired two engineers from Fairchild manufacturing, Tom Rowe and Gary Hart. Rowe would be critical in Intel's mastery of silicon-gate technology, which proved quite challenging. In describing Rowe's role at Intel, Bassett [2002, p. 184] noted, "Although Rowe took no written materials with him to Intel, he carried much in his head. For any straightforward process needed at Intel, he used procedures from Fairchild. And the basis for innovation frequently came from experience at Fairchild."

This is a story heard many times about semiconductor spinoffs—indeed, it is the norm. While silicon-gate technology was not protected by patents, that does not mean it was not afforded legal protection. In recent years, legal scholars have brought to the attention of economists the importance of trade secret laws. Trade secrets are ideas that firms work to keep secret because they are valuable but that they choose not to patent. Employees cannot use such secrets in other firms. Was Rowe's knowledge a trade secret? Fairchild did not challenge Intel regarding how it went about mastering silicon-gate technology, so we will never know how the courts would have ruled. Other cases are easier to adjudicate. When Ewart Baldwin left Fairchild to found Rheem, he took with him Fairchild's production manuals and many of the employees he had previously hired from Hughes. He was successfully sued by Fairchild for theft of trade secrets. Lécuyer [2006, p. 275] noted that, in the late 1960s, these kind of suits grew exponentially in the semiconductor industry in Silicon Valley.

In many states, Fairchild would not have needed to resort to trade secret law to prevent Rowe from using knowledge he acquired at Fairchild on Intel's behalf. It could have prevented Rowe from moving to Intel for some period of time if it had required him to sign a suitable non-compete covenant when he was hired, which would have prevented him from moving to a competitor for a stipulated time period. Even a one-year delay might have made his knowledge obsolete in the fast-moving semi-conductor industry. But Fairchild and any other company could not do that in California. It is one of a small number of states that do not allow employers to enforce non-compete contracts or covenants.

California is the home of Silicon Valley, which is famous (or infamous to some) for "job hopping" in which employees frequently move from one employer to another, often in the same industry. Would Silicon Valley as we know it today even exist if employee non-compete covenants could have been enforced? This will be discussed further in the next chapter on indus-try clusters. For now, it is worth noting that increasingly scholars are ad-vocating that states consider changing their laws to stop non-compete covenants from being enforceable. From the historical perspective of the automobile, semiconductor, and laser industries, this is certainly an idea that merits serious consideration. If it were adopted, it would probably bring even greater scrutiny to the law on trade secrets. Should the kind of knowledge used by Rowe at Intel be protected by trade secret law? If so, it would certainly have slowed down innovation at Intel and conceivably could have undermined its pioneering of both semiconductor memories and the microprocessor. What would be the upside to society of afford-ing Fairchild this kind of protection? These issues will be revisited in the concluding chapter of the book.

The final chapter will also examine the question of whether the U.S. environment is especially conducive to spinoffs and what policies coun-tries, including the United States, can institute to improve the environment for spinoffs. First, though, the importance of spinoffs in the formation of industry clusters is considered in the next chapter.

CHAPTER 4

THE VALLEY THAT SHOCKLEY BUILT AND THE SCHOOLMASTER OF MOTORDOM

WHAT HAS BEEN THE MOST INNOVATIVE AND DYNAMIC INDUSTRIAL region in the world over the last 50 years? Most people would likely name Silicon Valley.

Silicon Valley, which is pictured in figure 4.1, is located at the southern end of the San Francisco Peninsula in Santa Clara County, California. Even after many years of growth, Silicon Valley is tiny, with Santa Clara County in its entirety only containing about one-half of 1% of the total U.S. population as of 2010. Yet Silicon Valley is home to an extraordinary number of famous technology companies, nearly all of which originated there in the last 50 years. Just a small sampling of Silicon Valley companies, listed alphabetically, reveals what an incredible engine of high-tech activity the region has been.

- Adobe
- AMD
- Apple
- Cisco
- Ebay
- Google
- Hewlett Packard
- Intel
- Oracle
- Yahoo

Apple is currently the most highly valued publicly traded firm in the world. Google, Intel, Microsoft, and Oracle are not far behind. The other companies are hardly slouches themselves, household names among technology devotees. Many people became millionaires when these companies went public, and a few became billionaires. And this is just a short

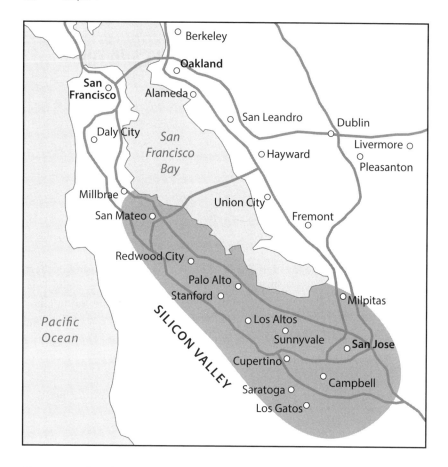

Figure 4.1: The Silicon Valley Region
(Source: https://intelligentcommunity.org/index.php?src=blog&year=2012&
category=Innovation&srctype=lister&pos=10,5,15)

list of the leading Silicon Valley high-tech firms. How could such a tiny
region generate so much high-tech activity and wealth? Every region and
country would like to know the Silicon Valley secret.

The silicon in Silicon Valley's name reflects the region's extraordinary
concentration of semiconductor producers. Few would dispute that the
region's emergence as a high-tech center was catalyzed by the semiconductor industry. But that just moves the key question back one notch—
how did the semiconductor industry become so concentrated in Silicon
Valley? It certainly was not because Silicon Valley had natural advantages for semiconductor producers; silicon is one of the most plentiful

resources on the planet, and there were not many electronics producers in the region before the semiconductor industry started there.

Economists and geographers have an answer for how industries like this end up so concentrated in one region. They envision a self-reinforcing process at work. Once an industry cluster forms in a region, it benefits the firms there. They have more workers to choose from to match their needs. Suppliers move in close to producers, making transactions less costly. Proximity makes it easier for firms to learn from each other about the latest technological advances. All these benefits make firms in clusters stronger competitors. As a result, they thrive at the expense of their competitors, taking over a greater share of their industry's output. In effect, once a cluster forms, it will naturally grow until slowed down by congestion or some other factor.

The evidence seems to line up with this view (Rosenthal and Strange [2004]). Firms in clusters are more productive and survive longer than their rivals. Entry also tends to be greater in clusters. Less is known about how clusters get going in the first place, but that is really not critical. Any random event can trigger a cluster to start. Curiously, though, not many industries become nearly as clustered as the semiconductor industry. In the typical manufacturing industry, plants are located closer together than would be expected by chance, but clustering is still modest, especially when there is no natural advantage possessed by any region (Ellison and Glaeser [1997]). Perhaps the initial event starting a cluster has to be dramatic to unleash the self-reinforcing forces envisioned as causing clusters to grow. Or perhaps something further is needed for clusters to grow, such as one or more exceptional early performers. Not much is known about this.

Michael Porter, the Harvard Business School professor of corporate strategy, has given a lot of thought to the importance of clusters in his book, *The Competitive Advantage of Nations* (Porter [1990]). In his view, the prosperity of developed countries depends on their ability to compete in innovative industries, which is enhanced by clustering:

> Proximity [i.e., clustering] increases the concentration of information and thus the likelihood of its being noticed and acted upon. Proximity increases the speed of information flow within the national industry and the rate at which innovations diffuse. At the same time, it tends to limit the spread of information outside because communication takes forms (such as face to face contact) which leak out only slowly. Proximity raises the visibility of competitor behavior, the perceived stakes of matching improvements, and

the likelihood that local pride will mix with purely economic motivations in energizing firm behavior. [1990, p. 157]

In Porter's view, nations that develop strong clusters in innovative industries are likely to prosper in international competition. Regions like Silicon Valley are not only regional assets, but they also enhance the ability of U.S. firms to compete internationally.

If clusters are important sources of a nation's competitive advantage, as Porter calls it, then understanding how they emerge and grow is of compelling importance. Among the six featured industries, two others besides semiconductors historically were heavily clustered: the automobile industry around Detroit and the tire industry around Akron. Although Detroit has suffered greatly in recent times with the decline of the U.S. auto industry, and there is little trace today of the tire cluster around Akron, in their heyday the Detroit and Akron clusters were even more extreme than the cluster of semiconductor producers in Silicon Valley. And like Silicon Valley, neither region had any compelling natural advantages for their industry. The central focus of this chapter is on what caused these three industries to become clustered.

Unlike most studies of clusters, the analysis here will focus on how each of these clusters started and evolved. Each will be dissected nanoeconomically, looking for common patterns in the evolution of the firms that populated them. The TV receiver industry will be similarly dissected. It is hardly an industry well known for clustering, but at first it was heavily clustered and then became much less so over time. The evolution of its firms will also be analyzed nanoeconomically, searching for clues about why it evolved so differently from the other three heavily clustered industries.

There is a general belief that the clustering of the semiconductor industry in Silicon Valley represents a fundamental change in the character of capitalism, a new model for innovation and the creation of wealth (Lindgren [1971], Sporck [2001], Moore and Davis [2004]). The nanoeconomic analysis of autos, tires, and semiconductors suggests the opposite—they are all part of a common process that dates way back, perhaps even to the beginnings of capitalism. Key to this process is spinoffs. All three clusters were distinguished by a much higher fraction of entrants that were spinoffs than other regions, and spinoffs were instrumental in the success of each cluster. The conventional view of clustering put forth by economists and geographers today does not address spinoffs as a potent clustering force, nor is it clear why mainly spinoffs would be especially well positioned to take advantage of any regional advantages conferred by clustering. Indeed, evidence will be presented that questions whether firms in the three clusters generally performed better because of advantages from being located in a cluster.

In autos, tires, and semiconductors, the process of reproduction and inheritance underlying spinoffs resulted in a buildup of top producers around early successful firms, which was instrumental in the clusters that formed in each industry. Autos and semiconductors exemplified how spinoffs drove clustering, with each experiencing a veritable explosion of spinoffs spurred by the decline of a once-great firm. The spinoffs more than made up for the lead firm's decline, suggesting that spinoffs do not grow merely at the expense of their parents. The TV receiver industry was different because spinoffs were not potent competitors, undermining the key force responsible for clusters.

Semiconductors, autos, and tires were unusual industries in terms of how extreme their clusters were. This is precisely why they were studied— extreme examples of a phenomenon can be especially illuminating about why it occurs. They are hardly the norm, though, which would explain why the kind of extreme clustering they experienced is uncommon. Rarely, for example, do we see the explosion of so many successful spinoffs in one region that occurred in Detroit and Silicon Valley. Indeed, industries like TV receivers in which spinoffs are inert and clustering does not flower are more common. Penicillin was like TV receivers, and lasers was an intermediate case regarding spinoffs and geographic clustering. They will also be discussed, but more briefly than the other four industries because they break no new ground.

Many questions are raised by the findings in this chapter. Porter and others have described clusters as being important aspects of a country's ability to compete internationally based on the putative benefits of firms locating close to each other. Is it possible that clusters could still play their conjectured role even without these benefits being terribly salient? Porter repeatedly notes the importance of spinoffs in spurring the performance of clusters, but his observation is not directly connected to his logic about how clusters contribute to a nation's prosperity. Yet if spinoffs are potent enough to spur the growth of clusters even when their progenitor declines, could they be the force that makes clusters important elements in a nation's international competitiveness? And if so, what does this imply about public policy to promote clusters? These and other questions will be grappled with at the end of the chapter and then picked up again in chapter 7 when lessons from all the chapters are synthesized.

• • •

Silicon Valley is one of the modern industrial wonders of the world. So we begin the analysis of clustering with how the semiconductor industry came to be so concentrated there. It is a remarkable story of how a potent combination of great talent and dysfunction can generate extraordinary prosperity.

The success of Silicon Valley can be traced back to one man, William Shockley. Shockley was the Babe Ruth of his industry. Ruth was perhaps the greatest baseball player that ever lived. He was a prodigious home-run hitter whose reckless lifestyle off the field was as well known as his exploits on the field. The New York Yankees acquired his talents in 1919 and a few years later took a big risk by building a gigantic new stadium. The Yankees went on to win a number of World Series and drew enormous crowds, and Yankee Stadium came to be known as "the house that Ruth built."

Like Ruth, Shockley was a giant in his field but less impressive outside of it. He was an esteemed physicist who shared the Nobel Prize for the invention of the transistor and founded the first semiconductor firm in Silicon Valley. He was also infamous for his racial views and paranoid in his management style, which doomed his company. But he was an extraordinary recruiter, and the failure of his firm unleashed a torrent of talented semiconductor spinoffs that galvanized Silicon Valley. If Yankee Stadium was "the house that Ruth built," then Silicon Valley can rightfully be thought of as "the valley that Shockley built."

Shockley's association with Silicon Valley dates back to his boyhood. His mother was one of the earliest female graduates of Stanford University in Palo Alto, and his family moved there in 1913, three years after his birth in London. As a boy, Shockley was subject to uncontrollable fits of rage, a harbinger of what was to come. He needed special attention not available in public schools and until age 8 was home schooled. His father, who died when he was 15, stimulated his interest in nature and science, while his mother taught him mathematics. In 1923 his family moved to Los Angeles, where he attended high school and then majored in physics at Cal Tech. After graduation, he headed east in September 1932 to enroll in a doctoral program in physics at MIT.

Shockley was determined to learn quantum mechanics, the burgeoning field in which particles of energy and matter were conceptualized to behave like waves and waves were conceptualized to behave like particles. Four years later, with his doctorate in hand, Shockley was the first physicist hired by Bell Labs (AT&T's research arm) after it lifted its Depression-era freeze on new hires (Riordan and Hoddeson [1997, pp. 4–5]). With the encouragement of Bell's research director, Mervin Kelly, Shockley set out to develop a solid-state device (i.e., one made of solid materials) to replace the balky and unreliable switches and amplifiers used in phone equipment. Shockley soon presided over a study group of scientists and engineers from Bell Labs and surrounding universities who were seeking to uncover the inner secrets to the strange behavior of semiconductors and how the modern theories of solids could explain that behavior. Success would await greater understanding of how electrons move in semiconductor materials such as germanium and silicon, which conduct electricity better than insulators such as rubber or glass but not as well as metals. Advances in solid-state electronics during World War II provided some of this understanding, and after becoming vice president of Bell Labs, Kelly organized a new solid-state physics group at Bell in New Jersey in 1945 with Shockley as its co-leader.

Two members of Shockley's group, John Bardeen and Walter Brattain, made the first breakthrough with the invention of the point-contact transistor toward the end of 1947. Bardeen was a theoretical physicist who began working at Bell Labs in 1945. He came up with the key ideas, which were implemented by Brattain, who had worked as an experimentalist at Bell Labs since 1929. Bardeen and Brattain worked shoulder-to-shoulder for nearly a month to get their new device to operate. It was fashioned out of a slab of germanium. Two electrical leads were soldered to a small strip of gold foil glued to a plastic wedge pressed onto the surface of the germanium. When it was powered up, it amplified electrical input signals manyfold, which Brattain demonstrated by speaking a few impromptu words into a microphone. In an experiment likened to Alexander Graham Bell's first successful test of his telephone apparatus 70 years earlier, Brattain's voice boomed in the ears of a headphone connected to the circuit.

The point contact transistor was a crude device that was difficult to manufacture, but it demonstrated the potential of semiconductor solid-state devices to serve as amplifiers. Shockley was elated with his group's success but chagrined by not being one of the inventors. The prior two years had been a time of ferment. Many ideas had been discussed by Shockley's group, typically with Shockley as the ringleader. But it was Bardeen and Brattain, on their own, who made the breakthrough.

Galvanized into action, Shockley spent nearly all of his free time trying to design an even better solid-state amplifier that would be easier to manufacture and use than the point contact transistor. Within a month or so he came up with an idea for a device that involved two wires attached to the ends and one wire to the middle of a small strip of semiconductor material, which could be either germanium or silicon. His device, named the junction transistor, was based on junctions established within the semiconductor material through the diffusion of chemical impurities, which eliminated the need for the delicate point contacts in Bardeen and Brattain's unwieldy device.*

It took a few years to translate Shockley's ideas into practice and prove their worth. But Shockley had great confidence in his ideas and rarely missed an opportunity to convey this to Bardeen and Brattain, whose relationship with their boss soured. After the invention of the point contact transistor, Shockley's group mainly worked on his theoretical ideas, which members of his group then investigated experimentally. Since Bardeen was also a theorist, he was effectively enjoined from contributing to his group "unless I wanted to work in direct competition with my supervisor, an intolerable situation" (Riordan and Hoddeson [1997, p. 185]).

Bardeen complained to Shockley's superiors, but they took no action until Bardeen decided to move to the Physics Department at the University of Illinois. Although Bardeen and Brattain would share with Shockley the Nobel Prize for the invention of the transistor in 1956, back in 1951 he wrote a three-page letter to Kelly explaining how the transistor led to his decision to leave Bell Labs. "My difficulties stem from the invention of the transistor," which "led to the semiconductor program being organized and directed in such a way that I could not take effective part in it" (Riordan and Hoddeson [1997, p. 192]). Bardeen would go on to win a second Nobel Prize in physics in 1972 for his work at Illinois on superconductivity.

After Bardeen's departure, Shockley was passed over for promotions within Bell Labs. Bardeen's complaints about Shockley had not gone unnoticed. Other world-class physicists had also complained about his overbearing competitiveness and heavy-handed approach to managing

---

* Not to be outdone by Bardeen and Brattain's 1949 *Physical Review* article "Physical Principles Involved in Transistor Action," Shockley published an article, "The Theory of P-N Junctions in Semiconductors and P-N Junction Transistors," in the *Bell System Technical Journal* (1949) and would soon complete the manuscript for his classic treatise of 1950, *Electrons and Holes in Semiconductors*, which clearly laid out the role of minority carriers (or holes) in the behavior of semiconductors.

people. According to his biographer (Shurkin [2006, p. 145]), Shockley experienced a bit of a mid-life crisis, which "reached its apex early in the summer of 1955. In two months, Shockley, aged 45, got a divorce, left his job, and decided to start a company of his own. He even sold his car, his beloved MG."

Shockley sought financing for his new firm, which he planned to focus on producing silicon junction transistors using recent advances developed at Bell Labs. Eventually Arnold Beckman, a fellow Cal Tech graduate who Shockley knew, agreed to finance Shockley's company, which was christened Shockley Semiconductor Laboratory. Beckman had founded a successful firm in Southern California in the 1930s to produce a pH meter he invented, and he wanted Shockley's company to be located there. Shockley preferred the San Francisco Bay area where his mother was living and he had grown up. When he heard of Shockley's plans, Frederick Terman, the provost and dean of engineering at Stanford, encouraged him to locate near Stanford. They shared a similar philosophy of recruiting first-rate people and paying top salaries, and Terman became a close ally in Shockley's efforts to found his company. The recruiting advantages from being near Stanford eventually convinced Beckman to allow Shockley to locate his company nearby in Palo Alto.

Shockley's fame and connections helped him recruit what proved to be an exceptional staff. At first he tried to hire men he knew well from his research department at Bell Labs, but they all turned him down. Disappointed, he redoubled his efforts. Shurkin [2006, p. 169] recounted how "he traveled from one end of the country to the other and to Europe, placed ads in publications such as *Chemical & Engineering News*, and scoured other labs. He went to one meeting of the American Physical Society in Pasadena ostensibly to give a speech. Actually, he told the audience, he was recruiting. He had arrangements with some places, such as Lawrence Livermore Laboratory, to get the names of people who had refused jobs there. That is how he found Gordon Moore."

He found Robert Noyce, a recently minted physics PhD from MIT, at Philco in Philadelphia, where he was working on transistors. Noyce was frustrated with Philco and awed by Shockley. When Shockley called him, "it was like picking up the phone and talking to God," Noyce recalled. "He was absolutely the most important person in semiconductor electronics" (quoted in Riordan and Hoddeson [1997, p. 237]). Shockley had intelligence tests administered to all his potential recruits. He even devised his own questions to test creative thinking. One of his favorites: If 127 people entered a conventional (i.e., single elimination) tennis tournament, how many matches had to be played to crown a winner? Shockley was looking for an elegant solution, and Noyce gave it to him. With only one winner, 126 people had to be eliminated, which required 126 matches (Berlin [2005, p. 60]).

Shockley recruited many other brilliant scientists and engineers, nearly all of whom were under 30. Initially he concentrated on producing silicon transistors using new techniques developed at Bell Labs to diffuse chemical impurities into silicon to create alternating layers with an excess or surfeit of electrons. Things did not go smoothly. Shockley was frequently on the phone with scientists at Bell to get direction and occasionally one or two flew out to Palo Alto to consult in person. It proved to be difficult to form good junctions between the diffused silicon layers. At a certain point, Shockley inexplicably decided to change course and put all his efforts into making a new, more complicated device of his own invention that was even more difficult to produce than diffused silicon transistors. Many of his employees thought this was not a good direction for the firm. But to Shockley, scientific advance was the result of solitary genius or at most a small number of geniuses, and he was unmoved.

This decision created considerable tension with his staff, which was compounded by Shockley's dysfunctional management style. He conducted some of his projects, including work on his new device, in secret, with only some of his staff allowed to participate. He did not trust his employees and would call up Bell Labs to check if their work was correct. He accused one of his employees of being a pathological liar and screamed insults at another, which led some of the other employees within hearing distance to threaten to quit. Things really degenerated after one of his secretaries cut herself on a pin left in a door. He was sure it was done deliberately, and in one account of this episode (Shurkin [2006, p. 176]) every employee was told to take a polygraph test up in San Francisco. After one went and was exonerated the rest refused to go, and Shockley had to back off. According to Shurkin [2006, p. 175], Shockley's problems stemmed from his competitive nature. "[H]e could not keep himself from believing that he was in a competition. Just as he had set himself up against Brattain and Bardeen at Bell Labs, he now exhibited the same behavior against his own employees, the very people he hired because they were so bright. He just didn't want them to be as bright as he was."

The precise chronology of the mutiny that ensued is unclear, but it was not long before the so-called traitorous eight left to form Fairchild Semiconductor. Included in this group were Noyce, Moore, Jay Last,

Jean Hoerni, C. Sheldon Roberts, Victor Grinich, Eugene Kleiner, and Julius Blank. They were all in their late twenties and early thirties. All but Kleiner and Blank, who were mechanical engineers with significant manufacturing experience at Western Electric, had PhD's. Despite various overtures they made to get Beckman to bring someone else in to manage the firm and attempts by Beckman to address their concerns, ultimately Beckman declared Shockley to be the boss. Everyone was told to "take it or leave it" (Riordan and Hoddeson [1997, p. 250]).

Backed into a corner, the group of eight felt they had to leave. They tried to find another employer nearby for the whole group. When that proved impossible, they were receptive to an overture from Alfred Coyle and Arthur Rock of Hayden Stone, a small investment banking firm in New York, to form their own firm. As discussed in the prior chapter, they were able to secure funding from Fairchild Camera and Instrument, a Long Island company then getting involved in missiles and satellite systems. With initial funding of $1.3 million, they founded Fairchild Semiconductor in 1957 in Mountain View, California, only a mile from Shockley Semiconductor Laboratory's original site. Their plan was to produce the diffused silicon transistors that they had originally worked on at Shockley Semiconductor.

Among the founders, only Noyce had any management experience to speak of, and he assumed the position of head of research and development. Ewart Baldwin, an experienced manager from Hughes Semiconductor with a PhD in physics, was brought in as general manager, and Thomas Bay, who had experience selling components to military avionics firms, was hired as manager of sales and marketing. Baldwin knew how to organize a semiconductor firm and ramp up production of new products to high volume. He also had a good sense of the military market for semiconductors and the size of the potential market for diffused silicon transistors.

The industry had initially produced germanium transistors, but germanium has a lower melting point than silicon and cannot operate at temperatures greater than 90°F, which was critical for military applications. Germanium transistors also do not completely turn off and continue to "drip electrons" like "a maddening faucet that you can never quite shut off completely" (Riordan and Hoddeson [1997, p. 221]), which limited their use in the Bell Telephone system. Texas Instruments, which started out as a small company producing seismographic equipment for oil prospecting, had developed the first silicon junction transistors in 1954. Subsequently they had a monopoly over the military market, but their transistors had significant limitations for certain military applications, which provided an opening for Fairchild.

Sherman Fairchild, Fairchild Camera and Instrument's head, was the largest stockholder in IBM. He convinced IBM to contract with Fairchild to produce silicon transistors for the advanced digital computer it was designing for the B-70 bomber. Securing such an order and actually delivering diffused silicon transistors that would meet IBM's exacting standards was another matter. The founders decided to divide up the required tasks. As Moore recounts:

> We divided the work to fit the backgrounds of the group. Roberts took responsibility for growing and slicing silicon crystals and for setting up a metallurgical analysis laboratory. Noyce and Last took on the lithography technology development, including mask making, wafer coating, exposure, development, and etching. Grinich set up electrical test equipment, consulted with the rest of the group on our electronic questions, and taught us how to measure various transistor parameters. Kleiner and Blank took charge of the facilities and set up a machine shop to make the equipment and fixtures we could not purchase. I took on the diffusion, metallization, and assembly technology development. Hoerni, our theoretician, sat at his desk and thought. [1998, pp. 55–56]

Fairchild's founders came up with numerous innovations to solve challenges encountered at each stage, and by August 1958 the first transistors were delivered to IBM. They had better performance characteristics than TI's silicon transistors, and sales took off. Then a crisis arose that threatened Fairchild's very survival. Tapping the cans in which its transistors were packaged could cause the transistors to malfunction. After months of unsuccessful efforts, it was finally discovered the transistors were shorting out due to loose particles being attracted by electric fields at the junctions between the diffused silicon layers. Tapping tests at the end of the production line were used to reduce the failures, but they could not be eliminated.

Fairchild's theorist and thinker, Hoerni, came to the rescue. He devised an unorthodox solution to the problem that led to a landmark innovation, the planar process. Building on new results reported by Bell Labs and prior experiments in which he had been involved at Shockley Semiconductor, Hoerni grew a layer of silicon dioxide on the top of the silicon wafer at the very beginning of the manufacturing process. Although silicon dioxide was considered harmful to transistors, he left the silicon dioxide layer on at the end of processing to protect the transistor junctions where shorting occurred. This not only solved the tapping problem but provided the transistor with much improved electrical characteristics.

Translating Hoerni's ideas into practice, however, was challenging. Early yields on planar transistors—the percentage of produced devices with acceptable performance—were very low, not exceeding 5% (Lécuyer [2006, p. 152]). Bell Labs had apparently invented a similar process to Hoerni's but "decided to forego its further development because of its seeming lack of manufacturability" (Lécuyer [2006, p. 153]). Fairchild did not have such a luxury, and over the next year, "Noyce and Moore devoted very substantial engineering and financial resources to the further development of Hoerni's fragile process and the design of planar products" (Lécuyer [2000, p. 175]). These efforts paid off, and the planar process made Fairchild a leader of the industry. It also solidified silicon as the main material for semiconductors and established the main developmental path that the rest of the industry has pursued since the late 1950s.

The success of the planar process made it an easy decision for Fairchild Camera and Instrument to exercise its option to buy the company for $3 million in October 1959 and convert it into a wholly owned subsidiary. This put ultimate control of Fairchild Semiconductor in the hands of a firm with little appreciation for the emerging semiconductor industry. On top of this, just before the planar process was revealed, Ewart Baldwin, along with many of his recruits from Hughes, left the firm to form his own firm, Rheem Semiconductor. Rather than look for a replacement to Baldwin, Noyce assumed the position of general manager, and Gordon Moore replaced him as head of research and development. As Lécuyer and Brock [2010, p. 32] portentously noted in their documentary history of the integrated circuit, "The business and fate of the firm was now in the hands of relatively inexperienced managers." A perfect storm was brewing within Fairchild that would lead to a veritable explosion of spinoffs.

The planar process led naturally to the integrated circuit, but as noted in the prior chapter, neither Noyce nor Moore fully appreciated its significance. Plans were formulated to build a new facility for the company's R&D lab some distance from production. This would exacerbate tensions that would arise in the next round of innovations based on metal-oxide semiconductors (MOS), which would greatly expand applications for ICs (Bassett [2002]). A strong leader could have headed off those difficulties, but that was the antithesis of Noyce's management style. When Fairchild Semiconductor's parent firm needed to hire a new CEO, Noyce was viewed as too soft, and Lester Hogan was brought in from Fairchild's rival Motorola. He brought with him over 100 managers from Motorola, who were dubbed "Hogan's heroes" after the popular, eponymous TV program at the time. Meanwhile, Moore's R&D unit was inventing new or improved devices so rapidly that neither Fairchild's manufacturing director nor or its sales manager wanted to hear about them.

These conditions caused Fairchild to implode. By the time the dust settled from the MOS era in 1972, 19 spinoffs had emerged from Fairchild, and 10 more would follow over the next 12 years. The greatest damage was done between 1961 and 1969 when a number of very successful spinoffs were formed by Fairchild's talented founders and top staff. As recounted in chapter 3, it all began with the founding of Amelco and Signetics to produce ICs, which took away Last, Hoerni, Roberts, and Kleiner and four of Fairchild's top research scientists and engineers. Two years later, a group of its best microcircuit engineers left to found General Micro-electronics (GM-e) over a dispute about the best way to respond to Signetics's success. Although GM-e ultimately was not successful, two of its spinoffs were, including AMI, which was founded by the first sales employee hired by Thomas Bay at Fairchild, Howard Bobb. As noted in the previous chapter, in 1967 some of Fairchild's top production managers, including Charles Sporck, the head of manufacturing, left in frustration over its parent's stingy compensation policies to reconstitute National Semiconductor in Silicon Valley. Intel was formed one year later after Noyce was passed over as the parent company's CEO and he and Moore grew weary over not being able to get new products out the door because of internal friction between Fairchild's R&D and manufacturing divisions. The following year Jerry Sanders, Fairchild's head of marketing, founded American Micro Devices (AMD) after he got into a dispute with the newly hired Lester Hogan.

Pooling data from the *Electronics Buyers Guide* (*EBG*) on transistor and IC producers, the producers on the ICE lists, and the Silicon Valley Genealogy, figures 4.2 and 4.3 present family trees for all the (confirmed) spinoffs in the Silicon Valley area and elsewhere through 1987.* The spinoffs of each firm are listed chronologically from left to right, with only the most significant spinoffs named to economize on space. The top half of figure 4.2 depicts what have been cleverly called the "Fairchildren," or all of Fairchild's spinoffs and the four generations of spinoffs descended

---

* The Silicon Valley area is broadly defined as the Consolidated Metropolitan Statistical Area (a delineation used by the Census Bureau to define labor markets in urban areas) around San Francisco encompassing the San Francisco Peninsula.

from them, nearly all of which were located in Silicon Valley. Among Fairchild's 29 direct spinoffs, six made it into the top 10 and two more into the top 20 largest (merchant) producers at some point between 1974 and 1990 based on the ICE sales data. Another three spinoffs founded by ex-Fairchild employees, including one founded by Jean Hoerni (Intersil), were successful, with one making it into the top 10 and the other two into the top 20 producers. Seven other second- and third-generation spinoffs of Fairchild also made it into the top 20 producers, with four of the seven coming out of top ten parents.

The bottom part of figure 4.2 lists the firms in Silicon Valley not connected to Fairchild that had spinoffs. Of these six firms, only Hewlett Packard was significant with six spinoffs, one of which made it into the top 20 producers. Fifty-six other firms also entered in Silicon Valley, but none made it into the top 20 producers.* As reflected in figure 4.3, one spinoff of Texas Instruments (TI) located in Silicon Valley and made it into the top 20 producers, but otherwise firms outside Silicon Valley played little role in its success. Thus, nearly the entire story of the semiconductor industry in Silicon Valley is about Fairchild and its descendants.

In contrast, outside Silicon Valley spinoffs were not nearly as plentiful or important. Figure 4.3 indicates that the most significant source of spinoffs outside Silicon Valley was TI. It had six direct spinoffs and 15 descendants in all, which pales relative to Fairchild's 29 direct spinoffs and 94 total descendants. The total number of spinoffs outside Silicon Valley was 75, or 11% out of the 686 total semiconductor entrants established outside Silicon Valley, whereas spinoffs constituted 66% of the 163 total semiconductor entrants located in Silicon Valley.† Moreover, unlike Silicon Valley, many of the leaders in other regions were diversifiers, including TI, General Instrument, Motorola, and Hughes, the four leading spawners of spinoffs outside Silicon Valley. Clearly, what distinguished Silicon Valley from everywhere else was the extraordinary number and quality of spinoffs descended from Fairchild.

*The backgrounds of most of these firms could be traced, but others could only be identified as new firms based on their date of incorporation. Conceivably some of these firms might also have been spinoffs, but no evidence turned up regarding their heritage.

†The Silicon Valley Genealogy made it easier to identify spinoffs in Silicon Valley than elsewhere, so the percentage of spinoffs outside Silicon Valley might be understated relative to the percentage in Silicon Valley. If the comparison of the percentage of spinoff entrants is restricted to the (larger) firms on the ICE annual lists, all of whose backgrounds could be traced, the same patterns emerge, with Silicon Valley having a much higher percentage of spinoff entrants than elsewhere.

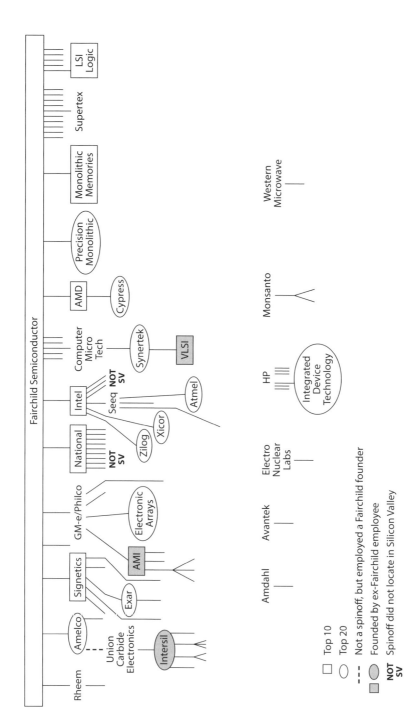

Figure 4.2: Family Trees of Silicon Valley Firms

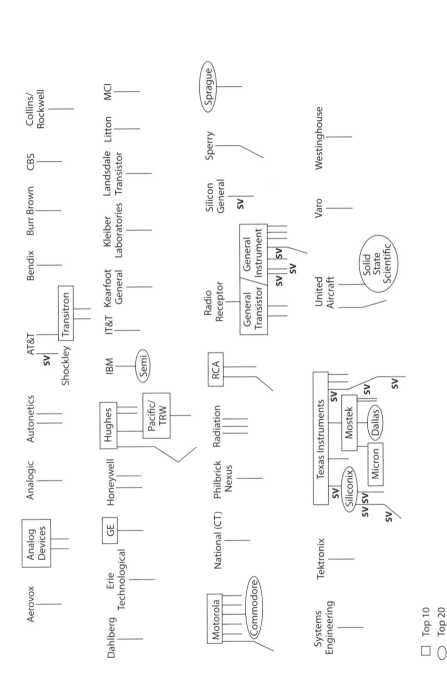

Figure 4.3: Family Trees of Firms outside of Silicon Valley

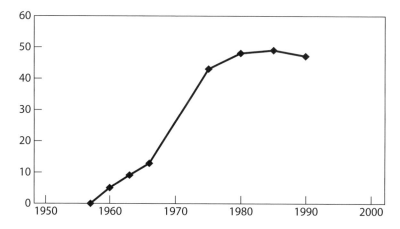

Figure 4.4: Market Share of Silicon Valley Firms as a Percentage of the Sales of U.S. Semiconductor Firms

The effect of all these spinoffs on the locus of geographic activity in the industry was dramatic. Figure 4.4 presents the percentage of the sales of U.S. semiconductor producers accounted for by firms based in Silicon Valley from the start of the industry in 1949 until 1990. The figures are based on the firm market shares reported in table 3.3 of chapter 3 and the annual sales of the other Silicon Valley firms on the ICE lists. At first, no firm was located in Silicon Valley, and the industry was mainly concentrated around New York, Boston, and Los Angeles, which accounted for 51%, 15%, and 15%, respectively, of the transistor producers listed in the *EBG* in 1961 (Klepper, Kowalski, and Veloso [2011]). Fairchild's success put Silicon Valley on the map. It was the only Silicon Valley firm listed among the leaders in 1963 and 1966, when its market share peaked at 13%. Although Fairchild's market share declined to 9% by 1975, Silicon Valley firms collectively increased their market share to 43%, reflecting the great success of the early spinoffs descended from Fairchild. Subsequently Fairchild declined further, but the market share of Silicon Valley firms continued to increase to 48% in 1980 and 49% in 1985 before falling back slightly to 47% as of 1990. Both the number of U.S.-based transistor and IC firms and the percentage located in Silicon Valley steadily increased over time, but Silicon Valley's percentage never exceeded 30% of all firms in the industry (Klepper, Kowalski, and Veloso [2011]), a number well below the collective market share of the Silicon Valley firms.

Between the talent amassed at Fairchild, its initial success, and then its implosion, there's no need to go any further to explain the clustering of the semiconductor industry in Silicon Valley. But is it possible that the clustering of the industry in Silicon Valley also reflected benefits from being located in a cluster, which might also have played a role in the high rate of spinoffs of semiconductor firms in Silicon Valley? It is always difficult to rule out a factor, but all the evidence suggests that the Silicon Valley cluster of semiconductor producers stemmed mainly from spinoffs and not from any benefits associated with locating in the cluster. There were 55 entrants in Silicon Valley that were not spinoffs, but none made it into the ranks of the top 20 producers, whereas a number of the non-spinoff entrants established elsewhere were leading firms. If there were benefits—what economists call "agglomeration economies"—from locating in Silicon Valley, all types of firms might have been expected to prosper there. But this was not the case. Moreover, the growth in the market share of Silicon Valley in semiconductor industry output was driven mainly by Fairchild's early spinoffs and was largely complete by the early 1970s, which precedes the main buildup (large-scale entry) of semiconductor firms in Silicon Valley. Last, most of the successful spinoffs in Silicon Valley had distinctive pedigrees, suggesting it was their background or heritage and not any underlying benefit of being located in a cluster that contributed to their success.

Given the mass exodus of top people from Fairchild, it is not surprising that the firm steadily declined after the 1960s and was eventually acquired and then sold to National at a distressed price. What is surprising is that its descendants more than made up for its decline, amassing a collective market share far in excess of Fairchild's market share at its peak. In large part this seems to have been due to the pioneering role that Fairchild's descendants played in developing new markets for semiconductors, particularly ones opened up by MOS and later CMOS (complementary metal-oxide semiconductors). For example, Intel pioneered MOS semiconductor memories, which opened up a large new market for semiconductors. Later it played a similar role with microprocessors. Lécuyer [2006, pp. 273–283] recounts similar roles played by other Fairchild descendants such as Intersil, which pioneered CMOS ICs for watches. By opening these new markets, Fairchild's descendants not only contributed to the growth of the industry but also expanded the share of the industry accounted for by firms in Silicon Valley.

The semiconductor industry largely represented a break from Silicon Valley's past. A few of the early recruits at Shockley Semiconductor

Laboratory came directly out of Stanford, but otherwise they came from other parts of the United States and beyond. Judging by its early patentees, whose backgrounds my students and I traced from various sources, Fairchild hired more of its inventors locally, including from Stanford, Berkeley, and some of the electronics firms that had either started or set up branches in the Stanford area after World War II. But Fairchild also recruited heavily from outside Silicon Valley, including from various Eastern electronics companies and universities located throughout the United States. It all got started with the eight founders of Fairchild hired by William Shockley, who forever changed the face of Silicon Valley. As Riordan and Hoddeson conclude:

> [Shockley] recruited a critical mass of first-rate scientists and engineers to the Stanford area, encouraging them to drink the life-giving waters of silicon and diffusion. They left his struggling band to start a dizzying succession of new semiconductor firms and turn a dry, sleepy valley of lush apricot orchards into the greatest fount of wealth on the planet. The brash entrepreneurial spirit that began with those 1957 defections from Shockley Semiconductor Laboratory multiplied a hundredfold, as job-hopping and the piracy of trade secrets became commonplace. In the process of turning silicon into gold many others became millionaires—and a few billionaires. But due to fate and his own obstinacy, Shockley never got to enter the Promised Land himself. This is why he truly deserves the title given him by his long-time friend and old traveling companion, Fred Seitz: the Moses of Silicon Valley. [1997, p. 275]

Like Silicon Valley with semiconductors in the 1950s and 1960s, Detroit and Akron were not likely places for the auto and tire industries to cluster during the first part of the twentieth century. As reflected in figure 4.5, Detroit and Akron are located in the Midwest, somewhat distant from the main population centers of the United States at the turn of the century, which were mainly in the East. Furthermore, neither region had any compelling natural advantages for their industry. Could it be that, like Silicon Valley, Detroit and Akron also sprung from the efforts of one or a few individuals like Shockley whose legacy far transcended their individual accomplishments? To that question we now turn, examining first the concentration of the automobile industry around Detroit.

To many observers, the wave of semiconductor spinoffs in Silicon Valley represented a fundamental change in the character of capitalism brought on by modern technology. Yet by turning back the clock 50 years before the rise of Silicon Valley, we can see that the automobile industry

Figure 4.5: Detroit and Akron in Perspective

followed a remarkably similar path. Not only did spinoffs play a prominent role in Silicon Valley's development, but they were also the driving force in the clustering of the automobile industry in Detroit. And just as William Shockley unleashed the spinoff process in Silicon Valley, one man, Ransom Olds, played a similar role in galvanizing spinoffs in Detroit.

Similar to Silicon Valley, at first no automobile producers were located in the Detroit area. Between the start of the industry in 1895 and 1900, 69 firms began producing automobiles in the United States, but none were located in the Detroit area. In 1901, Olds Motor Works, which was headed by Ransom Olds, began producing the Curved Dash Runabout, which took the industry by storm. Just as Fairchild took advantage of the shift from germanium to silicon transistors, Olds exploited the transition from steam and electric to internal combustion cars and by 1904 was selling an unprecedented 5,000 cars per year.

Although Olds Motor Works had been an engine producer prior to diversifying into automobiles, it subcontracted the production of all of its parts, including engines, to meet the demand for its cars. Its two main subcontractors for engines and transmissions were Leland & Faulconer and the Dodge Brothers, both local machine shops that produced parts for other companies. Another one of its subcontractors, the Briscoe Brothers, were sheet metal manufacturers that supplied Olds with radiators, gas tanks, and fenders.

In 1902, the skilled machinist and machine tool designer Henry Leland of Leland & Faulconer was brought in to advise the stockholders of Henry Ford Company about the value of their assets after they ousted Henry Ford as head of the company. Ford had been unable or unwilling to get finished cars out the door, and the stockholders wanted to close down to staunch their losses. Leland suggested that instead they could produce their own cars using an improved version of Olds's engine that he had developed but Olds had declined to use because it would have involved costly retooling. The newly reconstituted company was named Cadillac and soon became one of the leading producers in the industry. As discussed in chapter 3, in 1903 the Dodge Brothers agreed to produce engines, transmissions, and axles for Henry Ford at the outset of his new company, the Ford Motor Company, which was instrumental in its success after the failure of Ford's prior two ventures. In 1903, Briscoe Brothers helped finance Buick, which was eventually sold to William Durant and became the cornerstone of General Motors.

Like the developments that occurred at Fairchild, this set the scene for a perfect storm that would lead to an explosion of spinoffs in the Detroit area. As recounted in chapter 3, when he had to sell stock to diversify into autos, Ransom Olds lost control of his company to outsiders with little feel for managing a manufacturing company, similar to Fairchild Camera and Instrument's ownership of Fairchild Semiconductor. Henry Leland and Henry Ford were both rigid men with a singular focus who could be unreceptive to proposals from their top employees. William Durant was a manic organizer but a poor manager who could not maintain control of his company, twice being ousted from General Motors. The result was numerous spinoffs from Olds, Cadillac, Ford, and Buick/GM, which were the most prolific spawners of spinoffs in the industry. In total they had 22 collective spinoffs and 41 total descendants, most of which located in the Detroit area. Their family trees are presented in figure 4.6, including information about how long each spinoff produced (through 1936 to economize on space), whether it exited by being acquired, and whether it ever attained the ranks of the leading producers (through 1925).

Similar to Silicon Valley, spinoffs accounted for a disproportionate number of entrants in the Detroit area—48% of the entrants in the

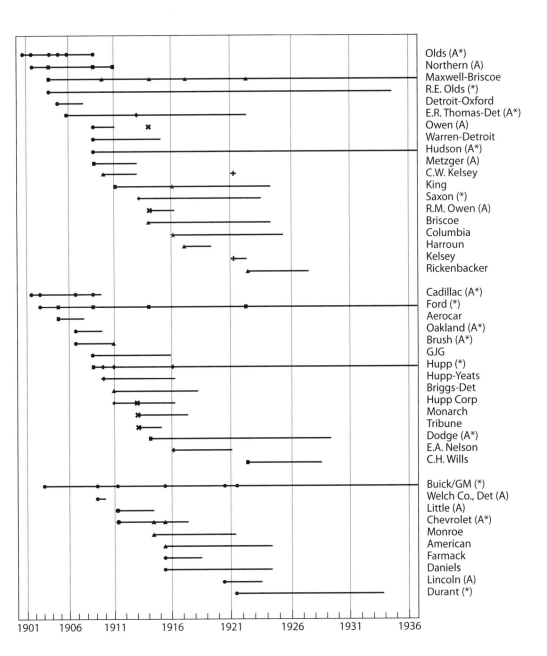

Figure 4.6: Family Tree of Leading Parents and Years Produced between 1901 (1) and 1936 (36).

Markers during a timeline denote a spinoff (indicated by a timeline below that begins with a marker of the same shape).

* indicates that the firm attained ranks of leaders by 1924

A indicates that the firm exited by being acquired by another automobile firm

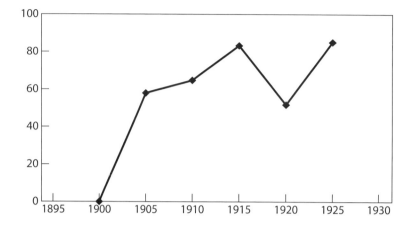

Figure 4.7: Percentage of U.S. Automobile Output Accounted for by Firms Based in the Detroit Area, 1900–1925

Detroit area were spinoffs versus 15% of the entrants elsewhere.* Also similar to Silicon Valley, the early great Detroit firms and their descendants accounted for nearly all the leading firms in the Detroit area listed in table 3.2. Almost without fail, these firms had distinguished pedigrees, similar to the Silicon Valley semiconductor spinoffs, with parents that were themselves leaders of the industry.

The effect of the spinoffs on the collective market share of the Detroit area firms is presented in figure 4.7 based on the firm market share data in table 3.2. Similar to Fairchild, Olds Motor Works put Detroit on the map and then the collective market share of the Detroit area firms rose sharply as Olds declined. By 1910 the market share of the Detroit firms had risen to 65%. It rose even further subsequently, reaching 85% by 1925 as the industry consolidated in the Big Three, Ford, GM, and Chrysler. As discussed in chapter 2, the total number of automobile firms peaked at 272 in 1909 and then steadily fell. The number in the Detroit area peaked soon after that as well, but the share of firms in the Detroit area rose steadily over time, although, similar to Silicon Valley, it never exceeded 30% through 1925.

Thus, similar to Silicon Valley, one does not have to go beyond spinoffs from the leading firms to explain the clustering of the automobile indus-

* While many firms in Michigan were located in Detroit, others were located nearby in other Michigan towns and cities. Sometimes firms in Detroit established branches or moved to nearby locations in Michigan, and vice versa. Accordingly, the Detroit area was defined as the area within 100 miles of Detroit within the state of Michigan.

try in the Detroit area. But like Silicon Valley, firms located in the Detroit area spawned spinoffs at a higher rate than firms located elsewhere (Klepper [2007, 2010]). Might this reflect that the clustering of the industry in the Detroit area was not just driven by spinoffs but also by the possible benefits from being located near other auto producers?

The automobile industry is much older than the semiconductor industry and data are available for all the automobile entrants on how long they produced. These data are particularly useful in addressing the question of whether there were advantages to locating in the Detroit area. According to my theory, the spinoffs in the Detroit area would be expected to produce longer than the spinoffs located elsewhere due to their exceptional pedigree. If it was also advantageous to be located in the Detroit cluster, then other types of entrants (i.e., diversifiers and de novo firms) in the Detroit area should also have produced longer than their counterparts elsewhere.

To assess this theory, table 4.1 reports the percentage of automobile entrants through 1924 that produced over 5, 10, 15, and 20 years for spinoffs and for all other entrants, broken down by whether they were located in the Detroit area or elsewhere.* If a firm was acquired by another automobile firm before it could produce some number of years then it was excluded from the computation—e.g., the percentage of firms producing over ten years was computed only for those firms that were not acquired before they could produce for over ten years.

As expected, the Detroit spinoffs produced markedly longer than spinoffs located elsewhere. Among those not acquired earlier, over half of the Detroit spinoffs produced for over 5 years and 17% were still producing after 20 years, whereas only 32% of the spinoffs located elsewhere produced for over 5 years and just 2% produced for over 20 years. But among the other types of entrants, those in the Detroit area are very similar to their counterparts elsewhere, with slightly more than 30% producing for over 5 years and around 5% producing for over 20 years. These rates are markedly lower than the spinoffs in the Detroit area and comparable to the spinoffs elsewhere. These patterns suggest that what made Detroit distinctive was its spinoffs and not any underlying benefits from being located in the Detroit cluster per se.

This conclusion is reinforced by table 4.2, which reports the percentage of Detroit spinoffs producing beyond each age separately for those

---

* A few firms moved in and out of the Detroit area. The location of these firms was based on where they produced for a majority of their years in the industry.

TABLE 4.1:
Percentages of Automobile Firms Producing > 5, 10, 15, and 20 Years by Background and Location

Background & Location	> 5 years	> 10 years	> 15 years	> 20 years	Number of firms
Spinoffs in Detroit	55	24	19	17	52
Spinoffs not in Detroit	32	12	6	2	90
Other firms in Detroit	32	12	10	4	60
Other firms not in Detroit	34	15	9	6	511

TABLE 4.2:
Percentages of Detroit Spinoffs Producing > 5, 10, 15, and 20 Years by Type of Parent

Parent Type	> 5 years	> 10 years	> 15 years	> 20 years	Number of firms
Leader	74	30	26	22	30
Not a leader	32	16	11	11	22

with and without a leading parent. As expected by my theory, those *with* a leading parent had markedly higher rates of production beyond each age. Among the Detroit spinoffs *without* a leading parent, they had rates of production beyond ages 5 and 10 similar to the spinoffs elsewhere and to the non-spinoffs in both the Detroit area and elsewhere. They did have somewhat higher rates of production beyond ages 15 and 20 than these other groups of firms, but this was based on just two long-lived spinoffs, one of which was founded by a prominent ex-Olds Motor Works employee (after he had founded another firm). If this spinoff is thought of as having a leading (grand) parent, the Detroit spinoffs without leading parents would look just like the spinoffs outside of Detroit and the other entrants in Detroit and elsewhere.

In terms of their joint market share, spinoffs in the Detroit area more than compensated for the decline of Olds Motor Works, just as semiconductor spinoffs in Silicon Valley more than compensated for the decline of Fairchild. The reason seems to closely parallel what occurred vis-à-vis semiconductors. The Detroit spinoffs pushed the boundaries of the industry, greatly expanding the demand for automobiles. Brush, Hupp, and Saxon produced popular low-priced small cars. Ford pioneered a car for the masses, which subsequently Chevrolet surpassed. The Dodge Brothers produced an upscale and modernized version of the Model T with an inexpensive closed body that was instantly popular. Reo, E.R. Thomas-Detroit/Chalmers, and Hudson developed larger cars with higher price tags that also garnered substantial sales. Similar to the semiconductor industry, this diversity of offerings brought many new buyers into the industry, and much of their business was captured by the leading Detroit spinoffs.

While Detroit was a big city before the advent of the automobile, the population of Wayne County, the home of Detroit, grew sixfold from 1900 to 1930, which is comparable to the growth rate of Santa Clara County (the home of Silicon Valley) from 1960 to 1990. Just as William Shockley galvanized Silicon Valley, the same could be said about Ransom Olds and Detroit. Unlike Shockley, Ransom Olds did get to the Promised Land even after he was ousted from his original company. But like Shockley, his contributions to the automobile industry far transcended his own accomplishments, and he was instrumental in Detroit becoming known as the Motor City. So if Shockley deserves to be known as the Moses of Silicon Valley, Ransom Olds deserves the title given to him to commemorate all the famous automobile people in the Detroit area who benefited from his tutelage: "the School Master of Motordom" (Doolittle [1916, p. 44]).

Recall that data on the backgrounds of tire producers were only collected for the 126 entrants in the state of Ohio, and limited market share data were available for the leading producers, which limits the analysis of the cluster of producers that emerged around Akron, Ohio. The Akron cluster was also different from the Silicon Valley and Detroit clusters in that the leading Akron producers emerged early on in the industry and never declined. But similar to the Silicon Valley and Detroit clusters, one man, Dr. Benjamin F. Goodrich, was instrumental in the success of the region, and spinoffs from the leading producers played a prominent role in fueling the growth of the Akron cluster.

Trained as a physician, Goodrich found his fortune in business, though not without difficulty. He acquired a failing New York rubber company at a young age and moved his company to Akron in 1871 in exchange for a sizable loan from local businessmen to keep it afloat. By the time he died in 1888, the B.F. Goodrich Company was prospering. Subsequently it capitalized on the bicycle craze in the 1890s by introducing a profitable line of pneumatic bicycle tires. It followed that up in 1896 by producing the first pneumatic tire for an automobile and went on to become one of the leading pneumatic automobile tire producers in the United States.

Goodrich's success played a role in the founding in Akron of Goodyear and Firestone, resulting in three of the top four tire producers being located in Akron (the fourth was U.S. Rubber, which had plants in Hartford, Connecticut and later, Detroit, Michigan).* Goodyear was founded in 1898 by two sons of one of the Akron industrialists who initially supported Goodrich. Impressed by Goodrich's success, they quickly moved their company into the production of bicycle tires, which was soon followed by a move into automobile tires. Before coming to Akron, Harvey Firestone, who was born in nearby Columbiana, Ohio, had extensive experience as a salesman for Chicago and Akron manufacturers of rubber carriage tires. Originally he came to Akron to work for a local carriage tire producer, Whitman and Barnes, and then in 1900 set up his own firm to sell and mount carriage tires of other manufacturers. In 1903 he began manufacturing his own rubber tires using supplies of prepared rubber and fabric from B.F. Goodrich. Another successful Akron rubber and tire company, Diamond, was founded in 1894 by employees of Goodrich. It was acquired by Goodrich in 1912.

Unlike the Silicon Valley and Detroit clusters, Akron got into the automotive and truck tire industry on the ground floor with the early entry there of Goodrich, Goodyear, and Firestone. Moreover, unlike Fairchild Semiconductor and Olds Motor Works, these firms did not implode but prospered and remained dominant in the industry for many years along with U.S. Rubber. Early firm market share data are lacking to trace the evolution of the Akron cluster, but data from the Census of Manufactures can be used to get a sense of the growth of tire production in Ohio. Figure 4.8 presents data from 1899 to 1919 on the share of U.S. tire and rubber production (combined) accounted for by plants in Ohio, and then from 1921 to 1935 on the share of just tire production accounted for by the Ohio plants (the Census Bureau broke out the tire industry separately beginning in 1921). The Ohio share of production steadily rose, peaking at 67% in 1935. Similar to the growth experienced by Wayne and Santa

* See Blackford and Kerr [1996] and Buenstorf and Klepper [2009] for the early evolution of the tire industry in Akron.

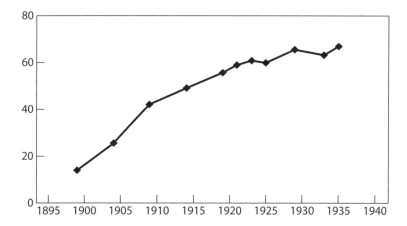

Figure 4.8: Percentage of U.S. Rubber and Tire Production Accounted for by Establishments in Ohio, 1899–1935

Clara counties, the population of Summit County, the home of Akron, increased fivefold from 70,000 in 1900 to 350,000 in 1930.

While much of this growth reflects the growth of Goodrich, Goodyear, and Firestone, Buenstorf and Klepper [2009] estimated that as of 1921 the next tier of Ohio producers, many of which were located in and around Akron, accounted for about one-third of the Ohio output. In addition to tracing the intellectual backgrounds of the 126 entrants in Ohio, Buenstorf and Klepper [2009] also traced their geographic origins. Diversifiers were classified as originating from where their previous production was based, spinoffs from where their parents were located, and startups from where their founders previously resided. Startups were the most difficult to trace; sometimes all that could be determined was that there was no evidence they originated from the county where they located or from Summit County. For nine of the 126 Ohio entrants, their backgrounds (both in terms of founders and geographic origin) could not be determined at all. In total, 103 of the 126 Ohio entrants were determined to have originated in Ohio. Figure 4.9, which is reproduced from Buenstorf and Klepper [2009], shows the counties in Ohio where they originated.

The 103 firms originated mainly in Northeastern Ohio. The largest number, 36, came from Summit County, the home of Akron. The next largest number, 16, came from Cuyahoga County, which is located next to Summit County and is the home of Cleveland, the largest city in Ohio and center of a large automotive supply industry. The map of the counties

Figure 4.9: Origins of the 103 Firms from Ohio

where the 126 Ohio firms located looks very similar (cf. Buenstorf and Klepper [2009]), reflecting that the Ohio firms generally located close to their origins, with 37 and 16 locating in Summit and Cuyahoga Counties, respectively. In total, over 70% of the producers in Ohio through 1930 (and beyond) were located in Northeastern Ohio around Akron.

Similar to the Silicon Valley and Detroit clusters, the best performing tire producers in Ohio originated in Summit County (and also located there). To illustrate, after Goodrich, Goodyear, and Firestone had entered, 29% of the entrants originating in Summit County produced for over 20 years versus 9% of the entrants originating elsewhere. The source of this strength is clear when the entrants originating from Summit County

TABLE 4.3:
Percentages of Ohio Spinoffs Producing > 5, 10, 15, and 20 Years by Geographic Origin

County of Origin	> 5 years	> 10 years	> 15 years	> 20 years	Number of firms
Summit	76	50	42	39	21
Elsewhere	27	14	0	0	23

and elsewhere are broken down by their backgrounds. Among the 36 entrants originating from Summit County, 21 (58%) were spinoffs, 8 (22%) were startups, and 7 (19%) were diversifiers. In contrast, among the 81 entrants originating elsewhere, 23 (28%) were spinoffs, 48 (59%) were startups, and 10 (12%) were diversifiers. Clearly, spinoffs were much more prominent in Summit County than elsewhere, similar to the higher incidence of spinoffs in Silicon Valley and Detroit than elsewhere in the semiconductor and auto industries.

All but 3 of the 21 spinoffs originating in Summit County were directly or indirectly descended from Goodyear, Goodrich, and Firestone, meaning that their founders at some point worked at one of these firms. In contrast, among the 23 originating elsewhere, only four were descended from these firms. Given the differences in their pedigrees, it is not surprising how much better the spinoffs originating from Summit County performed, as reflected in table 4.3.

These differences are even more pronounced when comparing the spinoffs that located (as well as originated) in Summit County versus elsewhere in Ohio. Among the 21 spinoffs originating from Summit County, eight located nearby in a contiguous county or just beyond the border of a contiguous county, and one spinoff that originated just outside Summit County located across the border in Summit County. Among the eight, only one produced for over 10 years, so the percentages in table 4.3 are even higher if the comparison is restricted to spinoffs that located in Summit County versus elsewhere. The most long-lived spinoffs that originated in Summit County also located there, including General, Seiberling, Amazon, Mohawk, and Swinehart. These firms composed most of the next tier of leading companies in the Akron cluster after Goodrich, Goodyear, and Firestone.

Apart from Goodrich, Goodyear, and Firestone and spinoffs descended from them, the other entrants in Summit County did not perform markedly better than their counterparts elsewhere in Ohio. The only other entrants in Summit County that produced for over 20 years were diversifiers, including three of the eight (other than Goodrich) located there. Elsewhere, diversifiers also performed well, with two of the eight located outside Summit County also producing over 20 years, and four of the startups outside Summit County producing for over 20 years as well. Similar to the Silicon Valley and Detroit clusters, what distinguished Akron from the rest of Ohio, and most likely the rest of the United States as well, was the large number and quality of its spinoffs. While the Akron cluster was distinctive in that its leading producers entered there early and prospered over time, like the Silicon Valley and Detroit clusters, the buildup of successful spinoffs from its early leaders helped drive its growth.

The TV receiver industry, to which we now turn, is intriguing because it provides an opportunity to see what occurs geographically when spinoffs are not a potent competitive force. As noted in chapter 3, about a third of the entrants into the TV receiver industry were diversifiers from the radio industry, and these firms dominated the ranks of the leading TV receiver producers. To drive home how dominant radio producers were, consider the performance of the 177 firms that entered into production of TV receivers between 1946 and 1989. Of these 177 firms, 58 or roughly one-third diversified into TV receivers from the radio industry. Among these 58 firms, 14 or 24% survived for over 20 years, including 9 of the 14 diversifiers that were among the top 16 radio producers as of 1940. Although it was not possible to comprehensively track the backgrounds of the other 119 entrants, most of them entered in the first eight years of the TV receiver industry. Generally a longer gestation period is required for spinoffs, suggesting that most of these firms were probably startups rather than spinoffs. Among the 119 firms, only one (or less than 1%) produced for over 20 years.

What makes this dominance particularly significant is that radio producers themselves were highly clustered in the three cities in the United States where television was commercialized: New York, Chicago, and Los Angeles. Among the 266 radio producers between 1945 and 1948, 55% were located within 25 miles of the three cities. Not surprisingly, 55% of the diversifiers of the radio industry that entered into TV receiver production were also located within 25 miles of these same three cities. What is more surprising is that the other 119 TV receiver entrants clustered in these three cities to an even greater extent—81% located within 25 miles of each of the cities. As a result, 73% of all the 177 firms that ever entered the TV receiver industry were located within 25 miles of these three cities, with New York alone accounting for 44% of the entrants. In

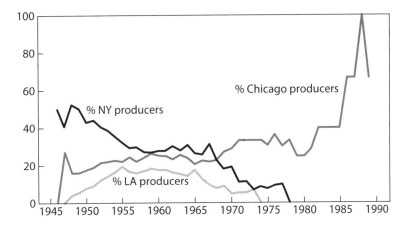

Figure 4.10: Percentage of Television Producers in New York, Chicago, and Los Angeles, 1946–1989

the semiconductor, automobile, and tire industries, the entrants were far more dispersed geographically. If there was ever an industry destined to be clustered, this was it.

Figure 4.10 plots the annual percentage of TV receiver producers in New York, Chicago, and Los Angeles from the outset of the industry in 1946 until 1989, when only three U.S. firms were left. It indicates that the industry never realized its cluster potential. Given the concentration of entrants in the three cities, one might expect that the three cities would dominate the industry throughout its evolution. International competition, initially from Japanese firms, may have thrown a monkey wrench into that expectation. Even before the Japanese invasion began in the latter half of the 1960s, though, the three city clusters did not exhibit robust growth. The percentage of firms declined in New York from a high of 50% to 30% by 1965, with Los Angeles and Chicago stable with 20% of the producers each.

In the next five years, color TV became popular and competition from Japanese firms with lower wages induced the leading U.S. firms to start transferring much of their low-skilled assembly operations offshore, mainly to Taiwan and Mexico. New York's share of producers continued to decline to 20% and Los Angeles's share of producers declined from 20% to 5%, with Chicago's share rising to 30%. In the next ten years, as competition from Japanese producers heated up and many of the remaining U.S. firms exited, New York and Los Angeles lost all their producers and Chicago's share increased and then dropped back below 30%.

Subsequently Chicago's share rose sharply, but only as the U.S. industry continued on its death march to three producers in 1989, two of which were located in Chicago.

The leading U.S. TV producers, all of which were diversifiers from the radio industry, were in the vanguard of transferring their operations to low-wage countries. Given their greater size, they could amortize the costs of moving offshore over a larger level of output, just as they could amortize the costs of R&D over a larger level of output as depicted in the theory of shakeouts featured in chapter 2. Surely New York and Los Angeles were not favored by these developments; only 19% and 13% of the entrants in New York and Los Angeles were diversifiers from the radio industry, with only one diversifier in the two cities among the top 16 radio producers in 1940. In contrast, 54% of the 26 entrants in Chicago were diversifiers from the radio industry, including five of the top 16 radio producers as of 1940. Consequently, only Chicago, with three of the leading TV receiver producers, Zenith, Motorola, and Admiral, maintained its presence in the industry over time. If there were any benefits from being located in a cluster, they were overwhelmed by broader competitive forces. And without spinoffs mounting any challenge to the leaders of the industry, there was little to prop up the fortunes of New York and Los Angeles, which were destined to lose all their TV receiver producers.

In the short story "Silver Blaze," Sherlock Holmes solves the mystery by recognizing the significance of the expected not occurring—a dog that did not bark. The TV receiver industry was destined to be clustered given the extraordinary clustering of its entrants, but then it did not bark—it did not spawn potent spinoffs. Without the buildup of successful producers around early entrants, the initial clusters that formed in the industry did not flourish, nor did any other geographic clusters arise. If there were any benefits from locating in clusters, they were not strong enough to offset the broader forces operating on the industry.

Penicillin followed closely in the path of the TV industry. All of the firms that succeeded in the industry were part of the World War II effort sponsored by the federal government. Their location, which mirrored where they were based before the war, largely determined where penicillin producers were ultimately located in the United States. Without spinoffs, no cluster formed around any successful producer(s).

Lasers offer an intermediate case in which the industry clustered around Silicon Valley, largely driven by spinoffs. Spectra Physics and its spinoff, Coherent, were the longtime leaders of the industry. Both were located in Silicon Valley.* They were the only two early leaders in the region to remain as later leaders, as shown in table 3.5 of chapter 3, but the region's cluster was replenished with five additional later leaders, four of which were spinoffs. Two of these spinoffs, Uniphase and Lexel, came out respectively from Spectra Physics and Coherent, which were the top two spawners of spinoffs during the period 1961–1994 (when firm backgrounds were traced) with six and five, respectively. (Hughes, located in Southern California, also had five.) Overall, spinoffs were heavily concentrated in Silicon Valley, with 23 of the 79 total spinoffs in the years 1961–1994, or 29%, coming out of parents located there. Like autos and semiconductors, the percentage of firms that became later industry leaders located there, 41%, was greater than the percentage of all firms located in the region, which settled down to around 15% after the industry's early years. Lacking a single spawner of spinoffs as prolific as Fairchild or a cadre of top spawners like Olds, Buick/GM, Ford, and Cadillac, the Silicon Valley cluster was substantial but less impressive than the leading clusters in semiconductors, autos, and tires.

• • •

Today Silicon Valley is one of the industrial crown jewels of the United States. It is a tremendous engine of entrepreneurship and economic growth that has helped the United States maintain its high-tech preeminence. In their time, the clusters of automobile producers around Detroit and tire producers around Akron also helped make the United States the high-tech center of the world.

These three clusters are among the most extraordinary regions without any obvious natural advantages that have emerged in modern times. As such, they provide an ideal laboratory to study how clusters emerge and grow. Consistent with the conventional view that clusters are driven by a self-reinforcing process benefiting their denizens, entry was heavily concentrated in each of the clusters, and firms located therein outperformed firms in their industries located elsewhere in the United States.

However, through labor-intensive digging beneath this patina, my nano-economic analysis of each of the clusters reveals that only one type of firm prospered in these clusters: spinoffs and, more specifically, spinoffs that emerged from the leading producers. It was these firms that were primarily responsible for the high rate of entry of new firms in these clusters. In

---

* As with semiconductors, the Silicon Valley area was defined broadly to be the Consolidated Metropolitan Statistical Area around San Francisco.

contrast, in the TV receiver industry, spinoffs were not potent compet-itors. In their absence, clustering did not flourish even though entrants were heavily clustered in the three largest cities in the United States. These findings drive home the importance of spinoffs for the phenome-non of clustering. While it is difficult to rule out entirely the presence of self-reinforcing benefits associated with clustering, the main force behind the Silicon Valley, Detroit, and Akron clusters was not these benefits but spinoffs. Nature—genetic endowments—not nurture, or "agglomeration economies," governed the histories of these three regions.

Surely the kind of explosion of spinoffs that occurred in each of the clusters, especially in Silicon Valley and Detroit, is rare. In each of these latter two clusters, one person turned out to be highly influential, which makes it hard to predict where such clusters will emerge. Early on, in-dustries tend to be led by diversifiers from related industries. But if a new industry represents a sharp break from prior technologies, even these firms will have limited advantages. The potential exists for an unexpected development, and when the stars are aligned, a dazzling industry cluster can arise in a span of 10 to 20 years.

One of the most intriguing aspects of this spinoff-driven process, ex-emplified by semiconductors and autos, is how it can be spurred by a great success followed by organizational dysfunction and decline. In both semiconductors and autos, this was linked to a diversity of new product offerings developed by spinoffs. But why is this diversity tied to spinoffs? Why can't it flower within incumbent firms? For example, why was Texas Instruments's success after the development of the IC insufficient to make Dallas as dynamic a semiconductor region as Silicon Valley? TI certainly spawned far fewer spinoffs than Fairchild. But why did its continued suc-cess not compensate for its lack of spinoffs in terms of Dallas's prospects relative to Silicon Valley?

This is not an easy question to answer, but the issues have long occu-pied economists. Leading incumbents in industries rarely are the source of major innovations in their product lines. Jane Jacobs, one of the great scholars of cities and their sources of growth, provides an intriguing di-agnosis of the problem:

> When large organizations actively try to add new goods or services to those they already produce, they create, like special reproductive organs, spe-cial divisions of labor for that purpose called research and development departments . . . [B]y definition, the parent work on which R&D can build, in comparison with the organization's total work, is exceedingly limited.

And even within these limitations, the new work that the researchers find it logical to develop frequently turns out to be irrelevant or hostile to the interests of the organization as a whole. Hence we have the paradox of useful inventions neglected by the very organizations that have "taken the trouble" to develop them. (Jacobs [1969, pp. 76–77])

Further insights into this phenomenon can be gleaned from a study by Chesbrough [2003] of 35 spinoffs that emerged from Xerox in the 1970s and 1980s, mainly from its Palo Alto Research Center (PARC) that it set up in Silicon Valley to engineer the "office of the future." PARC was famous for many innovative ideas that it developed but Xerox did not exploit internally. Xerox varied greatly in its involvement in these 35 spinoffs. In some it owned most of the stock and filled most of the seats on the board of directors, and in many of these spinoffs it also appointed the CEO from within its ranks. In others such as Adobe, which was very successful, Xerox took no equity at all, enabling venture capitalists (VCs) to participate to a much greater degree.

Chesbrough [2003] studied the performance of the 35 spinoffs based on whether they went public and what the market value of their stock was at that point. His main finding was that the more Xerox was involved in the spinoffs, the worse they performed. Chesbrough and Rosenbloom [2002] focused on six of the spinoffs, including two of the most successful, Adobe and 3Com, to understand why Xerox's involvement was so harmful. They found that all six of the spinoffs initially did not have a successful business model. Apparently VCs were more adept than Xerox's management in helping the spinoffs to productively change their business models, but the more involved Xerox was in a spinoff, the less room there was for VCs to participate. Seemingly, Xerox was handicapped in developing new ideas by a narrow mind-set it had developed from its copier business. As Smith and Alexander [1988] described this phenomenon, Xerox was "fumbling the future."

From society's standpoint, it would have been better off if Xerox had not been involved in any of the spinoffs. Clearly that would not have been optimal from Xerox's standpoint. So when an incumbent is myopic or downright dysfunctional and lets productive ideas be developed by spinoffs, the region in which it resides, and more generally society as a whole, benefits. In this view, Silicon Valley and not Dallas became the center of the semiconductor industry because Fairchild imploded whereas TI was well managed. TI aggressively pursued many of the new types of ICs that were developed over time, leaving little opportunity for spinoffs and limiting the extent to which the potential of these ideas was fully exploited. Silicon Valley, on the other hand, prospered by having many of the ideas that originated in Fairchild developed in separate spinoff companies that were better suited to fully exploit the ideas.

It is noteworthy that Powell, Packalen, and Whittington [2012] independently came to a similar conclusion regarding the success of three regions in the biotechnology industry: San Francisco, San Diego, and Boston. They found that what distinguished these three regions from other regions that also possessed the requisite characteristics to be successful in this industry was openness of their lead organizations to collaborations and sponsored spinoffs, and in the case of San Diego an acquisition of its lead organization that led to an explosion of spinoffs à la Fairchild. Alternatively, when the lead organization in a region mainly exploited the ideas it developed internally and did not foster the development of new organizations, its region failed to grow.

Of course, ideas getting out of leading organizations will only fuel the growth of its region if the new firms that arise to exploit the ideas also locate in the region. By and large, this seems to be generally true—new firms don't seem to venture far from their geographic roots. Certainly this was true of the spinoffs in Silicon Valley, Detroit, and Akron—nearly all the successful spinoffs in these regions were indigenous. Many factors may keep new domestic firms from venturing far, but one that deserves special consideration in high-tech industries is the hiring of researchers. Cheyre, Klepper, and Veloso [2015] found that semiconductor spinoffs hired about a third of their initial inventors from their parents. Nearly all of these spinoffs located close to their parents, and it seems doubtful that they could have hired all of these people if they had located elsewhere.

Some economists have theorized that new firms might not want to locate in clusters to avoid having their labor poached by their rivals (Combes and Duranton [2006]). But such poaching will only be relevant once firms get started and have labor that other firms want to hire. Given the high failure rate of firms when they are young, such concerns are likely to be trumped by the benefits of locating close to their parents, whether their parents are in clusters or elsewhere. If firms are successful, they could move out of clusters later to limit the poaching of their workers. But this rarely occurred in Silicon Valley, Detroit, or Akron, probably because it would have required the firms to replace much of their specialized labor force. Thus, even though it might not be desirable to be located in a cluster once a firm is successful, inertial forces may well keep firms in place. This would explain how firms like TI and Motorola remained successful over many years even though they were located far from the center of their industry in Silicon Valley.

What do we learn from all this about public policies regarding industry clusters? One lesson is that merely bringing firms in an industry together in a region is not likely to yield significant dividends. The European Union has long supported the development of industry clusters, as reflected in the title of one of the Commission of the European Communities' (2008) communications: "Towards world-class clusters in the European Union: Implementing the broad-based innovation strategy." Russia has embarked on a costly project to develop an ambitious high-tech cluster akin to Silicon Valley in Skolkovo on the western outskirts of Moscow (Gage [2010]). But the findings in this chapter suggest that, on their own, such efforts will do little to galvanize dynamic economic growth. Clusters prosper when they are driven by spinoffs. But merely bringing together firms in an industry will have little effect on spinoffs, as evidenced by the TV receiver industry. Clusters have to grow organically and cannot be engineered merely by bringing together like kinds of firms.

Might it be possible to influence the organic growth of clusters? One thing that a region could do is to ensure that if the stars were aligned for spinoffs to occur, intellectual property laws would allow them to form without legal restraints or barriers. In the last chapter it was noted that laws regarding the enforcement of employee non-compete covenants could prevent spinoffs from occurring. Stuart and Sorenson [2003] studied the formation of spinoffs after biotechnology firms were acquired. As we saw in the last chapter with LSI Logic and VLSI, acquisitions often spur spinoffs. This was certainly true in Stuart and Sorenson's study. They found that spinoffs were more likely to form after biotech acquisitions in states that restricted the enforcement of employee non-compete covenants. Regions might also want to give some thought to laws regarding trade secrets. Intel has used such laws to inhibit spinoffs (Jackson [1997]), and regions might want to limit the conditions under which this could occur.

Can regions do more than simply insure that conditions are conducive to the formation of spinoffs? For example, the Taiwanese government was instrumental in starting a semiconductor industry based in Taipei that was largely fueled by spinoffs. Thus, government can play a part in getting a high-tech industry started, in this case in a developing country.

Government also played a role in getting some of the six high-tech industries started in the United States, including semiconductors. Next we turn
to the fundamental question of whether government has a useful social
role to play in getting high-tech industries started in developed countries,
and if so, what form that role should take.

CHAPTER 5

THE GREATEST GOOD FOR THE GREATEST NUMBER

THE WARTIME PENICILLIN PROGRAM WAS USED TO OPEN THIS BOOK because it raises fundamental questions about the role of government in galvanizing the formation of high-tech industries. Government initiatives also played a fundamental role in starting the semiconductor, laser, and TV receiver industries. The main question analyzed in this chapter is what we can learn from these initiatives about how government support for new industries can potentially promote the long-term welfare of society.

The main initiatives in the four products came from the federal government and the military. The initiatives were not generally undertaken as part of some kind of over-arching industrial policy. Rather, they were designed to promote narrower goals. The wartime penicillin program, for example, was undertaken to strengthen the military's ability to participate in World War II. Both semiconductors and lasers were products important to the military, and it purchased them in great numbers. TV receivers were of marginal importance to the military, but radio communication was of enormous importance to the U.S. Navy, especially during World War I, and the navy played a major role after the war in the creation of RCA, which later propelled the TV industry forward.

Although these initiatives were mainly undertaken to satisfy parochial goals, this does not mean that we cannot learn important lessons from them about how government policy at the outset of new industries might be used to promote society's welfare. In each of the four products, the initiatives had quite long-lived effects, helping to create vibrant industries for the United States. The main question addressed in this chapter is whether the initiatives might have made sense as part of a broad-based government industrial policy.

Many of the initiatives involved, in one way or another, the support of early research related to the products. Research, particularly basic research, is a domain long recognized as worthy of government support.

Consider, for example, the invention of the transistor. It was made possible by theoretical advances in quantum theory that were mostly worked out by professors at universities rather than by employees of private firms. The advances mainly occurred well before the invention of the transistor. Knowledge is notoriously difficult to keep secret, and if the advances had been developed in private firms, it is likely that the underlying knowledge would have become widely known well before the invention of the transistor was possible. Consequently, the firms that financed the advances would have been no better positioned to invent the transistor than their competitors. No firm would have been willing to conduct research under these circumstances, so the transistor might never have been invented if research had been left entirely to private firms. And the transistor is hardly the only invention to come out of the advances in quantum mechanics. Without government finance of basic scientific research, technological progress would surely be slower.

The general principle behind government funding of basic research, or for that matter any kind of research, is as follows. If the long-term benefits to society, measured in dollars, outweigh the costs of research, then it would be in the interest of society to have the research conducted. If private firms would have difficulty capturing the full social value of the research, then it is possible the benefits to private firms of conducting the research would be less than the costs of the research. If so, private firms will not conduct the research even though the social benefits of the research outweigh the costs. It is precisely in such circumstances that government support for the research may be warranted.

This is not an idle concern, as the social benefits of research generally outweigh the private benefits. Research gives rise to innovations whose benefits are realized forever, but private firms reap the benefits only for a limited time. For example, the wartime penicillin program yielded a way to produce penicillin inexpensively. As a result, penicillin has been available to multiple generations since the war. But if the wartime program had been financed solely by private firms, it would have been just a matter of time before the discoveries would have been imitated by competitors at little or no cost. Even if private firms had been granted patents on the discoveries, this would only have afforded them a monopoly over the ideas for 17 years. After that point, all firms would have possessed the knowledge about how to produce penicillin inexpensively, and competition would have ensured that the benefits would have been passed on entirely to consumers. Society would have continued to reap the benefits of the research in the form of inexpensive penicillin, but the private firms that financed it would not, causing the private returns to research to fall short of the social returns.

The case for government support of research may be especially strong when industries are young. In the typical industry with good opportunities for innovation, over time the price of the industry's product falls and its quality rises as the innovations are realized. Typically, this brings new buyers into the market. For example, consider automobiles. As noted in the introductory chapter, in 1904, nearly ten years after the start of the U.S. industry, the number of cars sold annually was 23,400. By 1929 this had increased to 5.3 million cars through numerous innovations. If a firm innovated before 1904, initially it would have only reached at most 20,000 or so customers versus over 5 million later. Clearly, the potential returns from innovation would have been far greater later in the industry's history. Yet from a social standpoint, any innovation introduced early on would eventually have reached the much greater number of customers later even if by that time private firms were no longer reaping the benefits of the research. Consequently, the difference between the social and private returns to innovation would have been far greater when the industry was young. This is when government support for research can be especially influential.

This whole discussion has been at the level of "theory." Government is notoriously inefficient; government bureaucrats do not have the same incentives as private firms to act efficiently. Consequently, even when private firms fail to pursue innovative opportunities that could promote society's welfare, it does not mean government should jump into the fray.

Rather than continue this abstract discussion, the role that the federal government and the military actually played early on in penicillin, semiconductors, lasers, and TVs is considered. The key question asked is whether government support for these products could be rationalized based on the simple theory sketched out above about when government support for research is warranted.

The wartime penicillin program demonstrates the role government could play in galvanizing technological progress when private firms, on their own, were moving too slowly to realize the potential of penicillin as perceived by the government's wartime research leaders. As such, it is the first case considered, followed by semiconductors, lasers, and TV receivers. Each product is considered from the perspective of the intellectual environment surrounding its development, the initiatives, or lack thereof, undertaken by private firms, and the nature and effects of early government policies that influenced the formation and success of the industries that came to manufacture the new products.

• • •

Before the wartime penicillin program and the earlier discovery of the sulfa drugs in the 1930s, the medical profession had practically no tools to cure bacterial diseases. Following Pasteur and others, vaccines had been developed to prevent diseases, but actually treating them with chemical agents had proved elusive. Paul Ehrlich, the Nobel Prize–winning chemist from Germany, had developed the receptor theory of drug activity that is still the foundation of the modern pharmaceutical industry, and he set as a goal the synthesis of chemicals, which he called magic bullets, to treat each type of harmful bacteria in the body without harming the host tissue. One of the few successful applications of Ehrlich's ideas at that time was the 1910 development of Salvarsan to treat syphilis. This only reinforced the views of many in the medical community that any chemical toxic to microorganisms would also be toxic to host cells and "hunting microbes with magic bullets was little more than fantasy" (Sheehan [1982, p. 27]).

One influential member of the community who forever remained skeptical of using chemicals to treat diseases was Almroth Wright. He was Alexander Fleming's boss at St. Mary's Hospital in London where Fleming carried out his penicillin research in 1928. In his 1929 paper reporting the results of his penicillin research, Fleming speculated that penicillin might be an efficient antiseptic in humans to treat areas infected with penicillin-sensitive microbes (Fleming [1929, p. 236]). Wright adamantly opposed this conclusion and ordered it stricken from the paper (Baldry [1965, p. 71]), but Fleming resisted Wright's directive. Is it any wonder that in the face of such opposition Fleming was not able to make further progress on isolating penicillin and exploring its therapeutic properties?

If not for Howard Florey and Ernst Chain, Fleming might never have ascended to the pedestal he attained during his lifetime, including being knighted in 1944 and sharing the Nobel Prize with Florey and Chain in 1945. When Florey and Chain began work in 1938 on the isolation and purification of penicillin after reading Fleming's 1929 paper, their expectations were modest. Chain [1980, p. 21]) remarked, "There was nothing in Fleming's paper which justified the hope that his penicillin was a substance or mixture of substances of extraordinarily high therapeutic power which, for some reason, was neglected by everyone for many years."

Exploiting a sample of Fleming's *Penicillium* mold that had been sent to Florey's predecessor at Oxford University some years earlier for a different project, Florey and Chain used modern techniques to isolate a small amount of partially purified penicillin. After seeing encouraging results on mice, they tested it on a woman dying of breast cancer to determine whether it was safe for human use. While penicillin was not expected to help her, she developed a high fever and other signs of an adverse reaction. It turned out that the observed toxicity was due to impurities in the penicillin. When these were removed, it worked on the second patient, the Oxford policeman with abscesses all over his body. Although he died due to inadequate supplies of penicillin, enough additional penicillin was laboriously prepared to give to five other patients suffering from bacterial infections that had not responded to other treatments. Four recovered and the fifth died from a spontaneous rupture of a blood vessel after being brought out of a comatose state by the drug (MacFarlane [1979, pp. 328–333]).

These experiments suggested that penicillin had great potential to cure infections, but it was a devilish substance to produce (Baxter [1946]). Spores of the *Penicillium* mold were sowed in one-liter glass flasks or flat earthenware pans containing about one inch of a cultured broth. As the mold grew, a tiny amount of penicillin accumulated in the broth. It was unstable in liquid form, so a laborious process was devised in which the penicillin "was extracted into relatively small volumes of organic solvents, re-extracted from the solvent into still smaller volumes of water, purified by adsorption into alumina from which it was removed by ether and, finally, extracted into the watery solution from which it was dried" (Baxter [1946, pp. 343–344]). All told, 300 flasks yielded a powder that was 97% impure and just sufficient to treat one man for half a day, a rather paltry harvest for such a complex effort.

No wonder that when Florey visited the United States in July 1941 with another of his collaborators, Norman Heatley, only a few U.S. firms were exploring penicillin. Merck, Squibb, and Pfizer did have fledgling research efforts devoted to penicillin. However, these efforts were far from churning out practical dividends beyond making available meager supplies of penicillin for clinical testing (Hobby [1985, p. 79]). Florey visited various firms in the United States to see if he could interest them in producing penicillin on a larger scale. He was generally discouraged by their response and was "made to feel like a carpet-bag salesman trying to promote a crazy idea for some ulterior motive" (MacFarlane [1979, p. 341]).

Gladys Hobby was part of an early research team at Columbia Medical School investigating the therapeutic properties of penicillin. In her book, *Penicillin, Meeting the Challenge*, she speculated on why the U.S. pharmaceutical firms were slow to gamble on penicillin:

> Fear—that the penicillin-producing mold would contaminate other products on which they depended for sales and revenue. Fear—that the ease of contamination of penicillin-producing cultures, the instability of penicillin in the presence of an enzyme produced by some of these contaminants, and the still too low yields of penicillin then obtained in culture fluids would lead to excessive production costs. Fear—that penicillin would be synthesized so rapidly that equipment installed in 1942, even in 1943, would soon be obsolete. Fear—that the I.G. Farbenindustrie and Farbwerke Hoechst in Germany, with their remarkable ability to synthesize compounds as "606" [i.e., Salvarsan], Prontosil and related compounds, would take control of the market. Fear—that the substance would prove to be more toxic or less effective when used in large numbers of persons than was apparent in the few patients treated prior to December 1941. (Hobby [1985, pp. 109–110])

To all these fears needs to be added that the capabilities needed to make progress on the various fronts were distributed across a wide range of organizations, including universities, research institutes, government laboratories, and various firms. In their article on how the United States was able to meet its wartime production goals for penicillin, Greene and Schmitz [1970, p. 83] attributed the success to the collaboration of hundreds of "biochemists, chemists, bacteriologists, chemical engineers, biologists, mycologists, physicians, toxicologists, pharmacologists, and pathologists (to name but a few disciplines) on both sides of the Atlantic, managed and coordinated by industrial executives, academic administrators, and government leaders." No single U.S. firm came close to having the capabilities on its own to pull off the requisite advances.

Only an organization with the authority and resources of the federal government could make the wartime production of penicillin a reality (Stewart [1948]). The U.S. government was still in an isolationist mood in the late 1930s and as a result had gotten a late start in preparing for World War II. The National Defense Research Committee had been formed in 1940 at the urging of Vannevar Bush, the head of the Carnegie Institution in Washington. Its goal was to mobilize the research and development capabilities of the United States to enhance the military's ability to fight the war. Bush's efforts were supported by the presidents of Harvard, MIT, and Bell Laboratories (the latter was also the president of the National Academy of Sciences), and he became the chair of the committee. In 1941, when the Office of Scientific Research and Development (OSRD) was created, the NDRC was made a division of it. Under Bush's leadership, OSRD's mission was greatly broadened, including military medical research. Bush created the Committee for Medical Research (CMR) as a division of OSRD and selected A.N. Richards, a professor of pharmacology at the University of Pennsylvania who for ten years had also been a consultant to Merck, to head the CMR.

Although other government organizations would also play important roles, the CMR would prove to be the key actor in the wartime penicillin program. Richards was impressed with the work at Oxford, and it did not hurt that Richards had known Florey for many years and trusted his judgment (MacFarlane [1979, p. 341]). He immediately supported the kind of collaborative effort that Florey envisaged. At its sixth meeting on October 2, 1941, the CMR approved a resolution for a concerted research program on penicillin that would pool the information and resources of various organizations and also arrange a conference on the subject.

The conference took place on October 8, 1941, with Bush presiding. The research directors from Merck, Squibb, Pfizer, and Lederle Laboratories attended along with Richards, his vice-chairman, the chairman of the Chemistry Division of the National Research Council, and Charles Thom, the chief mycologist of the Department of Agriculture (mycologists study fungi like the *Penicillium* mold). At that point Merck had done the most research on penicillin production, while Pfizer had the most experience in large-scale fermentation processes, having for some years produced citric and other acids by fermentation.

Not much was accomplished at this meeting or the next one held about a month later. This all changed with the third meeting on December 17, 1941—10 days after the Japanese bombardment of Pearl Harbor—that was attended by the heads of the companies as well as their research directors. Also present was Robert Coghill, director of the fermentation group at the National Regional Research Laboratory (NRRL) of the U.S. Department of Agriculture at Peoria, Illinois. He reported that use of corn steep liquor in the culture medium to grow the *Penicillium* mold had increased yields twelvefold. As noted in chapter 1, this was the breakthrough that galvanized U.S. firms into action and later led Coghill to declare that a new industry was born.

Coghill was present at the meeting because, almost miraculously, within days of their arrival in New York, Florey and Heatley had been directed through a series of chance encounters to the U.S. group that could most help their cause. Initially they met with their benefactors at the Rockefeller Foundation, which had financed their trip, after which they visited Florey's children in New Haven, Connecticut. The children were staying with John Fulton, a Yale professor of the history of medicine and an old friend of Florey's, to avoid the dangers of the war in Britain. During their visit, Florey and Heatley met with Ross Harrison, president of the National Academy of Sciences. He sent them to the Department of Agriculture in Washington, DC, to see Charles Thom, who many years earlier had correctly classified Fleming's mold. Thom took his guests to see H. T. Herrick, who was in charge of the four recently opened regional labs of the U.S. Bureau of Agricultural Chemistry and Engineering that Congress had set up to develop new uses for surplus farm products (Hobby [1985, pp. 80–87]).

Herrick had hatched a scheme whereby directors of the four regional labs temporarily served one-month stints in Washington so that he could get away and indulge his passion for travel. When Thom brought Florey and Heatley to see Herrick, he was traveling, and his seat was reluctantly occupied by Percy Wells, who was the head of the Bureau's Philadelphia lab. As luck would have it, Wells was an expert in mold fermentation. Before heading the Bureau's Philadelphia lab, he had worked for nine years with the group that was exploring the use of deep fermentation techniques to grow natural products at the Bureau's Peoria, Illinois, regional lab. Wells immediately arranged for Florey and Heatley to visit the Peoria lab and work with scientists there on improving the yield of the *Penicillium* mold (Wells [1975]).

Within days of their visit, it was decided that the fermentation division of the lab should concentrate on three fronts: exploring the medium, temperature, and other environmental conditions in which penicillin was produced using the surface-culture method; searching for new mold strains with higher penicillin yields; and investigating whether penicillin could be produced through submerged methods (Raper [1948]). It was also agreed that Heatley would remain at the lab for two months to familiarize the staff with the work at Oxford. By September 1941 considerable progress had been made, and the Rockefeller Foundation provided additional funding to enable Heatley to stay at the lab for another three months. After the report of the lab's encouraging findings at the December 17, 1941 meeting, Richards saw to it that the OSRD provided funding for the lab to continue its work for six months beginning February 1, 1942.

The lab made substantial progress during those six months (Raper [1948]). Improvements in the culture medium increased penicillin yields in surface-culture production. A mold strain that initially had not appeared promising in surface cultures gave good results when grown submerged. Methods for testing the potency of the penicillin produced were improved. Over the next two years, the OSRD provided additional funds for continued work at the lab, with its total support estimated to be $27,000 ($365,000 in 2015 dollars). This was more than matched by support from the Department of Agriculture, which was estimated to be $100,000 ($1.35 million in 2015 dollars) (Raper [1948, p. 726]). Additional personnel were also assigned to the lab's penicillin efforts, enabling it to expand its agenda to examine the recovery, concentration, and purification of penicillin. Reflecting the lab's importance, progress reports by all the participants in the war effort were sent to it for distribution. Coghill also served as a consultant to help coordinate all the wartime penicillin efforts financed by the U.S. government [p. 727].

The lab's findings were widely used by the firms that produced penicillin during the wartime program. The formula it developed for the culture medium for surface production was used by all the firms before this method was displaced by more efficient submerged fermentation. The research it conducted on submerged fermentation using rotary drum and larger vat fermenters was instrumental in the United States meeting its wartime goals (Raper [1948, p. 730]). Pfizer was the pioneer in submerged production, but at first its yields were worse than with surface fermentation. According to Mines [1978, p. 76] in his history of Pfizer, "this might have dealt a fatal blow to submerged fermentation had not an unexpected break come their way, a double discovery." He was referring to the discoveries at USDA's NRRL of the superior mold strain for submerged production and the use of corn steep liquor in the fermentation broth. Merck, another of the leaders in submerged production, also acknowledged its debt to the NRRL in the development of Merck's submerged process (Helfand et al. [1980, p. 43]).

Despite the ultimate triumph of submerged fermentation of penicillin, the CMR's main effort during the war was devoted to the synthesis of penicillin in the laboratory (Helfand et al. [1980, pp. 48–49]). At the start of the wartime program, this was thought to be the most promising route toward the large-scale production of penicillin. After a positive report by a special committee, the CMR organized a synthesis program that included 15 firms, nine universities, five government agencies, and four research institutions in the United States and Britain. The total cost of the program was $3.27 million (more than $44 million in 2015 dollars), including $270,000 ($3.6 million in 2015 dollars) borne by government. A staunchly maintained position by an imperious British chemist that proved to be wrong slowed down progress, and by the close of the war the synthesis effort had not succeeded and was abandoned, although it did produce some useful findings about penicillin.

One researcher at Merck, John Sheehan, continued work on the synthesis of penicillin after the war as a professor at MIT with support from the drug firm Bristol Myers. On the eve of Sheehan's successfully synthesizing penicillin after many years of frustration, a British firm, Beecham, came out of nowhere to challenge his great accomplishment. Beecham had been trying to break into the antibiotics business and made a fortuitous discovery that enabled it to isolate the nucleus of the penicillin molecule from the fermentation broth, where it had resided unknowingly for many years. Building the full penicillin molecule by starting with this nucleus was cheaper than synthesizing the nucleus using Sheehan's methods and also made it possible to add side chains to the nucleus in the laboratory to create so-called semisynthetic penicillins with improved therapeutic properties. Beecham and Bristol Myers agreed to form a joint venture to produce these new forms of penicillin, but a bitter patent fight broke out between Sheehan and Beecham that scuttled their collaboration (Sheehan [1982]). Nevertheless, many semisynthetic penicillins were developed by Bristol Myers, Beecham, and other firms, opening up a new frontier for work on penicillin.

The other important role of the CMR was in the clinical evaluation of penicillin. Through its auspices, a committee ultimately headed by Dr. Chester Keefer, a professor of medicine at Boston University, took charge of clinical tests of the efficacy of penicillin. At first, Merck, Squibb, and Pfizer provided all their limited production of penicillin free of charge to the CMR, which enabled it to treat 100 patients through February 1943. As the program subsequently expanded as more penicillin was produced, the committee purchased all of its needs at a total cost of $1.9 million ($26 million in 2015 dollars) (Stewart [1948, p. 105]). The committee carefully doled out its limited supplies of penicillin to approved investigators, who were only allowed to treat patients with conditions for which penicillin showed promise and served the military's interests.

As word began to spread about the miraculous qualities of penicillin, Keefer was besieged by requests for penicillin from civilians, politicians, and other dignitaries. He steadfastly maintained the committee's guidelines, but some penicillin leaked out for unauthorized uses, complicating his difficult position as a life and death arbiter of penicillin. Perhaps the most consequential leak involved Patricia Malone, a two-year-old child with staphylococcal sepsis, who on August 11, 1943, was given just seven more hours to live. She was treated with an unauthorized supply of penicillin released by the army and was soon cured, resulting in a wave of unwanted publicity (for Keefer). Hobby wondered aloud in her book about what made John L. Smith, the VP at Pfizer in charge of penicillin production, gamble that Pfizer had the necessary technology at hand in 1943 for the mass production of penicillin using submerged fermentation. As she wrote (Hobby [1985, pp. 189–190]), "some of us who remember that summer and John Smith's intense interest in the patients being treated with penicillin in Brooklyn and Manhattan have always credited Patricia Malone for his decision to go ahead. . . . This child aroused the interest of many of us, but particularly of John L. Smith whose sixteen-year-old daughter had succumbed to an infection prior to the development of penicillin."

Clinical trials demonstrated the extraordinary therapeutic properties of penicillin, and by May 1943, it became apparent that the military would need far more penicillin than was yet available. At a meeting of the army and navy, the OSRD, and the War Production Board, another government entity that was set up to allocate scarce supplies of resources during the war, it was agreed that the WPB would assume full responsibility for the future production of penicillin (Hobby [1985, p. 171]). It selected 21 firms that it thought were best qualified to assist in meeting its production targets.

These firms were eligible for accelerated depreciation allowances on their investments in production facilities. Of their total investment of $22.6 million ($305 million in 2015 dollars), $14.5 million ($196 million in 2015 dollars) qualified for accelerated depreciation. This offset some of the risk associated with the potential synthesis of penicillin in the laboratory, which could have rendered their investments obsolete (FTC [1958, p. 53]). The WPB also financed the construction of six plants at a cost of $7.6 million ($103 million in 2015 dollars) [p. 6]. Through its Office of Production Research and Development (OPRD), it also financed a series of research projects on common challenges faced by all the producers (Elder [1970]). The projects were conducted at various universities and research institutes and resulted in a number of benefits to the industry, including a new, irradiated mutant mold strain with a significantly higher penicillin yield (Raper [1948, pp. 738–739], McGuire [1961, p. 253]).

By the second half of 1944, supplies of penicillin were sufficient to meet all of the military's needs, and in 1945 producers began selling penicillin to civilians through normal channels. Innovations in production caused the price of penicillin to decline by over 90% between 1945 and 1950, which led to a twenty-nine-fold increase in output (Greene and Schmitz [1970, p. 86]). Prodded by the success of penicillin, searches were conducted for other organisms that produced what Selman Waksman termed antibiotics—chemical substances that inhibited the growth of or even destroyed other microbes. A search of organisms in soil led by Waksman resulted in the Nobel Prize–winning discovery in 1943 of streptomycin, which was used to treat tuberculosis. Many other antibiotics with new and enhanced therapeutic qualities have since been discovered through similar searches, virtually creating a whole new pharmaceutical industry. By 1972, wholesale sales of prescription drugs in the United States had become nearly a $5 billion business ($28 billion in 2015 dollars) (Schwartzman [1976, p. 27]).

Before the advent of penicillin, most of the drugs on the market were synthesized in the laboratory. Germany was the world leader in synthetic chemistry and was the source of Salvarsan and Prontosil, the first of the sulfa drugs developed in 1935. Subsequently, the industry shifted mainly to the United States, as U.S. firms vaulted into the forefront of the discovery and production of antibiotics. Achilladelis [1993] analyzed all the antibacterial medicines in the world introduced after Prontosil through 1987. Among the 23 companies that introduced at least four of these medicines, 13 or 54% were based in the United States, including four of the top five innovators. These 13 firms also dominated the ranks of the sales leaders at the end of the period (1986–1988). All but two of the 13 firms were involved in the wartime penicillin program, and the other two began producing penicillin soon after the war.

There is little question that the wartime penicillin program was a great success. The social benefits just in the United States have been enormous and have far outweighed the costs of the program. Not only did penicillin launch a revolution in medicine, but it also catapulted U.S. firms to the forefront of the pharmaceutical industry, where they have largely remained (until a recent wave of international mergers and acquisitions). The question looking forward is whether the program provides lessons about how to use government to nurture future new technologies.

Market disciples recognize the need for government and/or private foundations to finance basic research at universities and non-profit laboratories. Simply put, firms cannot capture enough of the benefits to make basic research profitable even when the social benefits of the research outweigh the social costs. Indeed, all the early work on penicillin in Britain and the United States was done outside of firms, in universities and medical schools. Judging by the actions of firms in Britain and the United States, this effort was not sufficient to lead to the commercialization of penicillin. Many fundamental issues made firms wary of pursuing penicillin on their own. What was the potential market for penicillin? How could its cost of production be reduced? Was it worth investigating the synthesis of penicillin and/or trying to lower the cost of producing penicillin via fermentation?

It turned out that the social benefits of exploring these questions far exceeded the social costs. Nevertheless, it is easy to understand why firms were slow to pursue the questions on their own. Assessing the potential market for penicillin, for example, required a systematic and costly clinical investigation along the lines of Keefer's committee. It seems unlikely that firms could have patented any of the findings, such as that penicillin could be used to treat syphilis or bacterial endocarditis, or keep such findings secret for very long. Consequently, any exploration of the market for penicillin would have benefited all firms equally, which is precisely the condition under which no firm wants to act on its own.

Similarly, many of the discoveries at the NRRL benefited all the firms involved in the wartime program. Although some of these might have been patentable or could have been kept secret for a while, judging by the desultory efforts of the firms before the wartime program, it seems unlikely they would have generated enough benefits to any one firm to justify the costs. For example, Merck was approached in 1942 to support the research that led to the improved irradiated mold strain that later emerged from the OPRD-sponsored effort, but it declined (Bud [2007, p. 38]).

The synthesis of penicillin was also unlikely to be pursued by any individual firm. It was conducted by a dream team in the wartime program, but to no avail. Is it any wonder that no firm showed any sign earlier of trying to synthesize penicillin on its own? Concerns over synthesis of penicillin also slowed down firms from investing in fermentation facilities. Surely it was in the interests of the United States to have multiple paths to the production of penicillin. But were it not for the efforts of the WPB to designate a set of firms eligible for accelerated depreciation allowances and investing in production facilities itself, it is unclear whether the production path that won out would have been pursued by any firm on a timely basis.

Was it possible to have anticipated in mid-1941 that penicillin was ripe for development but government support was needed to make it happen, or was the penicillin program simply a leap of faith in the face of the exigencies of war? Certainly no simple calculus could have justified the wartime program, much as most ambitious investments by firms in innovation cannot be easily evaluated quantitatively. In the end, reasoned judgments have to be made by those with the most knowledge. That is what occurred with penicillin. A. N. Richards was well positioned to make those judgments. He was a successful professor of pharmacology who for ten years also had a foot in industry as a consultant to Merck. He had broad connections, including a past history with Howard Florey that turned out to be significant. He did not act alone but got input from the leading firms, from experts like Robert Coghill of the NRRL and Charles Thom of the Department of Agriculture, and from Vannevar Bush and others in the wartime scientific intelligentsia.

It seems doubtful that anyone could have anticipated that the wartime program would have benefited U.S. firms so much, shifting the power base in the pharmaceutical industry from Germany to the United States. But if anyone was in a position to anticipate it, it was Richards and Bush. Germany's hegemony in the chemicals industry prior to World War II was based on its support for academic research and the exploitation of that research by its chemical firms, which conducted extensive internal R&D. In the 1920s and 1930s, U.S. pharmaceutical firms were beginning to develop their own research capabilities and were forging links to academia (Parascandola [1985]). Richards was an important go-between for Merck with the academic community and a staunch supporter of university-industry cooperation (Swann [1988, p. 66]). Vannevar Bush was the head of an important private research institute situated in Washington, DC, and devoted to basic research, providing him with an unusual position from which to judge the potential influence of science on industry. Bush's pre-war tenure as chairman of the National Advisory Committee on Aeronautics (NACA, forerunner of NASA, established in 1916 to conduct research for the nascent U.S. aircraft industry) was also key to his expansive view of the role of government in promoting research-based innovation. These experiences were reflected in the famous report he issued near the end of the war, *Science: The Endless Frontier* (1945).

What would have been hard to anticipate, though, are the long-term opportunities for innovation opened up by the pioneering of submerged fermentation of penicillin in the United States. Submerged production made possible the inexpensive manufacture of other antibiotics, spurring searches for their discovery. It also provided the foundation for the semi-synthetic penicillins, which subsequently led to semisynthetic versions of other antibiotics. Just as early entry favored automobile, tire, and TV receiver producers as discussed in chapter 2, it also favored penicillin producers (Achilladelis [1993]), which were concentrated in the United States due to the wartime program. The emergence of the postwar dominance of the U.S. pharmaceutical industry would have been difficult to predict in 1940 or 1941. Certainly Germany's long dominance of the world chemical industry was testament to how a head start in innovation could impart an enduring advantage.

Through the lens of the institutional apparatus that governed the wartime penicillin program, some important lessons can be gleaned about how government can best be organized to manage a new technology (see Pursell [1979], Neushul [1993]). The impetus for the OSRD came from private citizens, who also ended up managing it. These citizens were distinguished members of the scientific intelligentsia who had come to occupy important administrative positions in the scientific world and were familiar with the push and shove of Washington politics. Their authority to make decisions for the U.S. government was repeatedly challenged in Congress and by members of the executive branch. They were accused of being elitists who only exploited a small percentage of the scientific and engineering talent in the United States. While perhaps true, it is not clear that opening up the wartime effort to broader participation would have been helpful. Moreover, Bush and his compatriots adroitly maneuvered the political system to avoid allowing political judgments to mar their efforts. Judging by current-day political maneuvering at the federal level, it is hard to escape the conclusion that this may have been an essential element of their success.

An overriding question is how much of the success of the penicillin program was owed to the patriotism of the heads of the various firms. Soon after Vannevar Bush was appointed to direct the OSRD in 1941, George Merck sent a telegram to him expressing his support for the wartime program: "Command me and my associates . . . if you think we can help you" (Helfand et al. 1980, p. 39]). Later, John [L.] Smith of Pfizer advocated for Pfizer's involvement in penicillin because "Fleming's discovery can alter the course of the War" (Mines [1978, p. 74]). To the extent that Merck and Smith were representative, conceivably other collaborative programs organized by government that did not face the exigency of war might be less effective.

But the cooperation of the firms should not be overstated. Coghill continually complained that the Big Three penicillin producers (Merck, Squibb, and Pfizer) were not regularly reporting progress to the NRRL for distribution to other participants (Sheehan [1982, p. 73]). At the end of the war, there was a flurry of patent applications regarding penicillin, suggesting that the firms were strategically withholding findings [pp. 72–73]. Patriotism may have been alive and well in the wartime penicillin program but probably was less crucial to its success than might be imagined. Moreover, as an examination of some of the other products will show, government intervention at their outset was also extremely beneficial without the exigencies of war. This comes through clearly in the semiconductor industry, to which we turn next.

In semiconductors, it was the military and not the OSRD or a similar organization run out of the White House that played the key role in galvanizing the industry. It directly supported research early on, just as the OSRD supported early penicillin research. But its most important role was as a buyer of advanced semiconductor devices, which it also used as a means to support research and development at targeted firms. It played this role for over 20 years, whereas the OSRD was under much greater time pressure in the wartime penicillin project to realize a return from its research support.

The military's support was instrumental in the development of the two most important innovations in the history of the industry, the planar process and the monolithic integrated circuit. Perhaps even more important, the military's support was critical in the emergence of Texas Instruments and Fairchild as early leaders of the industry. Nearly all the other leading firms in the industry descended from Fairchild, and secondarily TI, so the military was instrumental in seeding what evolved to be one of the most dynamic industries in the United States since World War II.

The semiconductor industry began with the transistor, which in many ways was the by-product of another important World War II OSRD-initiated program—radar. It was said that the atom bomb ended the war, but radar won it. The World War II radar initiative had a similar heritage to the wartime penicillin program. The British invented the cavity magnetron, a device capable of transmitting radio waves of much shorter wavelength than existing transmitters, enabling a more precise rendering of enemy aircraft. In August 1940, nearly a year before Howard Florey's visit to the United States, the British sent a technical mission to the United States seeking out help in perfecting and mass-producing the cavity magnetron and in developing detectors, antennas, and other components of radar systems.

With support initially from the National Defense Research Council and then the OSRD, the U.S. government set up a central laboratory at

MIT known as the Radiation Laboratory or Rad Lab to work on radar. The radar initiative grew to be bigger than the Manhattan Project (Gertner [2012, p. 66]), with the Rad Lab alone employing a staff of nearly 4,000 as of 1945, including ten future Nobel Laureates (Bruderi [1996, p. 130]). The second most important organization in the radar effort was AT&T's Bell Labs. Initially it was assigned the job of mass-producing the cavity magnetron at its Western Electric subsidiary, and it also played a major role in developing detectors for radar signals after they bounced off of their targets. This work opened up a number of fertile intellectual fronts related to quantum mechanics, the burgeoning field in physics concerning the atomic structure of materials. As discussed in chapter 4, Bell Labs set up a fundamental research program in solid-state materials in 1945 to exploit wartime advances in quantum mechanics with the ultimate goal of finding a way to substitute solid-state materials for mechanical relays and vacuum tubes in the telephone company's networks. Out of this work emerged the invention of the point-contact transistor in late 1947 (Buderi [1996, pp. 308–333], Riordan and Hoddeson [1997, pp. 88–141]).

Bell Labs recognized the importance of the transistor to the military and gave it the opportunity to classify it as a military secret. The military declined, but as anticipated, the military became a major buyer of semiconductor devices. The defense market grew from $15 million in 1955 to $294 million in 1968, accounting for between one-fourth and one-half of the total sales of semiconductors in this period (Tilton [1971, p. 89]). Moreover, the military constantly demanded better, more reliable devices and paid a premium to meet its needs. The military also provided research and development support to semiconductor producers in various ways. It contracted directly for R&D projects, it financed production refinement programs, and its appropriations for new weapons systems were passed on by contractors to semiconductor producers to support R&D and production improvements (Tilton [1971, p. 92]). Military programs also drove the initiative for "miniaturization" of circuits for rockets and other weapons, which resulted in multiple approaches to that end, including further R&D on semiconductors and support for the integrated circuit once that invention occurred (Holbrook et al. [2000], pp. 1034–1037).

Initially transistors were fabricated mainly from germanium, but the military preferred silicon devices because they could operate at higher temperatures. Its support for silicon transistors was instrumental in Texas Instruments's emergence as an early leader of the industry. When it was founded in 1930 as Geophysical Service Incorporated, TI specialized in oil-exploration services and equipment. During World War II its technologies for remote sensing and location generated $1.1 million in equipment sales to the military. Anticipating that geopolitics would dictate aggressive military spending after the War, TI's top management cultivated a substantial military business in new electronic technologies such as submarine detection equipment and radar (Nebeker [1994, pp. 106–108]). The transistor promised great miniaturization and ruggedness, making it an ideal addition to its military product line. At first, lawyers from AT&T resisted TI's application in 1951 to license the transistor, amused at TI's conviction that it could compete in the transistor field given its limited electronics experience. After persisting for months, TI finally got its license. It sent its top personnel to the second Transistor Conference held by Bell Labs in 1952 to learn about transistors and how to produce them.

That same year TI was also able to hire Gordon Teal of Bell Labs to head its R&D. Teal was well known throughout the industry for his efforts at Bell to grow single crystals of germanium. Single crystals offered purer germanium, which was essential to precise doping of the germanium with the controlled impurities needed to make Shockley's junction transistor work. At first, though, Shockley had resisted Teal's proposal to grow single crystals, forcing Teal to work after hours with another colleague at Bell to perfect his crystal-growing technique. Eventually Teal proved the worth of his ideas. He was also anxious to return to Texas, where he had attended school as an undergraduate and thus accepted TI's generous offer to be its head of R&D.

Not only did this greatly help TI in recruiting talented members to its R&D staff, but it also launched an effort to grow single crystals of silicon for manufacturing transistors for the military. At the time most experts generally felt that the industry was years away from being able to produce silicon transistors. But capitalizing on work that Teal had done at Bell Labs, TI was able to produce silicon junction transistors by 1954, well before any of its competitors. TI's success with silicon transistors effectively gave it a monopoly on the military market for four years, enabling it to increase its sales from $27 million in 1953 to $233 million in 1960. In a retrospective article, Teal cited a 1961 piece in *Fortune* magazine on the importance of the silicon transistor to TI's success:

> The silicon transistor was a turning point in TI's history, for with this advance it gained a big headstart over the competition in a critical electronic product; there was not effective competition in silicon transistors until

1958. TI's sales rose almost vertically; the company was suddenly in the big leagues. [1976, p. 635])

Fairchild Semiconductor also owed much of its early success to military orders for silicon devices. As discussed in chapter 4, Fairchild was founded to produce silicon transistors based on the latest advances at Bell Labs on junction transistors and solid-state diffusion. Fairchild's founders had become familiar with Bell's work on diffusion at Shockley Semiconductor, though, as discussed in chapter 4, translating research into practice required many innovations. Fairchild's silicon transistors were the first to operate at high frequencies and were sought after by the military for digital-based guidance and control systems for jet aircraft and missiles. As such, the military's defense contractors were instrumental in Fairchild's initial success.

Fairchild's first contract was for transistors in the navigational computer produced by IBM for the military's B-70 aircraft. To meet IBM's exacting standards, Fairchild introduced important innovations in production, pioneering a new form of silicon manufacturing (Lécuyer [2000, p. 170]). Even greater challenges awaited Fairchild in a subsequent contract with Autonetics, a subsidiary of North American Aviation that was developing the guidance and control system for the air force's Minuteman missile. The system was expected to guide a missile to a target in the Soviet Union with a precision of a few hundred meters. It also had to be extremely reliable, putting unique demands on Fairchild.

At this stage a customer, possibly Autonetics, discovered the tapping problem discussed in chapter 4. Tapping Fairchild's transistor cans could make its transistors unfit for operation. This is where Jean Hoerni stepped in to develop the revolutionary planar process, which was widely adopted throughout the industry. Autonetics actively pushed Fairchild to develop the planar process. As Lécuyer emphasizes, "Crucial to the decision [by Fairchild to comply] was Autonetics' willingness to buy Fairchild's future planar transistors. Thereby the avionics contractor offered a large market for the new components, which would help Fairchild recoup its heavy investment in process and product engineering" [2000, p. 175].

The very high reliability standards Autonetics set also forced Fairchild to improve its quality control and testing procedures. These improvements were lavishly funded by Autonetics, which helped position Fairchild for new military business. "The Minuteman also sanctioned the firm as a manufacturer of high-reliability products—which gave it considerable visibility in the military sector in the late 1950s and early 1960s" (Lécuyer [2000,

p. 180]). As a result, Fairchild was well positioned to take advantage of the threefold growth in the military market for silicon components in the late 1950s. Its sales grew explosively from $500,000 in 1958 to $21 million in 1960. By early 1960 it employed 1,400 people. "In short," writes Lécuyer, "in less than three years Fairchild had become one of the biggest electronics manufacturers on the San Francisco Peninsula. The firm was the second largest manufacturer of silicon components after Texas Instruments, as well as the leading producer of diffused silicon components in the United States" [2000, p. 180].

The planar process led naturally to the development of the monolithic integrated circuit at Fairchild in which all the elements of a circuit were manufactured on a single piece of silicon. A few months earlier, TI's Jack Kilby developed its own version of the monolithic integrated circuit. Much work remained to be done to convert these developments into useful devices, and if not for the support of the military, it is unclear how long this might have taken. Miniaturization of electronic circuitry had been a long-standing goal of the military. Each branch of the military supported its own approach to miniaturization, including a wide range of approaches using discrete circuit elements and miniature vacuum tubes, transistor, resistors, and capacitors. But eventually the military embraced integration as the best solution to miniaturization.

The air force provided $1 million in direct R&D support to TI (Tilton [1971, p. 91]) in 1959, which was essential to keeping its IC program going (Pirtle [2005, p. 86]). Fairchild had a company policy of not accepting military R&D support, and at first, as discussed in chapter 3, it did not aggressively pursue integrated circuits. Only after the military started buying ICs from one of its spinoffs, Signetics, did Fairchild jump into the fray, soon becoming the largest producer of ICs in the United States. Other firms also started producing monolithic ICs. From 1962 to 1964 nearly all the ICs produced by TI, Fairchild, and their competitors were purchased by the defense sector, and at a substantial premium (Tilton [1971, p. 91]). As TI, Fairchild, and other IC producers improved their production processes with experience, the price of ICs fell and the number of components crammed onto them rose steadily, fueling a tremendous civilian as well as military demand for ICs.

After the development of the IC, TI continued for many years as a leader of the industry, but Fairchild faltered. As figure 4.2 in chapter 4 reflects, though, Fairchild's descendants more than made up for its decline. It was by far the most prolific spawner of spinoffs in the industry, and figure 4.3 indicates that TI played a similar role outside Silicon Valley.

Nearly all the firms that became leaders of the industry between 1960 and 1987 descended from Fairchild and secondarily TI. As such, the military's support for TI and Fairchild was critical in seeding the entire industry, which has proven to be one the most vibrant in the United States since World War II.

Similar to the federal government's involvement in the wartime penicillin program, the motivation for the military's support of the semiconductor industry was to promote its own goals rather than to generate a vibrant civilian industry. Also similar to the wartime penicillin project, anticipating the long-term effects of its policies on the civilian semiconductor industry would have been difficult. But like the wartime penicillin project, the military's support helped spur much early innovation in semiconductors when firms otherwise would have been reluctant to commit their resources to innovation because of difficulty in capturing the returns from such efforts. The military also was quite broad-minded in parceling out its support, as evidenced by its willingness to support two unproven new firms, TI and Fairchild, which together revolutionized the industry. Overall, military support was absolutely critical in creating a vibrant semiconductor industry in the United States, just as the wartime penicillin program was instrumental in galvanizing a vibrant U.S. pharmaceutical industry.

In many respects, the laser also grew out of the wartime radar effort. Its development was much more protracted than the transistor, but at every step of the way military research support was critical. And once a working laser was developed, the military provided broad research support that helped start many of the companies that became leaders of the industry and bred later generations of laser leaders.

Charles Townes was the prime mover and shaker in the work leading up to the laser. After getting his doctorate in physics at Cal Tech, he took a job at Bell Labs in 1939, where he expected to do fundamental research. In early 1941, however, he was assigned to Bell's effort on military radar. For Townes this was a disappointment, but out of a sense of duty he accepted his assignment. During his wartime stint, Townes became familiar with the challenges of developing the shorter wavelength radars demanded by the military, which later helped point him to the laser.

After the war, Townes returned to fundamental research in microwave spectroscopy. Spectroscopists study the internal structure of atoms and molecules according to how they absorb and emit radiation. On the electromagnetic spectrum, microwaves are radio waves with wavelengths between 1 meter and 1 millimeter, which include the wavelengths used in wartime radar. The postwar boon in physics brought a number of discoveries about energy levels of atoms and electrons, absorption, and emission that made microwave spectroscopy, which uses microwaves to probe the internal structure of materials, a hot field. Townes was in the middle of the action, and his reputation grew, leading the Columbia physics department to offer him a professorship in 1947, which he accepted.

The Columbia physics department was well endowed with military support. The military wanted to maintain the productive work that had been done during the war at the MIT Rad Lab and the Columbia Radiation Laboratory, which was part of the Columbia physics department. Three separate military units, the Office of Naval Research, the Army Signal Corps, and the Army Air Force, established the Joint Services Electronics Program in 1946 to provide funding to the two labs. Before the end of 1946, a JSEP program was also started at Harvard to unite residues of wartime electronics work there, and in 1947 a fourth JSEP lab was started at Stanford. For the military, the labs promoted the science and technology that might yield military breakthroughs, kept leading scientists in touch with the military's needs, and helped train future scientists. For their part, the universities received equipment and faculty and graduate student support (Bromberg [1991, p. 15]).

Townes and the military were both interested in developing new microwave sources. The military was interested in them for better communication systems and radar. Townes was interested in probing the inner workings of molecules in ways not possible with longer wavelengths (Bromberg [1991, p. 14]). He came up with a novel idea that was later named the MASER, for *Microwave Amplification* by the *Stimulated Emission* of *Radiation*. If molecules of a suitable substance were passed through a magnetic or electric field, the excited ones would be separated from the unexcited ones. In turn, the excited molecules would be passed through a suitable chamber, called a resonant cavity, with reflective walls. If the right material was selected—Townes settled on deuterated ammonia gas—the result would be a buildup of microwave energy focused narrowly on a single wavelength.

The idea proved difficult to implement in practice. Working with a Columbia graduate student, Townes persisted even in the face of demands by his department head, himself a Nobel Laureate, and another distinguished faculty member to abandon the effort because of its cost and unlikely success (Hecht [2005, p. 24]). After roughly two years, Townes and his graduate student succeeded in developing a working maser. It was a large, complex, and sensitive device that never made it out of the laboratory, but it attracted considerable interest among other physicists. Work at Harvard and at another military-supported laboratory associated with the University of Michigan resulted in masers based on solid state crystals, which were far more practical. Yet in the end, even solid state masers proved to have limited applications (Hecht [2005, p. 32], Bromberg [1991, p. 61]). But the maser opened the door for its newer cousin, the laser, which emitted much shorter waves in the visible light portion of the electromagnetic spectrum, justifying the substitution of the L (for light) for the M (microwaves) in the nomenclature.

The idea for the laser also came from Townes and his brother-in-law Arthur Schawlow, who was an employee of Bell Labs. Schawlow had gotten his doctorate in physics from the University of Toronto in 1949, after which he spent two years as a post-doctoral fellow with Townes before marrying Townes's younger sister and taking the position at Bell Labs. In the maser, the resonant cavity is a rectangular box of the same length as the waves it generates with holes in the sides for the microwaves to escape. This was not a practical design for light waves, which are much shorter than microwaves. Schawlow proposed solving this problem by discarding the sides of the box and placing mirrors at opposite ends of a tube to reflect light back and forth within the tube. The mirrors would control how light waves resonated within the tube, limiting the buildup of light waves to a single wavelength. In 1958 he and Townes compiled their ideas in a paper, which was published toward the end of the year.

The paper recognized key features that would define a laser but did not provide a blueprint to develop a practical device. It attracted a lot of attention and initiated a race to develop the first working laser. The winner was Theodore Maiman of Hughes Research Laboratories. Maiman had developed a compact solid-state maser based on a ruby crystal, but it was widely believed that ruby would not work in a laser. Maiman, who was a dark horse in the laser race, believed otherwise and surprised the field by generating pulsed laser light from a ruby crystal coated with reflective silver film at each end. Through a strange set of events, including an unjustified rejection of his article on the ruby laser at a leading journal and an obscure journal publishing it without his permission, Maiman was initially denied the credit for developing the first laser, which embittered him for the rest of his life.

Although Hughes was a defense contractor, Maiman's work on the ruby laser was supported by internal company funds. His success was rewarded by a contract from the air force for bigger and better lasers for use as optical radars (Hecht [2005, p. 194]). The military supported other participants in the race, including Townes and a Columbia graduate student, Gordon Gould, who would ultimately be issued fundamental patents covering the laser.

After Maiman's breakthrough, lasers with other desirable properties, such as continuous rather than pulsed operation, were developed. The military was instrumental in many of these efforts. Not only did it fund much of the laser R&D at universities and private firms, but "private firms that committed their own resources often intended their input as seeding in the hope of eventual military R&D or procurement contracts. The very existence of small laser firms often depended upon the fact that Department of Defense R&D contracts were easy to obtain. Money from DoD contracts provided a vital source of funding even for those fledgling companies, such as Spectra-Physics, that intended eventually to establish themselves in the civilian market" (Bromberg [1991, p. 102]). Indeed, most of the early leaders of the industry that entered by 1963 received support from the military (see table 3.5 of chapter 3). With many of the spinoffs (that later became leaders of the industry) descended from these firms, the military's support helped shape the success of the industry for decades.

As in semiconductors, the military's support for maser and laser research was based on its own agenda, but it was quite broad-minded in how to dispense that support. Initially it was willing to fund broad, often fundamental research at universities without a clear plan as to how this research would serve its interests, hoping to extend the bounty realized from the wartime radar program. It maintained its support for many years, even though the practical dividends were quite limited. When the laser was developed, the military was a major buyer of laser systems and munificently funded research at both universities and firms. Whether it ever earned a sufficient return on its investment to justify all of its support is unclear, but the social payoff from its efforts has been great—a vibrant industry that continues to find new and expanded uses for lasers to this day. In many respects, the military's support seems like a role model for precisely the kind of research and development that private firms would typically not fund on their own yet is very much in society's interests.

The influence of the government on the TV industry dates to the early days of wireless telegraphy, or radio, well before TV broadcasting was a commercial reality. As discussed below, the navy drove the creation of RCA to control radio communication in the United States. While the effects this would have on the TV industry surely were not anticipated, RCA became the dominant investor in electronic television R&D early on and propelled the industry forward in the United States. As such, the military's influence on the TV industry proved to be dramatic.

In 1919, when the victorious powers in World War I turned to rebuilding the shattered world economy, the reconstruction of the radio communications system came up on the agenda. The U.S. Navy had long favored government ownership of the communication system in the United States, but had never succeeded in getting Congress to adopt its position. Entertainment broadcasting was not yet on the horizon and radios were used mainly in communicating with ships and in long-distance communication. The British Marconi Co. was the dominant provider of long-distance and ship-to-shore radio communication in the world. During the war the U.S. Navy had seized the properties of its U.S. affiliate, the American Marconi Co., to manage communication with its fleet. It was not anxious to return control of radio communication in the United States to a foreign-controlled firm after the war.

Before the war the General Electric Co. had developed an expensive alternator capable of transmitting radio signals over extremely long distances, and British Marconi was anxious to purchase these transmitters after the war. Both entities were pressured into a deal by the U.S. Navy. British Marconi agreed to help arrange the sale of its American affiliate to GE in exchange for the right to purchase the GE alternator for its routes outside North America. A new company, the Radio Corporation of America, or RCA for short, was created to buy American Marconi and manage its assets. It was also granted patent licenses on all of British Marconi's technology and GE's radio technology.

GE, AT&T, and Westinghouse were the dominant producers of electrical equipment in the United States and for some time had been developing new technology related to radios. Their radio innovations overlapped considerably, leading to numerous patent infringement suits that the navy feared would undermine technological progress in radio. It helped broker a solution to this problem soon after the creation of RCA. AT&T agreed to license all of its radio technology to RCA in exchange for a share of the ownership of RCA. Westinghouse was also brought into the fold, licensing its technology to RCA in exchange for a share of RCA stock. RCA would not be a manufacturer but would act as a selling agent for the equipment of its parents. By controlling all the major patents in radio, RCA would break the impasse that had threatened to slow down technological progress in the industry (Aitken [1985, pp. 250–494]).

Much about this arrangement would prove dysfunctional, especially when radio broadcasting for entertainment purposes blossomed into an enormous business in the 1920s. The legal authority for the arrangement RCA had with its erstwhile parents was also challenged in an antitrust suit. By 1932 the suit was settled through a consent decree in which RCA acquired the manufacturing facilities of GE and Westinghouse (AT&T had already severed its links with RCA) and began to manufacture its own radio equipment in competition with them. Since the mid-1920s, it had been licensing its technology to producers of radio equipment at healthy royalty rates as a percentage of their sales, and now it would manufacture its own equipment as well (Aitken [1985, pp. 494–513]).

RCA had also maneuvered to control the TV technology of Westinghouse and GE, which was not yet ready for commercial development. Here was a company that was the leading producer of radio equipment in the United States, earned substantial royalty income from licensing its radio patents, and had every reason to expect to dominate the TV industry once it became a commercial reality. While the navy could never have anticipated this outcome, RCA stood alone at the start of the TV industry as its dominant firm. As noted in chapter 2, in the 1930s, before TV was a commercial reality, RCA accounted for nearly 80% of the total R&D in TVs by all U.S. firms. It was the unrivaled leader of the industry, the bellwether that the FCC had to fight back to prevent its dominance from suffocating competition in TVs early on.

This was quite different from the typical new industry. The market for a new product is typically small at first, and no firm has a sizeable share of output over which it can profit from R&D. As a result, technological progress is often slow for many years. Not so in TVs. By creating RCA, the navy ended up engineering a technology giant that was willing to invest heavily in R&D to build a market for TVs, confident that it could both profit from producing its own TV equipment and also license its TV technology to its competitors. As a result, RCA became the world pioneer in TVs, in monochrome TV and then in color TV when challenged by its arch-broadcasting rival, CBS.

Clearly, the navy could never have anticipated the effects of its actions on the TV industry—it had not even anticipated the rapid emergence of entertainment broadcasting and its profound effect on the radio industry. But by creating a dominant early radio producer with every expectation of dominating the nascent TV industry, the military's establishment of RCA provided a setting in which private action was sufficient to move the industry forward during its formative era. RCA's dominant position was reinforced by its participation during World War II in the development of guided antiaircraft missiles, a project funded by the Office of Scientific

Research and Development. This project enabled it to develop a superior tube for its TV camera, on which it capitalized after the war as the TV industry took off (Bannister [2001, pp. 133–166]).

• ⁖ •

At the start of the chapter, a logic was presented in which government support for R&D in young industries was in society's long-term interests. In young industries, the initial producers have a small output relative to the output firms will produce later. This limits the output over which they can earn a return from R&D. Consequently, there might well be R&D projects for which the societal returns exceed the costs but the private returns are insufficient to cover the costs. Government sponsorship of such R&D projects could be in society's interests, promoting the greatest good for the greatest number.

This framework was used to interpret the initiatives undertaken by the federal government and the military in penicillin, semiconductors, lasers, and TV receivers, the four products where government involvement was most prominent. In each case the motive for government involvement was not to promote the welfare of society at large but to satisfy more parochial goals, typically of the military. But the key question asked for each product was whether the government's initiatives were consistent with policies that could promote the long-term welfare of society.

The nature of the government initiatives varied across the four products. In penicillin and lasers, the government classically financed R&D projects that any single firm or even group of firms would have had difficulty justifying on their own. In the wartime penicillin project, the government explored the potential uses for penicillin, it helped finance an attempt to synthesize penicillin in the laboratory involving a wide range of firms, and it both financed and coordinated efforts to improve the production of penicillin. These efforts widely benefited all the firms that eventually produced penicillin, which in large part was why no one firm would likely have pursued them on its own. In lasers, the military financed basic research at a number of university physics departments related first to the maser and then the laser without a clear conception of how this research would yield practical benefits. It seems unlikely that any one firm could have captured enough of the benefits of this kind of research to justify financing it on its own.

In semiconductors and TVs, government policy mainly influenced early R&D by influencing the R&D pursued by key producers. In semiconductors, the military supported considerable R&D early on (Misa [1985]), but its primary influence came as a "lead" consumer through defense contractors. They were charged with acquiring advanced semiconductor technology and were given ample funding to pay premiums to cover the R&D needed to achieve the requisite advances and product specifications. This policy was instrumental in many of the key advances introduced in silicon devices, including the planar process and the monolithic IC, two innovations that revolutionized the industry. The military was also instrumental in the early success of TI and Fairchild, from which most of the other leaders of the industry descended. In TVs, driven by national security concerns, the navy basically created RCA to centralize radio technology in a single U.S. firm. It also had the effect of centralizing early TV technology in RCA, which led to RCA's investing substantially in TV R&D and becoming the world pioneer of monochrome and color TV.

While these heterogeneous government policies were pursued for parochial reasons, would they have made sense as part of a concerted U.S. industrial policy? Certainly so if judged by their success in galvanizing vibrant U.S. industries. The wartime penicillin project shifted the locus of pharmaceutical production from Germany, where it had remained for many years, to the United States. Support for semiconductors led to one of the most vibrant industries in U.S. history. U.S. semiconductor firms have generated countless innovations and now lead the world in gigantic niches such as microprocessors. The industry has also given rise to Silicon Valley, one of the great industrial wonders of the world, a cradle of many new high-tech industries not related directly to silicon, including the biotechnology industry. U.S. military support for masers and lasers basically created the laser industry, and the United States continues to have a major presence in that industry today. The creation of RCA was key to the United States' pioneering monochrome and color TV receivers.

Could the success of these policies have been anticipated at the time they were undertaken? Alternatively, were the policies successful mainly because we have concentrated on successful industries, so that any early government policies would look successful in retrospect? Is it possible that if a larger group of industries were studied, we would find a number of instances where similar kinds of government policies either failed to galvanize a vibrant U.S. industry or actually served as a barrier to such industries?

These are difficult questions to answer, largely because it is so time consuming to study individual industries. Amassing a larger, representative sample of industries to judge the efficacy of early government policy would be quite challenging. The best that can be done is to assess the kinds of policies undertaken by government in the products studied to see if they resonate with the theory about the kinds of government policies in young industries that could promote social welfare. In each product, it was argued that the policies did make sense as a means of promoting the long-term welfare of society. They led to R&D projects that were in the interests of society, yet firms were unlikely to pursue them on their own without government support of some kind. In each case, the "market" would have come up short and it would have taken much longer, if ever, for a vibrant U.S. industry to emerge.

Indeed, in retrospect it seems remarkable how influential early government policies were in galvanizing vibrant U.S. industries given the predominant military orientation of the policies. In all four products, the initiatives undertaken were mainly motivated by the interests of the military. Nevertheless, those policies had extraordinary effects on civilian as well as military interests. In many ways, this illustrates the weaknesses of market decision making when industries are young. Except under extraordinary circumstances, private firms usually forgo research on risky problems that, if solved, might generate large social returns in the long term in favor of low-risk short-term R&D with calculable private returns on those investments. Through a variety of mechanisms, military interests provide the means for firms to undertake the R&D necessary for the creation of radical innovations and, consequently, the evolution of vibrant, high-tech civilian industries.

This was the motivation for opening the book with a discussion of the wartime penicillin project. Our collective memory about this project is beginning to fade, yet it is extraordinary how a fairly modest investment by the federal government in just three years ended up planting seeds that have flowered ever since. Many observers have written off this success to patriotism, suggesting that firms cooperated because of the exigencies of war but would not do so in normal times. That is much too easy a way to dismiss the significance of the wartime penicillin program regarding its implications about government industrial policy. Patriotism surely was present, but the success of the program seems based mainly on the limitations of what private firms would do on their own in young industries, not the exigencies of war. The influence of government policies in the other three industries drives home this conclusion.

It is certainly the case that the wartime penicillin program and government policies in the other three industries when they were young are not generally thought of as models of government industrial policy. In large part this is because they were undertaken to promote military interests.

Yet one can only wonder how much more effective they would have been as industrial policy if undertaken to promote the long-term welfare of society. War has a way of galvanizing social action. The main lesson learned from studying the four products is that there is no reason to wait for war to involve government in the development of industries when they are young.

CHAPTER 6

THE HARDER THEY COME, THE HARDER THEY FALL

WE NOW COME FULL CIRCLE TO CONSIDER THE PERFORMANCE of high-tech industries when they get old and are dominated by just a few firms. Three of the six industries are featured: autos, tires, and TV receivers. Autos and tires are the two oldest industries in the group by far, dating back to the 1890s. The TV receivers industry is younger, having begun in 1946. However, its leading firms predated the industry, having cut their teeth in the radio industry where they competed for many years.

What all three industries in their mature eras have in common is that they were decimated by international competition. In autos, the Big Three firms of GM, Ford, and Chrysler not only dominated the U.S. industry for many years but had plants throughout the world. Yet over the last 40 years or so they lost nearly half of their share of the U.S. market to foreign competitors, and in 2008–2009 the federal government had to step in to manage the bankruptcies of GM and Chrysler to avoid an apocalyptic collapse. In the tire industry, Goodyear, Firestone, Goodrich, and Uniroyal long dominated tire sales in the United States and also had plants around the world. Yet today only Goodyear is left as an independent firm. The other three leaders, along with the number-five firm, General Tire, all sold out to foreign competitors. In the TV receiver industry, RCA was the pioneer of monochrome and then color TV around the world, and Zenith was its primary challenger. Yet RCA, Zenith, and every other major TV receiver producer in the United States either closed down or sold out to foreign rivals many years ago.

What happened to cause these once-vigorous industries to become devastated by international competition when they were mature? This is the main question addressed in this chapter. Of the three industries, the decline of the automobile industry has been written about the most, particularly the decline of its two leading firms, GM and Ford. In its time the decline of the TV industry also attracted considerable attention, although only a few unpublished doctoral dissertations have attempted to analyze the decline of the industry as it played out over 40 or so years. Much less has been written about the decline of the U.S. tire industry, but its decline was also precipitous. The challenge in this chapter is to marshal the studies that were conducted to gain insights into why all three industries declined so sharply in the United States after many years of success.

Rarely are declines like these attributable to a single factor. Indeed, different authors advance alternative reasons for the declines of each industry. Yet one theme comes through in all three declines—new technological developments hurt the leading U.S. firms in each industry. In autos, it was an entirely new method of production known as "lean production." In tires, it was the radial tire. In TV receivers, it was changes in the product and production process wrought by advances in semiconductors.

But why should major technological developments have been such a problem for the leading U.S. producers? Historically, their forte was innovation. Indeed, as discussed in chapter 2, they became the leaders of their industries by dominating innovation. When the modern technological developments occurred, they were all large enough to be able to profit handsomely from innovation. Certainly they were not taken by surprise. The major automobile producers conducted joint ventures with various Japanese firms that were in the forefront of the new method of production, including General Motors's venture with Toyota, the leading proponent of lean production. The leading tire producers had subsidiaries in Europe that produced the radial tire well before it was adopted in the United States. The leading TV receiver innovator, RCA, was also a leading semiconductor producer and early on set up an internal unit to exploit advances in semiconductors in TV receivers.

Part of the problem may have been that the leading U.S. firms were on top for so long they became complacent and arrogant. Certainly there were instances of such behavior. Another problem may have been that they were no longer headed by the entrepreneurs and great managers that catapulted them to the top. The importance of such factors notwithstanding, the problem was deeper.

A market structure in which an industry is dominated by a few large firms is not inherently conducive to innovation. The leaders can, and do, readily monitor each other's innovative efforts. If one makes a move, the others are likely to soon follow. But then competition will keep down the returns from innovative efforts, making it difficult to recoup the costs of major innovations. For example, it will be argued that if GM, Ford, and Chrysler had all invested in developing small cars in the 1950s and

1960s, competition among them would have driven the price of small cars down to their average cost of production, leaving them no room to earn the profits needed to cover their costs of developing the smaller cars. In effect, to be able to profit from innovation, firms need to have a monopoly from their innovations for a sufficient period of time, but this will not materialize if they all innovate at the same time. Recognizing their mutual interdependence and joint interests, the leading automobile firms eschewed developing small cars until forced to reckon with new challengers.

While each industry had a fringe group of domestic competitors, these firms were too small to be able to benefit from major innovations and as a result were not threats to the leaders. The only viable competitors were from other countries, but it was not easy to recognize the threats they posed at first. Once they got a foothold in the U.S. market, though, it was only a matter of time before they launched their full invasions. And when this happened, the U.S. firms were behind the eight ball, having to catch up quickly with formidable challengers.

Change is never easy, especially for organizations that have built up a certain competency over time that is embodied in their personnel and bureaucratic structure. As a result, it was not long before the challengers moved ahead of them in size. Once the challengers were larger, they had a larger output over which they could profit from future innovations, giving them a greater incentive to innovate subsequently. Recall from chapter 2 that this is just how the leaders emerged in autos, tires, and TV receivers when these industries were younger, exploiting the advantages of size to dominate innovation. Only now everything worked in reverse for the one-time U.S. leaders except for the few that were able to act decisively. For the rest, the harder they came, the harder they fell.

In many ways, the market strangled itself in each of the industries. The market structure that evolved in each industry was the natural outcome of a competitive process in which the rich got richer. But it inevitably dulled the incentives of the leading firms to innovate. Yet the leaders had accumulated abundant resources from their prior innovative accomplishments, which they could draw upon to try to deflect their challengers. In effect, they had been insulated from the day-to-day forces of the market that punish laggards. As they struggled, battles did occur to gain control of the leaders through hostile takeovers and initiatives aimed at the board of directors. While these efforts may have headed off the total ruination of the firms, they were not generally successful in preventing them from experiencing massive declines in value before they finally gave up the fight.

In some cases, such as Detroit in autos and Akron in tires, whole regions were dragged down.

By featuring innovation in the decline of the long-time U.S. leaders, I am not denying the importance of other factors that have also been cited as contributing to their decline. In two of the products, autos and TV receivers, Japanese firms initially had lower costs, especially lower wages, than U.S. firms. While this certainly aided them in establishing a foothold in the United States, in many ways it compensated for their lack of technology, which they had to license and/or copy from U.S. or other Western firms. Eventually, though, their cost advantages dissipated through exchange rate changes and other developments, but this did not dim the challenges they posed. Unions have also been implicated in the declines of once great U.S. firms. In the auto and tire industries, both the United Auto Workers and United Rubber Workers negotiated onerous work rules that handicapped producers. But that was just part of the baggage that hampered the ability of the leading auto and tire producers to respond to the technological challenges posed by their foreign invaders.

Other factors that may have played a role include the divorce of ownership and control in mature firms (no one "owns" the company to control management) and the difficulty of attracting top inventive and managerial talent in older, slower growing industries. These possibilities will be considered at the end of the chapter, after taking stock of what happened in each of the three industries. Also considered will be what the leading firms might have done to avert their declines and how public policy could be fashioned to cope with the vulnerabilities of mature high-tech industries.

• • •

The decline of the U.S. automobile industry is considered first, followed by the declines of the U.S. tire and TV receiver industries. Each story begins with a brief history of the pre-decline period to set the stage for subsequent events.

THE U.S. AUTOMOBILE INDUSTRY

The automobile industry was one of the great success stories of the United States. Although the automobile was mainly a European invention, it was American firms that took the lead in developing its potential during the first part of the twentieth century. Three of these firms, Ford, General Motors, and Chrysler, became household names. Known as the Big Three, they dominated the industry for over 40 years until challenged by foreign competition.

As discussed in chapter 2, between 1908 and 1914 Ford developed the Model T and the moving assembly line, enabling the company to capture half of the burgeoning sales of motor vehicles in the United States at its peak. Buoyed by the success of his company, Henry Ford assumed greater responsibility for its management, which had largely fallen on its brilliant business manager, James Couzens. Therein lay the basis of Ford Motor Co.'s near destruction. In his book on the decline of the U.S. automobile industry, *The Reckoning*, David Halberstam recounted how Henry Ford steadily lost touch with his workers and his customers beginning in the 1920s.

> Ford was a giant company run more and more by the whim of an aging, mean-spirited, often irrational eccentric. . . . On occasion he [Henry Ford] would talk about trying something new, and there would be a flurry of activity, and then he would completely forget what he had started, and the idea would slowly die. For its engineers and designers, the Ford Motor Company, only a decade earlier the most exciting place to work in America, was professionally a backwater. Sycophants rose, and men of integrity were harassed. [1986, p. 88]

This provided an opportunity for General Motors to move ahead of Ford. Between steady improvements in its Chevrolet car and the production of a range of models for different tastes, GM displaced Ford as the leader of the industry with around 40% of the market in the 1930s. For a while Chrysler, which emerged in the late 1920s as the number-three firm in the industry, even moved ahead of Ford in market share. Eventually Ford regained the number-two position when Henry Ford II was brought in during World War II to replace his famous grandfather and righted the company by bringing in a number of top managers from GM.

As of 1961, the U.S. market was still dominated by GM, Ford, and Chrysler. Their joint market share of U.S. vehicle sales was 85.3%, with GM's share 45.71%, Ford's 29.26%, and Chrysler's 10.37%.* They were each behemoths, ranking first, third, and seventh, respectively, in sales among Fortune's top 500 firms in 1961. GM was consistently one of the

---

*All market share figures are from WardsAuto, http://wardsauto.com/keydata/histori cal/UsaSa28summary.

most profitable firms in the United States, earning an average return on its assets from 1946 to 1967 of 14.7% compared to 9.9% for Ford, 7.6% for Chrysler, and 6.6% for the average manufacturing company (White [1971, p. 249]). The only substantive challenge to the Big Three came from small imported cars, epitomized by the Volkswagen Beetle, whose market share of 2.97% in 1961 would rise to over 5% at its peak in 1970.

While Japanese firms, led by Nissan and Toyota, would soon become the main challengers to the hegemony of the Big Three, they had little presence in the U.S. market in 1961. Nissan and Toyota started producing trucks and cars in Japan in the 1930s. Back then their operations were primitive, and the Japanese market was dominated by GM and Ford, which assembled cars mainly from parts produced elsewhere. But GM and Ford were pushed out of the Japanese market by a law requiring domestic automakers to be majority owned and managed by Japanese nationals. Subsequently, high tariffs on imported cars protected domestic manufacturers, giving them an opportunity to hone their skills. By the mid-1960s, Nissan and Toyota were beginning to make inroads into the U.S. market with their smaller cars.

At first their cars were not competitive in the United States. Halberstam [1986, p. 425] described Nissan's original U.S. car, the Datsun, as "simply terrible, crude and underpowered." Management back in Tokyo was unresponsive to suggestions by its American personnel to improve the car to suit U.S. tastes. But eventually they came around, and as sales of Nissan's cars boomed in Japan they were able to cut the price and raise the quality of their Datsun car in the United States. Nissan and Toyota gained steadily on the other U.S. imports. By 1968 they each accounted for over 0.5% of the sales of vehicles in the United States. While this was still far behind Volkswagen, it was precisely what was needed to begin an assault of the U.S. market.

Nissan and Toyota were aided by the ambivalence of U.S. makers regarding small cars. "The Big Three went into the compact market only when the import total began to rise beyond their estimates, and even then they did it only half-heartedly" (Halberstam [1986, p. 442]). For example, when in 1968 GM brought in its own foreign import, Opel, it was handled by its Buick dealers, "who had neither the knowledge nor the desire to sell it properly. For them, each Opel that was sold was a Buick that was not sold" [ibid.]. White [1971, pp. 177–188] studied the steps taken by the Big Three and the few other remaining U.S. auto producers after World War II regarding small cars. He attributed the Big Three's reluctance to aggressively pursue small cars to their recognized interdependence. "[T]he Big Three mutually contemplating a small car could only see lost profits from reduced sales of larger cars. Only after consumer tastes changed so that this minority [small car demanders] became larger *and* imports began satisfying these customers did the Big Three finally respond to this segment of the market. Low profit customers were better than no customers at all" (White [1971, p. 178]).

Unanticipated increases in oil prices in the 1970s brought about by the Arab Oil Embargo following the Yom Kippur War in the Middle East and then disruptions in oil production in Iran and Iraq spurred demand for smaller cars. Toyota, Nissan, as well as Honda—a latecomer to the Japanese market, all benefited. All three firms parlayed their early experience with small cars to expand subsequently into the mainstream U.S. market for larger cars, following U.S. firms as they profited from producing larger SUVs, minivans, and light trucks. Toyota captured 6.24% of vehicle sales in the United States by 1980, which grew to 16.73% by 2009, the year of the managed bankruptcies of GM and Chrysler. Likewise, Honda expanded from a market share of 3.28% in 1980 to 10.86% in 2009 and Nissan increased its market share from 5.49% in 1980 to 7.26% in 2009.

These inroads led to a steady loss in market share by the Big Three. For a time, it was just the Big Two, as Chrysler was acquired in 1998 by the German firm Daimler Benz, only to be sold off in 2007 (at a considerable discount) to the private equity firm Cerberus. By 2009, GM's market share had declined to 19.58%, Ford's to 15.29%, and Chrysler's to 8.79%. Beginning around 2005, all three members of the Big Three experienced staggering losses that compromised their financial viability (Ingrassia [2010, pp. 191–215]). Only Ford was able to raise enough money to stay afloat. GM and Chrysler went through managed bankruptcies in which they were saved from liquidation by large loans from the federal government. Both emerged as smaller and leaner companies, shedding substantial liabilities they had acquired over the years. Detroit, the epicenter of the industry, and the broader Midwest region were left devastated, although the damage could have been far worse without the intervention of the federal government.

Invariably, declines this precipitous have multiple causes. Initially, Japanese firms were aided by lower wages. In part this was due to exchange rates and in part to Japanese labor unions, whose demands were far less militant than the United Auto Workers union. But in time it became apparent there was a lot more to the Japanese advantage than wages. In the early 1980s, under considerable political pressure, Japan agreed to limit its export of cars to the United States. Coupled with the rising value of the yen beginning in the 1970s, this provided an impetus for Japanese auto firms to start producing in the United States, and today these "Japanese transplants" do much of their production there. The Japanese firms were determined to ward off the UAW, which necessitated paying comparable wages and benefits to their workers, negating any remaining cost advantages that Japanese producers might have enjoyed. Yet the leading Japanese firms continued to take away large chunks of market share from the Big Three.

Led by Toyota, the leading Japanese firms had developed a novel system of production that gave them a competitive advantage over their U.S. rivals. The U.S. production system dated back to Ford and the development of the moving assembly line. Workers each performed simple, repetitive tasks and were basically told to "check their brains at the door" (Hounshell [2003]). After the UAW came to power in the 1940s, an adversarial relationship emerged between management and labor. An elaborate set of work rules and grievance procedures were established to check management's power over labor. Productivity and quality both suffered enormously.

Toyota's production system evolved from very different conditions after World War II. It featured teamwork and "total quality management." Teams of production workers were given tasks to perform and told to work together to figure out how best to perform them. Checking for and repairing defects was done by the teams as cars were produced and workers were allowed to shut down the production line to find and eliminate the source of defects. Small inventories of parts were maintained to economize on space and costly work-in-progress. Suppliers were given information about how their parts fit into the broader production process and were expected to suggest changes to improve the overall system. The team concept was also applied to the design of new car models. The same team stayed with the design process over the four- to five-year design cycle and was empowered to make meaningful changes, whereas U.S. firms periodically handed off designs to new groups with limited power to implement change.

This system had many advantages over the U.S. system, particularly regarding the quality of cars produced. Cars were better designed from the outset to minimize production problems. Workers took pride in their work and were quick to spot defects and eliminate their source. This minimized rework at the end of the production line, which could take up to 20% to 25% of the labor and production space in U.S. plants. In their seminal study of the global automobile industry, *The Machine that Changed the World*, James Womack, Daniel Jones, and Daniel Roos assembled data on the efficiency of assembly plants around the world as of 1989. They found that on average the Big Three required 50% more assembly hours per vehicle and had about 50% more defects per car than producers in Japan, which translated into much higher ratings of Japanese than American cars in publications like *Consumer Reports*.

Not only did this provide Japanese automobile producers with a decided competitive advantage, it also proved challenging for U.S. firms to overcome. Ford suffered gigantic losses in the early 1980s, which may help explain why it was uniquely able to respond to the Japanese challenge. Its president and then CEO, Donald Petersen, embraced many aspects of the Japanese system and worked unceasingly to implement it within Ford (Petersen and Hillkirk [1991]). Chrysler also suffered gigantic losses in the late 1970s, requiring a government loan guarantee in 1979 to avert bankruptcy, yet it did not adapt very well, whereas General Motors adapted only slowly despite engaging in an ambitious joint venture with Toyota called New United Motor Manufacturing Inc. Its difficulties are instructive regarding how challenging change can be to a large, bureaucratic organization.

NUMMI was set up in 1983 to build a small car, the Chevy Nova, modeled after one produced by Toyota in Japan. It was to be built using the Toyota system of production in a GM assembly plant in Freemont, California, that had been closed since 1982. The plant was notoriously dysfunctional before it was shut down. "Daily absenteeism was regularly over 20%; beer bottles littered the parking lot; and even the slightest dispute had to go the bargaining table" (Keller [1989, p. 129]). The plan was to hire from the old labor force except for the biggest trouble makers. In exchange for job guarantees, the UAW agreed to abide by the Toyota production system. Job categories were reduced from 13 to 4 and the workers were organized into teams and initially were flown to Japan for intensive training.

Toyota was contemplating producing in the United States and wanted to use the joint venture to scope out the challenges of producing there. GM hoped to learn about what made the Toyota system so successful. Keller [1989] studied the NUMMI venture and its effects on GM. The venture was also featured in a two-part episode of the radio program *This American Life* aired on March 26, 2010, just before the venture was finally closed down. Workers at NUMMI were invigorated. They were proud of the cars they built and grievances and absenteeism plummeted relative to the prior experience of the plant. Managers were also invigorated and became proselytizers of the Toyota system. After three months of operation, GM ranked the plant among its top three in terms of quality with virtually no defects per car (Keller [1989, p. 131]). This was confirmed in the Womack et al. study [1991, p. 83], where NUMMI had an efficiency close to Toyota's plants in Japan, which was far greater than the average GM plant in the United States.

Despite getting a bird's-eye view of the Toyota system, GM had difficulty using the opportunity to close the competitive gap with Japanese producers. In part this was due to the lessons from the plant being unexpected. GM expected to discover some kind of distinctive technology Toyota was using to give it an advantage, but at its heart the Toyota system involved a novel way to organize and treat labor. Perhaps more fundamentally, the adoption of NUMMI principles required a whole different management philosophy and "company executives were no doubt reluctant to pursue this direction, for it touched at the heart of what was culturally wrong with GM" (Keller [1989, p. 135]). Teamwork in GM was certainly limited. GM was rife with power bases in which employees owed greater allegiance to their divisions than to the broader company. This doomed a number of ambitious programs undertaken in the 1980s by GM's CEO, Roger Smith, including a vast internal reorganization of the company [1989, pp. 99–123] and the establishment of its ill-fated Saturn Corporation, which had been conceived as a "different kind of car company" ostensibly modeled on the Toyota production system.

It appears that GM did gradually learn the lessons of NUMMI as more and more managers circulated through NUMMI and then relocated to factories where they could transfer what they learned (Keller [1989, p. 143]). But as automotive manufacturing expert James Womack noted in the *This American Life* show, it took too long for GM to embrace the lessons from NUMMI. By the time GM went bankrupt, he acknowledged that it was a much better company than it had ever been, but "it was too late, and that is really sort of hard to forgive—that if you take 30 years to figure it out, chances are you are going to get run over. And they got run over." Seemingly GM was not ready "to hear the real message of NUMMI—that management must change right along with everyone else. . . . Full implementation of Japanese methodology necessitated a behavior change by everyone in the company, not just the people on the factory floor" (Keller [1989, p. 246]).

THE U.S. TIRE INDUSTRY

The U.S. tire industry was dominated for more than 60 years by four domestic firms, Goodyear, Goodrich, Firestone, and U.S. Rubber (renamed Uniroyal in 1966), all of which entered the industry early on. Foreign firms had little impact on the industry, either through exports or direct investment in the United States, until the radial tire appeared on the U.S. scene in the 1960s. Ultimately, the radial created great challenges for American producers and led all the major tire firms but Goodyear to sell out their tire business to foreign rivals.

Before the advent of the radial tire in the 1960s, Goodyear and Firestone were the leading firms in the industry, followed by U.S. Rubber and Goodrich. These four firms and General Tire & Rubber, a 1915 spinoff of Firestone, were the only firms that sold tires as original equipment (OE) to the automobile manufacturers. To break into this market, tire producers had to have well-developed distribution and service networks and be at the forefront of innovation, and only these five firms qualified. Each of the automobile manufacturers bought from multiple suppliers to keep prices down, though they had their favorites based on historical relationships. The shares of sales of the five OE tire suppliers to the four main automobile manufacturers and their overall OE sales as of 1965 are listed in table 6.1.

OE sales accounted for around 25% of all tire sales, with the other 75% accounted for by replacement sales to consumers. Goodyear and Firestone were also significant players in this market, selling through their own stores and independent dealers. The other majors also participated in this market along with a set of fringe firms composed of mainly Armstrong, Gates, Mansfield, Cooper, Dunlop, and Mohawk. These firms also sold through their own and independent dealers as well as through chain stores such as Sears and Montgomery Ward, which sold their tires under their own brands. Sears was a particular power in this segment of the market. The overall sales of the majors and the other (fringe) firms as of 1963 are listed in table 6.1.

The bias ply tire was long the mainstay of the industry. It was composed of layers of rubberized fabric, called plies, running around the circumference of the tire, topped by a patterned rubberized tread. The cords of the fabric ran on a bias, or diagonal angle, to the direction of travel and in successive plies criss-crossed each other in a herringbone pattern. Innovations in the design of the tire and the materials used to produce it resulted in steady increases in its life expectancy and comfort (Warner

TABLE 6.1:
Estimated Firm Shares (percentage) of 1965 OEM Market and 1963 Total Market

Firm	GM	Ford	Chrysler	American Motors	Total 1965 OEM	Total 1963 Market
Goodyear	10	27.5	80	70	29	30.6
Firestone	25	43	5		26.2	22.7
U.S. Rubber	45	10			25.9	14.6
Goodrich	17.5	12.5	15	30	16.3	11.7
General	2.5	5			2.6	5.5
Others						14.9

Sources: Huber, *The Tire and Rubber Industry* (New York, Reynolds and Co., 1965) in Denoual (1980), p. 70, and Warner (1966), p. 26, in Denoual (1980), p. 7.

[1966]). Rosenbloom, Sull, and Tedlow [1996, p. 15] reflected on the advantages of the bias ply tire: "Bias construction provided flexibility in the face of bumps and potholes in the road, thus giving the American driver the feeling that he or she was driving a moving living room."

The radial tire did not begin to influence the U.S. tire industry until the 1960s, but it had a long history dating back to a patent issued to two Englishmen in 1914 (Denoual [1980]). It was pioneered by Michelin, which was based in France. In the radial tire, the cords in the plies run straight around the tire from one rim to the other, perpendicular to the direction of travel. An extra layered belt is also placed between the plies and tread. From the beginning, Michelin used steel wire for the belt, whereas other manufacturers, such as Pirelli of Italy, used a textile belt. A major capital investment in new production was required to produce the radial; existing bias ply plants could be retrofitted to produce it, but building an entirely new plant for its production was not much more expensive (Sull, Tedlow, and Rosenbloom [1997, p. 473]).

Radials were also considerably more expensive to manufacture than bias tires and required much more attention to detail in the manufacturing process. As Sull et al. [1996, pp. 16–17] relate, however, "The principal impetus for adoption of the radial design came from its undeniable benefits to the consumer . . . The life expectancy of a bias ply tire in the mid-1960s was about 12,000 miles, while radials lasted 40,000 miles. Although the radial cost more to manufacture—and its price to consumers was correspondingly greater—the cost per mile was markedly lower." It also provided better gas mileage and better safety and handling except at lower speeds, where driver and passenger felt the bumps in the road to a greater degree.

In 1946 Michelin filed its basic patent in the radial tire and in 1948 announced its first radial tire with three steel wire belts. Michelin owned the French automobile producer Citroën, which installed Michelin's radial tire on its Traction avant car in 1952 and then on its iconic Deux Chevaux car in 1953. Five years later Citroën introduced a car of completely different design, the DS 19, with a sophisticated suspension designed to accommodate the radial. Soon the radial was adopted by the other main French automobile producers, and by 1965, close to 60% of replacement sales in France were accounted for by radials. By then the radial also started making inroads in the United Kingdom, Germany, and the Benelux countries (Belgium, the Netherlands, and Luxembourg). In addition to Michelin, in 1951 Pirelli of Italy started producing its own radial tire with a textile belt, and in the late fifties, Continental of Germany, Dunlop of Britain, and the European subsidiaries of Goodyear, Firestone, and U.S. Rubber also started producing radials (Rajan et al. [2000, p. 61]).

The radial tire for passenger cars first received serious consideration in the United States in 1963 and 1964 when problems developed with bias ply tires. Increases in the life expectancy of bias ply tires had started to stagnate in the early 1960s. Around the same time, automakers, anxious to reduce tire weights and costs, had promoted the replacement of the traditional four-ply tire with a two-ply construction, arguing that quality improvements in cord materials permitted the elimination of two plies. At first things went well, but then safety problems surfaced in the two-ply tires, and improved tires became a priority. The radial tire was a natural alternative.

In many respects, though, the radial tire was an extremely unattractive innovation to the leading U.S. tire producers. A massive investment was required to develop the facilities needed to produce the radial, and the demand for tires would be expected to decline given the greater life expectancy of radials. Furthermore, historically GM, which accounted for about half of OE purchases, carefully managed its business to insulate the OE suppliers from sudden shifts in their market shares, which surely would limit the advantages to any one firm from aggressively pursuing the radial. Seemingly there were no firms on the horizon that could challenge the majors on radials. The fringe firms had never been in the technological vanguard and were extremely unlikely to pioneer the radial. Michelin and Bridgestone of Japan had made inroads into supplying radial truck tires in the United States, but both lacked the facilities in North America that would be required to compete in the passenger tire OE business.

This situation was analogous to the shift to small cars in the automobile industry. For the major suppliers of the OE market, radials promised to cannibalize their existing sales of bias ply tires at a massive cost in terms of new investment. How would they ever recoup the costs of learning how to design and produce radials? Not surprisingly, they resisted producing the radial. Between 1964 and 1967 they researched the prospects of the radial and submitted radial tires to Detroit for evaluation, but apart from Goodrich none went forward with its development. Concerns were raised about whether Americans were ready for the radial's high price and rougher ride at lower speeds. Indeed, Denoual [1980, p. 354] remarked that in all his interviews with tire executives of that era, they showed little appreciation of the technical benefits of the radial. Instead, "they talked mostly about increased costs, suspension changes and tire harshness." The radial suited Europeans, "okay perhaps for little doodle-bugs scooting around on cobblestones, but [it was] hardly appropriate for a hairy-chested, Gary Cooper-mobile" driven by Americans (Rosenbloom et al. [1996, p. 18]).

Goodrich's efforts focused on a textile belted radial that was based on technology it licensed from Pirelli. It launched a major campaign in 1967 to sell this tire on the replacement market. Sears, for its part, announced in late 1965 that it would no longer produce two-ply bias tires and would start to sell Michelin's steel belted radials under its Allstate brand. This galvanized Michelin to sell more radials through its own dealers in the United States, and between Sears's and Michelin's efforts a relatively limited but growing market opened up for radials in the late 1960s and early 1970s. Goodrich's radial was less successful, reflecting repeated quality problems it encountered between 1965 and 1970.

Unlike the other automobile manufacturers, Ford became interested in the radial around 1965 through its efforts in the late 1950s and early 1960s to improve both the life of OE tires and the suspension of some of its cars, particularly the Lincoln. As recounted by Denoual [1980, pp. 106–111], Ford investigated what its engineers called the vehicle/tire interface and ways the two systems could be optimized. By early 1965, a practical solution was found to all the technical problems of adapting radial tires to U.S. cars, including the rougher ride of radials at lower speeds. Requests for radial tires made to Ford's specifications were communicated to the five U.S. OE suppliers while development work continued in parallel with Michelin, which had approached Ford for the first time in 1961.

Neither Goodyear nor Firestone had much interest in supplying radials to Ford, and U.S. Rubber and Goodrich were unable to produce radials to Ford's satisfaction. Denoual [1980, p. 134] did not mention General, but noted that "Ford's options progressively narrowed down to Michelin," and in 1968 Ford contracted with Michelin to supply a limited volume of steel belted radials for Ford's 1970 Lincoln Mark III car. Now Michelin's foothold in the United States was secure. To facilitate the supply of radials to the U.S. market, it built a radial passenger tire plant in South Carolina in 1975 and simultaneously erected a rubber mixing facility nearby. By 1976, Michelin was supplying 10% of Ford's OE purchases (Denoual [1980, p. 287]), and subsequently it expanded its facilities both in the United States and Canada, where it had been producing radial truck tires for the U.S. market since 1971.

General Motors went in a different direction, supporting a new belted bias tire promoted by Goodyear as a solution to the safety problems of the conventional bias tire, that also increased its life expectancy. Goodyear added a stabilizing belt similar to the one used on radial tires to the conventional bias ply tire. It was not a new idea, but Goodyear capitalized on it by tying it to its past development efforts to use polyester as a cord material. It came out in 1967 with a belted bias tire with a polyester body and a fiberglass belt, which it called the Polyglas. In two years the belted bias tire accounted for 85% of OE sales, with all the majors developing their own versions of the tire.

But all was not well. Safety problems started to materialize with belted bias tires, prompting GM to reevaluate the radial tire in 1970. It formed an internal group to get tire producers to pool their knowledge in order to come up with a common radial tire that met GM's specifications. Soon GM committed to the radial, and starting in 1972 it gradually introduced steel belted radials on its cars. By 1976, 85% of its new cars were equipped with radials (Denoual [1980, p. 152]). Ford also committed to an expansion of the use of radials on its cars (Sull et al. [1997, p. 475]), and by 1975, 90% of Ford's cars were equipped with radials (Denoual [1980, p. 287]).

Once GM and Ford committed to radial tires, the OE suppliers had to conform if they wanted to maintain their OE business. Uniroyal (the renamed U.S. Rubber) followed Goodrich and began radial production in the United States in 1971. In the next two years it experienced various problems, including controlling its costs and finding a niche for its tire in the replacement market (Denoual [1980, pp. 156–161]). It was the most burdened with debt of the major tire companies, constraining how much it could spend on the radial. It had also had difficulties increasing the size of its European radials to satisfy the needs of the U.S. OE market (Denoual [1980, pp. 336–341]).

Firestone also ramped up its radial efforts in 1971. Initially it focused on finding a way to produce radials on its existing bias ply equipment. When that did not prove satisfactory, it started to develop a new generation of radial equipment, which in 1973 it announced permitted radial assembly operations to be completed at one work station. Its new radial tire, dubbed the Firestone 500, was developed under time pressure and proved to be a disaster, necessitating the biggest and most expensive recall in the history of the industry (Denoual [1980, pp. 162–169]).

Goodyear was the last to act. It continued to express confidence in the belted bias tire and developed a version of it with a steel belt, but these efforts failed to impress GM. Finally, in an abrupt shift Goodyear committed to produce radials in 1973, led by a new CEO with considerable radial experience at Goodyear's European subsidiary. Internal tensions arose at first concerning what technology to use to produce the radial, but eventually these were resolved. Between 1972 and 1974 the firm spent $347 million in capital expenditures in excess of depreciation on tires and followed this up with $377 million more between 1977 and 1979, while the tire capital expenditures of its rivals fell off sharply (Sull et al. [1997, p. 478]). This total investment of $3.25 billion (in 2015 dollars) by Goodyear enabled it to capture an unprecedented share of the OE market in the 1970s (Denoual [1980, pp. 169–175]), and in the 1980s it continued to invest as its rivals withered (Sull et al. [1997, p. 479]).

Tire producers had long earned returns on their investments not much different from the manufacturing average, but the conversion to radials depressed their profitability sharply after 1973 (Rosenbloom et al. [1996, p. 26]). Firestone was particularly hard hit and sold off much of its tire and other assets to remain afloat. Goodrich decided to restrict its losses and in 1981 abandoned the OE market entirely. Between 1985 and 1990, every major U.S. tire producer faced a hostile takeover bid, and all but Goodyear were acquired by foreign manufacturers. In 1986 Goodrich merged its tire business with Uniroyal's in a joint venture that was ultimately sold to Michelin in 1990. In 1987 Continental of Germany bought

General's tire business, and in 1988 Bridgestone bought Firestone. A new world order emerged in the tire business; as of 1993, Michelin was the largest tire producer in the world with a world market share of 19%, followed by Bridgestone with 18%, Goodyear with 17%, and Continental with 7% (Rajan et al. [2000, p. 57]). Akron had long been the center of the U.S. industry, although it reached its zenith back in the 1930s. The changeover to the radial, though, was its death knell, as all the old bias ply plants located there were closed.

Rajan et al. [2000] conducted a statistical analysis of data for U.S. tire plants collected by the U.S. Census Bureau to test whether the sell-offs were motivated by greater productivity on the part of foreign radial producers or the failure of U.S. firms to close their obsolete plants on a timely basis. Their findings suggested that neither factor was at work. U.S. plants that were sold off were no less productive than foreign-owned plants nor did their productivity increase after being sold off, and they were not more likely to be closed after being sold off than other U.S. plants. They conjectured the sell-offs were motivated by the high costs of maintaining an extensive R&D and marketing operation. Firms needed a large output over which to benefit from these costs, prompting the sell-offs of the U.S. firms to their stronger international rivals. Rajan et al. [2000] also cited the globalization of the automobile industry as a cause of the sell-offs, with tire firms needing operations throughout the world, including the United States, to match the needs of global automobile producers.

In retrospect, the sequence of moves and countermoves by the U.S. tire firms makes sense in terms of the incentives and capabilities of the participants. The prospect of switching over to the radial tire had to be depressing for all the OE suppliers. Is it any surprise that under these circumstances the major firms found reasons to dismiss the prospects of radials and latch on to new tires that preserved the viability of their bias ply capacity? Goodrich was the lone exception, which is understandable as it had the most to gain from radial tires given its small share of the replacement (and OE) market (Denoual [1980, p. 323]).

If Sears along with Ford and later GM had not taken the lead, the strategy adopted by the tire companies regarding radials might have been more effective. Certainly Michelin would have had a harder time getting a foothold in the U.S. market. Furthermore, if the belted bias tire had worked out, undoubtedly the widespread adoption of radials by automakers would have been delayed. In turn, this would have delayed the massive expenditures ultimately required to convert to the radial and the pain it caused in terms of the profitability of the tire companies.

Once the writing was on the wall in the form of the radial plans of GM and Ford, though, the incentives of the tire companies concerning the radial changed. It was only a question of how much to spend on developing the radial and how to manage the development process. At all but Firestone there was a changing of the guard, with executives from Europe brought in to manage the conversion to radials. Not surprisingly, this caused considerable tension, and many of the displaced executives left their longtime employers (Denoual [1980, pp. 362–368]). Goodyear had the largest market share and thus the most to lose by not acting, and it was the most decisive in investing in the radial. The other majors hedged in one way or another, and in a world where cost spreading of R&D and marketing were pertinent, the new world order left them little choice but to sell off to foreign rivals in the forefront of the radial revolution.

THE U.S. TELEVISION RECEIVER INDUSTRY

The TV receiver industry was another of America's once proud industries that were decimated by foreign competition. Created in 1919 to control radio communication and technology in the United States, RCA was the industry's pioneer in monochrome and later color TV receivers. Zenith was its main challenger. Together they typically accounted for 40% or more of U.S. sales of TV receivers even as imports began to invade the U.S. market. But like the rest of the firms in the industry, they ultimately abandoned the industry to foreign rivals.

The U.S. TV receiver industry began in 1946 when RCA introduced its model 630TS, which was known as the Model T of the TV receiver industry. TV broadcasting and production developed in Great Britain around the same time, and it was not long before firms from other Western European countries began producing TV receivers (Levy [1981, p. 178]). The European countries adopted a different transmission system than the United States, with France adopting yet a different system from the rest of Europe. While this facilitated trade of TV receivers within Europe, it insulated the European market from the rest of the world, particularly the U.S. producers, who were never aggressive exporters.

Japan was not very far behind Europe in monochrome broadcasting and receiver production, both of which began in 1953. It was also the second country after the United States to initiate color broadcasting and receiver production in 1960. It adopted the same transmission standard as the United States and licensed technology from RCA, Philips of the

Netherlands, and EMI of Britain. In the early 1960s Japanese manufacturers began to have an impact on the U.S. market with exports of smaller, portable monochrome sets with screen sizes less than 13 inches. U.S. firms were not very aggressive about producing sets for this market segment, which came to be known as "tinyvision." Many reasons were advanced for their sluggishness, including that greater returns were to be earned from larger sets, reminiscent of the failure of U.S. automakers to produce smaller cars before being challenged by imports.

Japanese firms were also able to make further inroads in the U.S. market in the 1960s through the production of "private-label sets," which accounted for between 15% and 30% of sales in the United States as of 1964 (LaFrance [1985, p. 223]). These sets were purchased mainly by major retailers, which branded them under their own label, obviating the need for Japanese producers to develop U.S. distribution networks. Most of the major U.S. firms did not produce these sets in the 1960s, which they viewed as "un-American" and "tainted." According to LaFrance [1985, p. 226], "For most [U.S. firms], it constituted too strong a break with traditional practices. While this outlook may have made sense in the late 1950s, the potential entry of Japanese sets through private-label channels in the 1960s should not have been ignored."

Japanese producers in the 1960s initially had a marked cost advantage over U.S. producers at the prevailing yen-dollar exchange rate, and once they got a foothold in the United States, they steadily expanded. By 1971 imports of monochrome receivers from Japan peaked at 36% of U.S. consumption,* although this figure understates Japanese competition as Japanese firms also operated in Taiwan and South Korea, from which they exported to the United States. To counter the cost advantage of Japanese producers, U.S. firms moved their assembly operations to low-wage countries, especially Taiwan and Mexico. By 1977, imports of monochrome receivers represented 82.3% of U.S. consumption, including sets assembled by U.S. firms outside the United States (Wooster [1986, p. 203]).

Monochrome receivers ultimately were displaced by color TV receivers, which began to take over the market in the 1960s. Japanese producers proved to be formidable competitors in color TV receivers as well. They lacked their own technology but licensed heavily RCA's color patents; as of 1981 they were still paying $50 million per year to RCA from color licensing deals struck in the 1960s (LaFrance [1985, p. 366]). Basically

---

*This was computed from tables 2-4 and 2-6 in Wooster [1986].

RCA decided to forgo conquering the world, instead capitalizing on its technology by licensing it to all comers:

> To a greater degree than any other American company, RCA reverenced the patent. It was the company's building block, even if originally tainted with illegality, providing the royalty income that in several depressed years during the thirties spelled the difference between profit and loss, a stream of bottom-line dollars that flowed into the research laboratories and nourished new technologies like color. Over the years a corporate culture emerged that held the licensing activity of RCA sacrosanct, and its principal disciple was Sarnoff. The slogan "world leader" was soon abandoned. The decision had been made to license the world rather than sell RCA products to its consumers. (Bilby [1986, p. 221])

Imports of color receivers from Japan steadily rose and peaked at one-third of U.S. consumption in 1977, leading to the imposition of voluntary quotas on Japanese imports from 1977 to 1980. With Japanese firms also operating in Taiwan and South Korea, quotas on imports from both countries soon followed. In the 1970s the yen increased relative to the U.S. dollar and Japanese wages also rose sharply, greatly reducing the advantage of Japanese firms producing in Japan. Sony was the first Japanese firm to invest in the United States in 1972. The import quotas hastened this process, with many more Japanese firms establishing a base in the United States after 1977 to get around the quotas.

The Japanese market for TV receivers was itself quite large, on the order of 70% of the size of the U.S. market. Initially, like automobiles the Japanese market was protected by high tariffs and restrictions on foreign investment and by various non-tariff barriers. This made it difficult for U.S. producers to export to Japan, although to most Japanese observers the problem was U.S. management, which was unwilling to design TV receivers for the Japanese market and sustain the losses needed to establish a market position there (LaFrance [1985, p. 282]). Later the trade barriers were lifted, but U.S. producers never became significant exporters to Japan. Between its own market, exports to the United States, and limited penetration of the European market (despite its different transmission standard), by 1970 Japan produced more TV receivers than any other country in the world. As of 1977, five of the ten largest producers in the world, including number one Matsushita, were located in Japan (Sciberras [1979, p. 8]).

The effects of Japanese competition on the U.S. industry were devastating. The number of U.S. TV receiver producers peaked at 105 in 1949.

By 1964, when Japanese exports to the United States began to take hold, the number of American producers was down to 42. As competition from Japan heated up, the number of U.S. producers fell to 21 as of 1970. It declined further to 8 by 1980 as Japanese competition in color TV receivers intensified. The profit margins of U.S. producers shrank greatly in the 1970s (Wooster [1986, p. 76]), and many of the early leaders of the industry had difficulty keeping up with technological change and exited. Wooster [ibid.] called 1974 the year of color television's "Great Reorganization," with a number of second-tier U.S. makers exiting or selling out. Motorola sold its TV receiver business to Matsushita, and Magnavox sold out to the number-two world producer, Philips. Philco ceased TV receiver production and sold its trademark to GTE, which had acquired Sylvania and its TV business in 1959. Admiral was sold to the U.S. conglomerate Rockwell International, which shut down its operations in 1978.

RCA, Zenith, GE, and GTE-Sylvania were the only major U.S. firms still in the industry as of 1980, but not for long. In 1981, GTE sold off its TV business to Philips. RCA had gone through turbulent times after its longtime leader, David Sarnoff, receded from the company and died in 1971 (Sobel [1986, pp. 199–260]). It embarked on a disastrous strategy in mainframe computing and invested $580 million in a video disc player that was abandoned in 1984 (Graham [1986, p. 213]). After many changes in top management, RCA was sold to GE in 1986, which bought the firm mainly for its subsidiary National Broadcasting Company (NBC). GE promptly sold off RCA's and its own TV receiver business to Thompson, France's leading company, claiming in its 1988 annual report that the two businesses together had lost $125 million in the 1980s (Carbonara [1989, p. 450]).

Only Zenith was left, and it was reported to have been ready to quit the TV receiver business in 1988 (Perry [1988]). Back in 1977, under difficult financial times, it had largely thrown in the towel. It fired a quarter of its workforce, including half of its R&D staff, and moved much of its operations overseas. It further cut its remaining R&D staff sharply in 1987 when it reported a corporate loss of $28.9 million. LG Electronics of South Korea acquired a controlling share of the company in 1995 and later acquired the rest of the company when it went bankrupt in 1999. With Zenith's exit, the whole industry was ceded to foreign producers.

It was mainly the competition from Japan that did in U.S. producers. Similar to automobiles, the Japanese producers began by marketing smaller TV receivers and exploited a wage and general cost advantage.

But this advantage did not persist as Japanese wages and the value of the yen rose and U.S. firms moved much of their operations to low-wage countries. Nevertheless, as was true in autos, Japanese firms continued to make inroads into the U.S. market. The main reaction of the U.S. firms was to claim foul—they were losing out because Japanese firms were engaging in unfair trade practices. Zenith was the industry leader in initiating numerous legal actions against the Japanese firms, including charges they dumped TV receivers at artificially low prices in the U.S. market and conspired to charge high TV receiver prices in Japan to subsidize their activities in the United States. Most of these charges were not sustained by the courts and did not appreciably slow down the onslaught from Japanese producers.

The onslaught appears to have been fueled by the ability of Japanese firms to develop a superior production system that yielded more reliable products, similar to the advantage of Japanese automobile producers. It stemmed from the faster adoption of solid-state components in the era of color TVs. Wooster [1986, pp. 68–69] noted that "the 1960s and 1970s witnessed a simultaneous advancement in the understanding of the principles of color television, and a revolution in the understanding of the fabrication and design of electronic circuitry." This revolution was brought about by the replacement of vacuum tubes by transistors and then ICs that packed ever more transistors and other discrete circuit elements onto a single chip. By reducing the number of components that could fail and the number of connections between them, ICs markedly improved the reliability of TV receivers. Reliability was also improved through the automated insertion of components and testing of assemblies, both of which were made possible by the use of ICs in TV receivers.

Managing the process of adopting discrete semiconductor devices and then ICs was where Japanese producers had a decided advantage. Until the mid-1970s, most American firms produced hybrid receivers composed of vacuum tubes, transistors, and other discrete semiconductor devices, using only a few ICs. In contrast, by 1970 most Japanese firms were producing all solid-state receivers (Wooster [1986, p. 73]). Subsequently, Japanese firms were quicker to adopt advances in ICs, consistently being a generation or two ahead of the U.S. producers in their level of component integration (Magaziner and Reich [1982, p. 175]). Evidence presented by Wooster [1986, p. 146]) indicates that in the mid-1970s American color receivers failed at five times the Japanese rate and by 1980 were still failing at two to three times the Japanese rate. This dovetails with data presented by Magaziner and Reich [1982, pp. 175–176] on service call rates, which were three times higher for American sets in the mid-1970s and two times higher at the end of the decade.

The leading Japanese producers were all highly integrated in semiconductor production and produced about three quarters of their components in-house, far more than the typical U.S. receiver producer (Sciberras [1979, p. 31]). Matsushita also developed automated insertion and quality control equipment, which it sold to other firms, and Hitachi made its own testing and packaging machines to enhance quality control (LaFrance [1985, p. 350]). Another advantage of Japanese firms was reminiscent of the Japanese automobile producers. In contrast to the United States, all management staff members were required to spend half of their first year or two in manufacturing and were trained in quality control techniques (Sciberras [1979, p. 33]). This enabled the Japanese firms to build greater reliability into their receivers. The Japanese firms also devoted about a third of their R&D budget to the production process, an amount that far exceeded their U.S. competitors [p. 30].

Some of the difficulties American firms encountered in adapting to semiconductor developments pertained to their small size relative to the Japanese producers as of the 1970s. As Wooster [1986, p. 150] noted, the high levels of R&D and capital investment required to adopt new solid-state technologies and the ramifications they brought for the production process "could only be justified if these costs could be spread over large volumes of output." Sciberras [1979, pp. 33–34] reached a similar conclusion: "Writing-off large capital expenditures over larger volumes of production makes the costs of attaining higher quality less severe for the Japanese than for the generally smaller US and European firms." This can help explain the ultimate failure of many of the leading U.S. firms, but not Zenith and RCA, which were the third and fourth largest producers in the world in 1977.

RCA is the more intriguing of the two firms, because like its Japanese rivals it was a semiconductor producer, an advantage that Zenith lacked. Indeed, RCA set up a unit in 1964 to develop specialized ICs for TV receivers. An article (Goldstein [1997]) on the career of Jack Avins, who was selected to head the unit, provides a glimpse into RCA's limitations. Avins was sent to Japan at the end of 1971 to trumpet to its Japanese licensees the virtues of a new color receiver RCA developed based on a novel IC design. During his visit, he toured the laboratories of all of Japan's leading TV producers. Upon his return, he sounded "the alarm bell that the United States was rapidly losing leadership in design and manufacture of color televisions. Avins observed that Japan was, to his surprise, beyond copying the Americans in circuit design. Pointing out that Japan continued to reduce labor content of receiver manufacture through increased integration and plant automation, he called for 'radical action on a wide front' for RCA" (Goldstein [1997, pp. 182–183]). Included in this radical action was greater automation of production and increasing the engineering staff from its "pitifully inadequate" levels [p. 184].

RCA does not seem to have embraced Avins's warnings, focusing instead on developing a solid-state receiver that was intended to establish a new standard for picture quality (Goldstein [1997, p. 184]). Perhaps it was just too much to teach an old dog new tricks, as it were. RCA's specialty was developing new product technology that it could license. It had never been adept at manufacturing, losing ground to its U.S. rivals after it pioneered both monochrome and color TVs. Despite its familiarity with semiconductor technology, it was an unlikely candidate to imitate the advances in production pioneered by the leading Japanese firms.

One other factor deserves to be mentioned about the source of the advantage of Japanese firms. Many authors (e.g., LaFrance [1985], Wooster [1986]) noted the importance of Japanese industrial policy in the success of its TV producers. Between protecting its home market, promoting exports, and supporting joint firm research on ICs, government agencies were seen as providing Japanese firms with a competitive advantage over their U.S. rivals. Some of these policies engendered the legal actions undertaken by Zenith and other U.S. firms alleging dumping and collusion. While Japanese industrial policy may have played a role in the decline of the U.S. TV receiver industry, Magaziner and Reich express a common view about the ultimate problems that plagued U.S. TV producers:

> Although some of the allegations against the Japanese companies did have merit, the U.S. companies ultimately failed because they invested in lawsuits, offshore production bases, and cosmetic features rather than in basic product design, process improvements, and export market development. Whatever dumping the Japanese may have engaged in was a minor aspect of their competitive success. The real basis was their well-designed investments to cut costs and increase quality and their designs for fundamentally new products [such as VCRs]. [1982, p. 179]

• • •

The argument advanced for the decline of the once-great U.S. leaders in autos, tires, and TV receivers can be broken down into four components.

(1) The leaders in each industry were not aggressive innovators. (2) This let foreign rivals get a foothold in the U.S. market, which they then exploited with superior products. (3) The leaders were not aggressive innovators because they recognized that mutually aggressive behavior would not enable them to recoup the costs of major innovations and because at times the major innovations on which they floundered challenged their core competence. (4) The size of firms had an important influence on their ability to profit from innovation, so once the U.S. leaders fell behind their foreign invaders in terms of size, they were relegated to playing a difficult game of catch-up.

Each of these elements can be evaluated on the historical record for the three industries. Consider first whether the leading U.S. firms were not aggressive innovators. The record is pretty clear. In autos, the U.S. leaders were slow to produce smaller cars and to adapt to lean production methods. In tires, they were slow to pursue the radial. In TV receivers, they were slow to produce small portable TVs and to incorporate the latest advances in semiconductors in their products. TV leaders were also reluctant to produce private label sets, and the industry leader, RCA, abdicated its role as a world competitor in exchange for licensing revenue.

Certainly this had competitive consequences. Japanese invaders were able to get a foothold in autos through small cars and in TV receivers through small portable TVs and private label sets. In tires, Michelin got a foothold with radials with Sears in the replacement market and Ford in the OE market. After getting these footholds, the invaders prospered because the U.S. leaders ended up producing demonstrably less reliable and lower quality products, exemplified (in the extreme) by the Firestone 500 radial tire.

Were the U.S. leaders slow to innovate because of their recognized interdependence? White [1971, pp. 177–188] certainly conjectured so regarding small cars based on his review of the historical record, and TV producers were noticeably absent from the small end of the market for portable monochrome TVs. The best case for this argument is undoubtedly the radial tire. If either of the top two firms, Goodyear or Firestone, had aggressively pursued the radial, surely the other majors would have soon followed. But all that would have gotten them was mutually smaller sales at a great cost in terms of new equipment/plants. How would they ever have recouped the costs of learning about how to design and produce radials? Is it any wonder that with the exception of Goodrich, the smallest of the top four, none of the other firms aggressively pursued the radial? Alternatively, Rajan et al. [2000] placed the blame for their sluggishness on the need to coordinate with auto manufacturers in terms of modifying their suspensions to accommodate the radial. Yet Sears successfully went ahead with Michelin's steel belted radial in the replacement market without the benefit of such efforts, and the major tire producers were not interested in, or able to satisfy, Ford's radial needs even after Ford made the necessary changes. Moreover, even after GM committed to the radial, Goodyear tried to temporize with a steel belted version of the bias belted tire.

This is only half the story, though, regarding the slowness of the U.S. leaders to innovate. The other half is that some of the innovations challenged their core competence. GM was composed of powerful, often-rivalrous divisions and like the other auto companies had a long-standing adversarial relationship with labor. NUMMI revealed how it needed to change to come into the modern world of lean production, but actually implementing the needed changes was challenging to its very being. In the TV receiver industry, semiconductor technology was not the forte of most of the producers, and the most qualified firm, RCA, was never adept at managing manufacturing. In tires, a changing of the guard at the level of top management was required to get the radial implemented in the U.S. leaders. Yet not every firm failed to adapt, as illustrated by Ford in the 1980s under Donald Petersen and Goodyear once it committed to the radial. These two cases illustrate a dictum that was featured in chapter 2 on shakeouts: where there is a will, there is a way.

Firm size played a prominent role in all three industries in conditioning the returns from innovation. All three industries had a fringe of second-tier leaders behind their long-dominant firms. But these fringe firms were even less impressive innovators than the leaders. In the tire industry, once the major auto manufacturers committed to the radial, it was only the largest firm in the industry, Goodyear, that invested decisively and survived. And in the TV receiver and tire industries, it was the largest firms in the world that ultimately prevailed in the new technological era.

Might other factors besides innovation also have been at the crux of the decline of the U.S. leaders? Japanese firms certainly had wage and other cost advantages at first in autos and TV receivers, and this was certainly helpful in breaking into the U.S. market. But even after the playing field was leveled through voluntary import restraints and the movement of TV producers off shore, the leading U.S. firms still floundered. Regarding unions, the UAW was notorious for the hindrances it placed on auto manufacturers. But when it came to NUMMI and similar ventures (e.g., Saturn), they were willing to play ball, and management can hardly be exonerated for the adversarial relationship that developed with labor. Could it be that once they were mature and slower growing, the auto, tire, and TV receiver industries were no longer attractive to the best talent the United States had to offer? Perhaps, but this did not seem to hamper the ability of Ford and Goodyear to parry their foreign invaders. Where there was a will, a way was found to compete with the available talent at hand.

A last factor that will be considered is the divorce between ownership and control that is characteristic of large, older firms. This has been a pervasive problem in modern American capitalism. Ownership of the company's stock is dispersed, so no one is able to directly control management. The board of directors, which in principle is supposed to represent the interests of owners, is often captured in some way by management. As a result, management may be free to pursue their own goals to the detriment of stockholders. In the context of the three industries, management may have shied away from cracking the whip—taking the steps needed to bring everyone in line to parry foreign invaders. Furthermore, they may have been inclined to compete too long even after it should have been apparent that they were overmatched. Rosenbloom et al. [1996] explicitly raised this argument in asking why some of the tire companies never even seemed to have entertained entering the radial market in the United States after GM and Ford committed to the radial.

It is hard to rule out this argument as having some bearing on the poor performance of the leading auto, tire, and TV receiver firms in modern times. Note, though, that a few firms in the mix were basically family owned and controlled—this was true of Ford Motor Company and Firestone. Clearly, family did not avert a major crisis at Firestone. Ford was the most able of the auto firms to address the challenges of lean production, but it does not appear this had anything to do with the Ford family's control of the company. Indeed, the Ford family did not favor Donald Petersen, the architect of Ford's comeback in the 1980s, and Petersen retired early, after which Ford eventually experienced harder times (Brinkley [2003, pp. 717–757]).

What can be done, both at the firm level and in terms of public policy, to avert drastic declines of other mature high-tech industries? One idea is to make the board of directors more independent of management. The board needs to demand that management have a well-planned strategy to cope with major new technological developments, especially when they are coming from another country. Such a strategy needs to be able to project long-term contingencies and how a firm intends to deal with them.

Ford had such a strategy under Donald Petersen. Goodyear also seems to have had such a strategy once it accepted the radial was here to stay. But most of the other leading firms did not have such a strategy and flailed away, experimenting with costly initiatives that were not systematically investigated before they were implemented. This only compounded their problems, as GM's struggles in the 1980s exemplify (Keller [1989]).

Another possibility is to weaken the ability of firms to ward off hostile takeovers. The tire companies were seemingly galvanized to sell off to foreign rivals in the 1980s after repeated overtures to take them over. All of these acquisitions failed, but they may have had the salutary effect of forcing the tire companies to take stock and sell off before sustaining further losses, preserving their remaining stockholder value. This did not happen in the case of General Motors, the largest of the U.S. automobile companies. Consequently, stockholders lost everything—over $50 billion in the value of GM stock as recently as 2009.

Corporate governance issues, such as the proper role of the board of directors and the ease of hostile takeovers, have occupied a lot of attention in recent years with the colossal failures of companies like Enron. Changing the ways companies are governed may be difficult to achieve, but from the perspective of mature, high-tech industries long dominated by a small cadre of producers, such changes may be long overdue.

CHAPTER 7

THE BEST OF TIMES, THE WORST OF TIMES

Editors' note: Steven Klepper was reworking drafts of this final chapter when he passed away. This chapter is constructed from the parts of the initial draft that were completed by Steven, notes that he either wrote directly or in collaboration with Joseph Plummer (a writer who worked with Steven during the final months of the project), and an extensive outline iterated numerous times by Steven. Our editing amounted to arranging these materials in the order specified by the outline, expanding some abbreviations where appropriate, and making some minor changes to improve clarity. This chapter provides insights into Steven's thinking about the implications of his research agenda. It includes novel ideas and policy suggestions that should stimulate future theories, empirical analyses, and policy debates about how to maintain and enhance the competitive advantage of high-tech entrepreneurship in modern economies. Even in its abbreviated form, this chapter provides a window into Steven's broader vision of "how societies can best tap their full creative, innovative potential to generate growth and prosperity for the greatest good for the greatest number."

This chapter includes two sets of notes, owing to the special nature of its contents. To distinguish them, the notes provided by Klepper will appear as footnotes, as they do in the other chapters. Notes that we revised, which include relevant material from Klepper's notes with our additions in brackets ([ ]), will appear as endnotes at the end of this chapter, following the appendix.

• • •

It is now time to step back and extract lessons for how to compete in this high-tech world. One set of lessons pertains to firms and individuals. A key question that will be addressed is: What are the novel aspects of how high-tech industries evolve that inform the strategies that firms and individuals should use to compete in the high-tech sector? Another set of lessons will be extracted for societies, whether they are nations, states, or localities. The fundamental question they face is: How should the rules of competition and the role of the government and military be set up to best tap a society's full innovative potential?

The study of the six industries from birth through maturity and beyond provides a unique picture of how competition and innovation evolve in high-tech industries. The government and military can be instrumental in getting new high-tech industries going. Eventually, many high-tech industries become dominated by a small number of competitors, but the continual creation of new submarkets can keep these forces at bay. If shakeouts are sufficiently delayed, industries develop their own leaders from within, in the form of spinoffs of incumbent producers. When the spinoff process is especially intense, geographic clustering thrives. Prolonged dominance can undermine incentives to innovate and make firms vulnerable to technological challenges mounted by foreign competitors.

The evolution of the six industries spans over 100 years, beginning with the auto and tire industries in the late nineteenth century. The great industrial historian Alfred Chandler wrote about the start of this era in his book *The Visible Hand*. Prior to the late nineteenth century, American capitalism mainly involved small firms performing specialized functions. But at the end of the nineteenth century these firms began to be displaced in the United States and Europe by a new order of national and global firms that performed internally many of the functions previously mediated by the market. They invested heavily in research and development and generated continual innovations that moved their technologies forward by leaps and bounds. The Big Three auto firms of General Motors, Ford, and Chrysler and the Big Four tire companies of Goodrich, Goodyear, Firestone, and U.S. Rubber epitomized this process and came to dominate their industries.

The other four industries came later, propelled forward by advances in electronics and chemicals. Early on, all four were galvanized by the federal government and the military. They helped contribute to a golden era of growth in the United States following World War II. Since 1970 or so, though, that growth has slowed down. Japan began to assert itself as a formidable competitor to the United States in the high-tech sector, and later South Korea and Taiwan, among other Asian countries, joined the pack. European firms also flexed their muscles in selected high-tech industries as they recovered from World War II. The oldest of the six industries, autos, tires, and TV receivers, showed the effects of this new competition. Long dominant U.S. firms struggled to keep up with foreign competitors as their industries declined to the point of extinction.

The new competitors from Asia seemingly benefited from proactive policies enacted by their governments, which were far more involved in the industrial sector than the U.S. government. As McKendrick, Doner, and Haggard [2000, p. 3] recounted, "[t]he challenge seemed deep and systemic: the American system of capitalism itself was seen as a liability. Asian forms of industrial organization and manufacturing, corporate governance, and industrial policy all pointed toward dominance in the battle for market share and economic growth." Those concerns seem somewhat dated now with the malaise Japan experienced over the last 20 years and the Asian financial crisis of 1997–1998, but concerns continue to abound today in the United States about how to use government to prime the pump for future industrial growth. One of the central concerns of this chapter is what can be learned from the six industries about the potential role that government can play in helping societies tap their full innovative potential.

Before offering any advice, the first order of business is to convince you that forces governing the evolution of the six featured industries capture the essential forces governing the evolution of high-tech industries in general. Six industries is not much of a sample from which to make generalizations, particularly regarding patterns that only hold for a subset of the industries. Fortunately, though, the main patterns found in the six industries hold broadly in high-tech industries, to which we now turn.

• • •

The nanoeconomic analysis of the six industries reveals a set of intertwined building blocks for how high-tech industries evolve. Some other high-tech industries have been similarly studied, but the total number is too small to reach confident generalizations. It turns out, though, that there are other ways to skin a cat to establish the generality of the findings for the six industries.

Consider first the evolution of a new industry's market structure—entry, the number of producers, and the share of output produced by the largest firms. Chapter 2 laid out two paths. Both begin with vigorous entry and a rise in the number of producers. In the more common path, innovation focuses on improving an industry's products and lowering their cost of production. Eventually entry dries up, a shakeout ensues, and the industry becomes dominated by its leading producers. Autos, tires, TV receivers, penicillin, and lasers in its later years fit this mold. In the other path, innovation mainly creates new variants of the industry's product appealing to new classes of buyers, opening up new submarkets.

The persistent creation of new submarkets provides opportunities for entry and a continued rise in the number of producers, keeping down the dominance of an industry by its leading producers. Lasers for its first 35 years and semiconductors fit this mold.

How general are these two patterns in high-tech industries? Consider first shakeouts. Gort and Klepper [1982] found a quick and dirty way to study the prevalence of shakeouts. They used a multi-volume compilation called *Thomas' Register of American Manufacturers*, which has been published annually (with a few skipped years early on) since 1905. For a very large number of manufactured products, *Thomas'* lists the names and addresses of all of their producers, which is convenient for marketing purposes. For a sample of 46 major new products introduced over the period 1887–1960, Gort and Klepper [1982] counted the number of producers annually of each product. Most of the products were high-tech, including five of the six featured products (all but autos); consumer products such as electric blankets, electric shavers, freezers, and phonograph records; military and space-related products such as rocket engines, guided missiles, and polariscopes; and intermediate products such as jet-propelled engines, nylon, cathode-ray tubes, and nuclear reactors.

Each product's evolution was divided by Klepper and Graddy [1990] into the three stages depicted in figure 7.1. Stage 1 corresponds to the rise in the number of producers to its peak.* Stage 2 corresponds to the shakeout stage in which the number of producers falls sharply. Stage 3 begins after the number of producers begins to level off (see Klepper and Graddy [1990] for the criteria defining stages 2 and 3). Data were collected for each product from its date of introduction through 1981. Some products were too young as of 1981 to reach stage 3, and others were not high-tech and thus would not necessarily be expected to undergo a shakeout. But of the 38 that had reached stage 3 by 1981, 22 had gone through a clear stage 2 in which, on average, the number of firms declined on net by 52%. This is not as extreme as autos, tires, TV receivers, and penicillin, but losing over half of an industry's firms on average is still a pronounced decline.[1]

The other main concept about shakeouts is the power of new submarket creation to forestall a shakeout. This was how the delayed shakeout in lasers and the absence of a shakeout in semiconductors was explained.[2]

---

*For products commercialized before 1905, stage 1 begins when the product was first commercialized and contains a gap reflecting that *Thomas' Register* was not published until 1905.

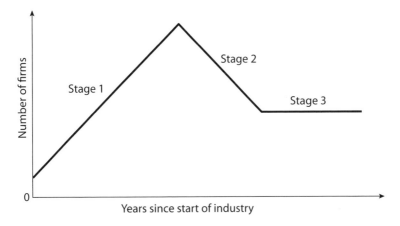

Figure 7.1: The Three Stages of a Product's Evolution

But two industries is not much on which to generalize. Fortunately, Sutton [1998, pp. 93–112] developed a clever way to test the influence of submarket creation on industry evolution without needing to reconstruct the evolution of any industries at all.

Sutton's basic idea reflects the way national census bureaus collect and report information about firms. They report aggregated information about industries, including the total sales of an industry and the share of its sales accounted for by its top four firms, called the four-firm concentration ratio. This information is reported at various levels of industry aggregation. Sutton isolated 55 U.S. manufacturing industries in 1977 (all the data he needed were available for this year) where firms spent over 4% of their sales on research and development. These industries, which are defined at a pretty disaggregated level, include the main high-tech industries in the U.S. economy. For example, one industry among the 55 was "Integrated Circuits," which was at the heart of the semiconductor industry for most of its history.

For each of his 55 industries, Sutton looked at the sales of even more disaggregated products within the industry. For example, in "Integrated Circuits," the sales of memory chips, microprocessors, various types of logic circuits (that performed different logical functions), and different types of hybrid ICs combining discrete elements with smaller ICs were reported. Each of these might be thought of as a submarket within the "Integrated Circuit" industry. Sutton computed the fraction of the industry's sales accounted for by its largest such submarket, which in the case of

"Integrated Circuits" was memory chips, which accounted for 28% of its sales. He conjectured that when this percentage was small, the industry was composed of many submarkets and would be expected to have a low four-firm concentration ratio. Otherwise, it would not be very segmented and would be expected to be dominated by its leading producers.

The figure for Integrated Circuits of 28% was on the small side for the 55 industries, which is consistent with the industry not being terribly dominated by its leading U.S. firms, as discussed in chapter 2. Overall, Sutton found that in industries in which the share of sales accounted for by its leading submarket was less than 20%, the industry's four-firm concentration ratio was between 20% and 60%. Alternatively, when an industry's leading submarket accounted for over 60% of its sales, its four-firm concentration ratio was typically greater than 60%. Thus, it appears that high-tech industries with a richer array of "submarkets" are less dominated by their leading firms, as might be expected if indeed submarket creation is key to forestalling shakeouts.

New submarkets creating opportunities for new firms to enter an industry can have powerful implications for incumbent firms if the new submarkets unexpectedly come to challenge existing submarkets at a later date. This will be featured in the discussion of firm strategy in high-tech industries. No doubt one of the leading proponents of this idea is Christensen [1997], who features the power of submarket dynamics to overturn even well-managed leaders of an industry. He uses the hard disk drive industry, which he analyzes nanoeconomically, to make his case. The industry is itself of considerable interest, as it shows off how profoundly an industry's evolution can be influenced by the creation of new submarkets, such as occurred in the laser industry. Unlike lasers, however, the creation of new submarkets repeatedly caused the leaders of the industry to be overturned.

Christensen [1997, p. 3] likened the study of the disk drive industry to the study of fruit flies by geneticists. In humans, it is hard to understand the causes and effects of any changes because new generations come along every 30 or so years. In contrast, fruit flies "are conceived, born, mature, and die all within a single day. If you want to understand why something happens in business, study the disk drive industry. Those companies are the closest things to fruit flies that the business world will ever see."

IBM was the pioneer of the modern disk drive, which is a magnetic storage device constructed much like an old record player. It uses a mobile arm to read and write information coded as 0s and 1s on magnetically coated disks. From 1976 to 1995, disk drives were improved at a frenetic pace. The amount of information packed into a square inch of disk drive surface increased by 35% per year, with the physical size of drives reduced at a similar pace" (Christensen [1997, p. 7]).

In the 1960s IBM marketed disk drives with its mainframe computers as did other mainframe computer makers. Then, in the 1970s an independent disk drive market emerged in which disk drive producers sold directly to manufacturers of smaller computers. By the mid-1980s the independent market accounted for about 75% of world production. Of the seventeen firms in the industry as of 1976, only IBM survived until 1995. An additional 129 firms entered the industry, of which 109 failed, and the industry experienced a sharp shakeout (Christensen [1997, p. 7]).

Christensen engaged in a nanoeconomic analysis of the industry to test whether the relentless pace of technological change was at the heart of the high firm failure rate. He concluded that there were two main types of technological changes in the industry, each with its own effects on the industry's leaders. One type improved the industry's products, whereas the other involved the creation of new, smaller drives that opened up new submarkets for disk drives. These smaller drives appealed mainly to the producers of new, smaller computers—first minicomputers, then personal computers, laptops, and notebooks—each with its own separate submarket. The industry's leaders were always in the vanguard of the first type of technological change, but the second type "*disrupted* or redefined performance trajectories—and consistently resulted in the failure of the industry's leading firms" (Christensen [1997, p. 9]).

At first, these smaller drives were not of interest to incumbent producers, as they had inadequate storage capacity to service the needs of their customers. But after each new type of drive was introduced, innovation steadily increased the storage capacity of drives of all sizes. At a certain point, the new, smaller drives began to appeal to previous buyers of larger drives. The smaller drives had enough capacity to service their needs, and the other virtues of the smaller drives, such as their lower cost and smaller size, more than compensated for their lower storage capacity. But the incumbents had largely ceded the lead in these smaller drives to new firms, often spinoffs from the incumbents. By the time their customers showed interest in the smaller drives, their slow start was hard to overcome. Consequently, each round of smaller drives that opened up new submarkets ushered in a new era of leaders. Unlike autos, tires, TV receivers, penicillin, and lasers, it was later entrants, mainly spinoffs, that prospered in the industry as a result.

This is hardly an isolated story, and Christensen recounts other industries that experienced a similar evolution. We will return to consider the implications of this kind of evolution for firm strategy in high-tech industries, but it is clear how threatening the creation of new submarkets can be. Submarket dynamics also can enrich the possible paths that new industries follow. The laser industry illustrates how a continual rise in the number of producers for many years can give rise to a shakeout. The disk drive industry experienced a classic shakeout, but rather than benefiting early entrants, it was later entrants that came to dominate the industry. In the computer industry, the creation of new submarkets related to smaller computers upset the dominance of the industry by IBM based on its prowess in mainframe computers and led to renewed entry and growth in the number of producers (Flamm [1988], Bresnahan and Malerba [1999]).[3]

Another aspect of the way new industries evolve concerns the origins of its leaders. In chapter 3, in four of the six industries—all but TV receivers and penicillin—the heritage of new firms profoundly affected their performance. Firms founded by employees of incumbent firms in the same industry—what we called spinoffs—far outperformed other new firms. Moreover, larger firms spawned more of these spinoffs, and their spinoffs were superior performers. Similar patterns have been found in the small number of other industries that have also been dissected nano-economically.* But do these patterns hold more generally?

A lot is at stake for societies in how they should structure policy regarding high-tech industries if these patterns hold generally. Basically, societies will have to depend on incumbent firms to generate the next generation of leaders. But as we saw, incumbent firms do not generally play this role willingly. Why should they be interested in breeding their potential competitors? But if the incumbent firms do not want to play their anointed role voluntarily, society needs to figure out how to structure its laws to ensure the creation of future generations of leading firms.

Researchers have been able to make headway on the question of whether spinoffs generally are superior performers using what are called matched employer-employee data sets. In some countries, particularly in Scandi-

---

*In the United States, spinoffs have been studied in hard disk drives (Christensen [1993], Agarwal et al. [2004], Franco and Filson [2006]) and medical devices (Chatterji [2009]), and to a lesser extent biotherapeutics (the part of biotechnology pertaining to humans) (Mitton [1990], Romanelli and Feldman [2006]). They have also been studied in law firms (Phillips [2002]). Outside the United States, spinoffs have been studied in the historical automobile industries of Great Britain (Boschma and Wenting [2007]) and Germany (Cantner et al. [2006], Von Rhein [2008]), in the German laser industry (Buenstorf [2007]), the Australian and New Zealand wine industry (Roberts et al. [2011]), and in the world ready-to-wear fashion industry (Wenting [2008]).

navia, the national census bureau not only collects data on every firm but also on every employee of every firm. Such data sets can be used to identify the founders of new firms and their work heritage.

Analyses of these data sets have consistently revealed the same pattern—the heritage of new firms profoundly affects their performance. This holds for all types of industries, not just high-tech ones. Among new firms, those founded by employees in the same industry are by far the best performers, especially when the impetus for firm founding was not the failure or imminent failure of their parent firm.*[4]

Chapter 4 established that spinoffs were key to geographic clustering in high-tech industries. With larger firms spawning more and better spinoffs and spinoffs not venturing far from their geographic roots, successful firms built up around early successful entrants, giving rise to clustering. The main reason for the emergence of clusters was spinoffs, not any benefits to firms associated from being located in a cluster.

These ideas fly in the face of conventional wisdom and have radical implications for public policy, which historically has promoted the formation of clusters. As such, it is imperative to investigate whether they can explain the formation of clusters in high-tech industries generally. Unfortunately, this is a daunting challenge. Studies of the location of manufacturing plants in the United States and the United Kingdom indicate that plants are more clustered than would be expected if they located randomly, but clustering is typically modest (Ellison and Glaeser [1997], Duranton and Puga [2005]). Consequently, extreme cases like autos, tires, and semiconductors are difficult to come by, making generalizations difficult. Similar to these industries, once clusters have formed, it does appear that production eventually shifts away from clusters (Dumais et al. [2002]), but exactly how clusters form in the first place cannot be readily explored in a large number of industries.

Traditional view of clustering [was] never tested within context of evolving industries. [I] looked at where [spinoff] firms located originally [and found that they] typically [stayed close to] their base of operations for many years; [that is, there was] little relocation of base [as one would expect to find if agglomeration effects were drawing firms to clusters, regardless of their heritage]. What we see in the above three industries [autos, tires, and semiconductors] was the importance of the high rate

---

*See Muendler et al. [2012] for Brazil, Denmark; Eriksson and Kuhn [2006], Dahl and Reichstein [2007], Sørensen [2007], and Sørensen and Phillips [2011] for Denmark; Hvide [2009] for Norway; Baptista and Karaöz [2007] for Portugal; and Andersson and Klepper [2013] for Sweden.

of spinoff creation. Fairchild was the most extreme example, but Olds Motors was also fertile, as were the three big Akron firms. We do not see spinoffs venturing very far for social as well as economic reasons.

Extreme clustering has been observed in a couple of other industries that have been dissected nanoeconomically—disk drives and biotherapeutics (the part of the biotechnology industry having to do with humans), which is encouraging. Indeed, the evolution of the geographic concentration of the disk drive industry is worth recounting because it closely resembles the geographic clustering of the semiconductor industry.* Similar to semiconductors, the disk drive industry ended up being clustered in Silicon Valley, but it did not begin that way. At first the industry was concentrated in Southern California around Los Angeles, Minneapolis, Colorado, and Silicon Valley. After about 20 years of evolution, though, over 70% of the sales of disk drive firms were accounted for by firms based in Silicon Valley. Most of these firms were spinoffs of leading firms in the industry that ultimately could be traced back to IBM, whose main disk drive operations were located nearby in San Jose, California.[5] The leaders were mainly based in Silicon Valley, but like other firms in the industry they increasingly moved their production to lower-cost areas, particularly Singapore (McKendrick, Doner, and Haggard [2000]).[6]

Chapter 5 established the importance of the federal government and the military getting four of the six featured industries started, and chapter 6 chronicled the similarities in the decline of the U.S. auto, tire, and TV receiver industries. Neither of these patterns can be easily generalized. When it comes to the influence of the military, numerous other examples of high-tech industries jump-started by the military will be advanced. In contrast, it takes considerable time for industries to become extinct, so there are not a lot of other examples of this phenomenon in the United States to draw upon. In both cases, we will have to rely upon a limited number of industries from which to generalize—that is simply the nature of the beast.

As already suggested, these issues bring into perspective the long-term importance of a firm's management of innovation at pivotal stages of market development. We can now step back and extract wisdom for innovators from our study. What are successful practices for the management of innovation? What processes in evolving high-tech industries should absorb the attention of innovators and guide business strategies?

---

*See principally Christensen [1993], Agarwal et al. [2004], Franco and Filson [2006], and McKendrick et al. [2000].

Editors' note: This is where the continuous text ended. The remainder of the material in this chapter follows the handwritten outline supplemented by whatever relevant notes we could find.

• • •

I. IF YOU GET ON TOP, MILK THE ADVANTAGE OF SIZE

A. Henry Ford's main problem: From the experience at Ford, we can see a behavior repeated many times throughout the twentieth century.

- Once on top of a market, the leading firm milks the advantage of its size at tremendous long-term cost to the innovation needed to maintain market leadership. However, Henry Ford's main problem was not a trade-off between size and innovation. The rate of price decline [measuring the rate of innovation] was going down anyway.

- Ford became a weakened organization when it lost James Couzens in 1919, the managerial genius who protected the company's capital and translated it into operations that delivered a product to satisfy the market.

B. In the subsequent tossing and turning of Henry Ford's mercurial passions, Ford Motor Co. dissipated the firm's historic advantage.

• • •

II. FIRM ADVICE

A. Submarkets create a great challenge to incumbents. Fundamental is the need to study and understand why firms in leading markets hesitate in the face of opportunities that later prove to have been unsurpassed. This reluctance occurs over and over again in industries of every sort and high-tech industries have no special immunity to it. Many high-tech firms struggle with the dilemma of a new submarket rising farther ahead on a path made passable by the incumbent's original technology.

- However, high-tech industries enjoy the capacities of well-trained workers. Many of them have the technical experience to create new technologies with their own imaginative ideas. This is part of what they learned while working near the edges of potential new submarkets. [Hence], if [incumbents] don't pursue [opportunities], [that] can be a basis for spinoffs.

- Submarkets can still be a basis for spinoffs resulting from other reasons.

- Spinoffs dilute top talent. For that reason alone, they tend to inspire caution when executives foresee internal support emerging for a spinoff. Various studies of the phenomenon suggest that modest losses of talent to a spinoff can be tolerated. However, patterns of multiple spinoffs from a single firm often reflect and even create sustained losses and decline in market position. The causality (common cause of multiple losses and decline) seems plausible.

B. How can [incumbents] avoid missing opportunities created by new submarkets?

Common reasons for not pursuing [submarket opportunities]:

1. Smallness—incumbent managers may dismiss the emerging submarket for its relatively small scale, when compared to the incumbent's balance sheets. Inside judges conclude the submarket will not achieve benchmark levels.
2. Un-relatedness—dismiss the submarket as beyond the firm's core mission and label the opportunity "not what we do."
3. Boss not in-tune: The boss who keeps a watchful eye on current operations may not see the future from the same perspective as an underling watching for new career opportunities.

Problem with these reasons:

1. [Smallness:] Who cares about current size of the submarket? It is the future that matters.

   - Integrated Circuits [were initially] viewed as a small submarket.
   - Smaller disk drives viewed as new submarket.
   - Miniaturized He Ne lasers [presented an] unclear submarket.

2. Un-relatedness: Why is this relevant—cost of managing diverse operations?

   - If so, [incumbent firms can] constitute and manage [the new submarket] as a separate operation.
   - What is unrelated at one moment may prove related due to latent substitutability of submarkets, à la lasers and disk drives.

3. Boss and underling don't see eye-to-eye:

   - Why [should there be the] same hierarchy about ideas and other decisions?
   - As an immediate patch, why not rely at least upon a court of appeal within the firm to air arguments and bring complete information to decision making?

C. [Ways] how to pursue "unnatural" ideas:

If the idea is perceived to be a small, unrelated opportunity, not favored by a boss, how to pursue without butchering:

1. [Set up a] separate entity with only partial ownership by firm.

- This minor interest in the new enterprise could include an option for later purchase at a suitable strike price.

2. [The firm can] get others involved with more knowledge about the new submarket, particularly potential customers from whom the demand for the innovation appears strongest. This seems to be the lesson from the Xerox spinoffs that wasted time and resources on ideas that other innovators have already developed.

- Such engagement can avoid typical marketing focus groups and involve seasoned decision makers with imaginative strategies for shaking up and refocusing unworkable business plans.

- Marketable innovation also requires venture capitalists as partners, which means ceding them ownership but perhaps even more so ceding decision making in excess of ownership. Perhaps [this] is where a buy option would provide a satisfactory inducement. Christensen's assessment of a firm's long-term interest in a market that appears to be driven by countervailing interests offers inspiring reading.

• • •

III. INDIVIDUAL ADVICE: WHEN INDIVIDUALS SHOULD LEAVE TO FOUND OWN FIRMS

A. Walking out the door is a formidable chore and the essential first step is an accurate assessment of when an employer is failing to pursue a good idea because it does not know how to evaluate its potential.

1. One common indicator of such a situation is the narrow scope of analysis that decision makers steeped in a specific technology apply to new ideas. Depending upon the character of the invention around which an incumbent company formed, some companies remain satisfied with profits from technology's version of a one-trick pony, a great performer in a limited arena. The firm fails to bring better business tools, gained in reputable MBA programs, to its analysis of markets, and operations usually don't grow. Such old-school management of a technology enter-

prise should raise a significant warning to any employee seeking new opportunities for submarket growth.

2. Another circumstance forcing the innovator to seek the fortune of a good idea elsewhere can be a consequence of an employer recently acquired by new owners. [This may result in] hubris.

3. The boss having a narrow view and the firm offers no court of appeal. Unfortunate as such roadblocks may be for the enterprise, the innovator may have no better recourse than his or her independent path away from the firm offering job security.

B. Accidental entrepreneurs. Gordon Moore

Heritage importance:

1. As Gordon Moore, a founder of Fairchild Semiconductor, the precursor of Intel, points out in "The Accidental Entrepreneur," heritage reflects the quality of a prospective worker.

   • Fairchild invented the integrated circuit to create the opportunity for a new submarket in the first place. For those who worked on the opportunity, that heritage was a golden predictor of things to come.

2. Also important in knowing how to solve problems, both technical and managerial.

3. Also important in gaining novel experience to exploit.

   • Intel [founders] not making [the] same error as Fairchild in doing too much research that [the firm] couldn't handle. Moore and his colleagues learned firsthand that no lasting value originates in ideas that cannot be marketed as useful products. Then they had gained experience with manufacturing and a real market before founding the firm that would create a huge segment of the modern electronics industry.

   • Don't start firms for negative reasons [thinking that one] can do better than the failing firm that had inferior managers: findings about worse performance of spinoffs of parents that fail in country studies, findings of best spinoffs from top firms in new industries.[7]

C. Test out a new market by seeking out others potentially better positioned to evaluate the market.

Seeking help from VCs and others able to place money on the table may mean a dilution of ownership. However, it is also a meaningful litmus test of whether the promising concept has reached the stage around which to build a new market.

1. Ideal if VC funding is required anyway.

How semiconductor IC spinoffs of Fairchild [were] financed.

• • •

IV. DEEPER QUESTION, MOVE LONG RANGE—CAN INDIVIDUALS POSITION THEMSELVES IN TERMS OF FIRMS THEY WORK FOR AND JOBS THEY PERFORM TO BEST POSITION THEMSELVES FOR AN ENTREPRENEURIAL CAREER?

A. Entrepreneurial career can include internally acting as an entrepreneur for a firm as well as leaving to found one's own firm.

- Top executives and managers in the early automobile industry, including major initial shareholders, followed this path. The top technology innovators in the first semiconductor firms followed this path. It was almost a job requirement for anyone holding a technical position in the laser industry. The tire industry developed almost entirely with the leadership of founders who had earlier joined the top firms from which they moved to create a startup.
- The history of pharmaceuticals is notable for the industrial innovation tied to the so-called Baxter Boys. Indeed, Baxter stands out as an ideal employer for individuals wanting to learn the fundamentals of entrepreneurship. Baxter recruited freshly minted MBAs and gave them lots of responsibility as a matter of company policy. From that internal dynamic, the firm became a fountain feeding founders and top managers into many pharmaceutical industry startups.[8]

B. Elfenbein et al. (2010)[9] especially useful for scientists and engineering entrepreneurs—explain sample.[10]

[The surveys employed by Elfenbein et al.] distinguish between founding own firm versus staying in for-pay employment.

- [They find that] size matters—smallness better breeder of entrepreneurship—workers in smaller firms have higher probability of leaving to start their own firms:

1. Similar to industry evolution studies—probability of a startup doesn't increase proportionately with size.

- Size also plays a role in success—smallness better—[which] is on surface at odds with nanoeconomic studies.

2. But in evolving industries, leaders [are] not so big on absolute scale during formative era.

- The type of job matters for the inside entrepreneur, whose skills more often need to grow with experience and insight that accrues to marketing and finance managers and corporate executives. This assumes, of course, depth of knowledge in the technology driving the new firm's product.

3. The technologist most readily gains such entrepreneurial skills on the job. Hence the value of small firms in providing experience across a spectrum of business functions, as seen so often in the careers of successful technologists.
4. Certainly defines the kind of person who left to found firms in case studies, [where having] opportunities [was key].

- Top people in autos, sometimes part owners.
- High-level tech people in semiconductors, top managers after acquisitions.
- Tech people of all levels in lasers.

C. Can see founding as part of broader entrepreneurial career path.

Tires make path most salient.
Can see in other industries like pharms—"Baxter Boys" [Higgins, 2005]. This analysis provides some idea about what kind of tacit knowledge is learned by top people so that they can use it to manage other firms or to start, organize, and manage their own firm.

1. [Baxter was an] ideal employer to learn entrepreneurial finance.
2. Company policy to take fresh MBAs and give [them a] lot of responsibility.
3. Common place to recruit top managers as well as source of founders.

Indeed, working for startups itself can be part of beneficial path if we look at wages—Campbell article.[11] Means thinking about employer as well as job may be relevant for individuals as they make their way up the corporate ladder aspiring to be top managers and possibly entrepreneurs. Might also want to strike the chord of being an accidental entrepreneur—be sensitive to biases and blind spots of decision makers to forge out on own, exploiting what a person's employer chooses not to pursue—don't be daunted by rejection of an idea. Can always see if one can drum up support elsewhere, which would be a sign about the value of a rejected idea.

D. [There is a] lot more to learn about entrepreneurial paths—non-accidental entrepreneurs—but clearly, being strategic is an important element in shaping one's own career path if one wants to be entrepreneur.

- Tires—wouldn't found firms out of big 4 unless were top person—did stint at top first.

• • •

V. SOCIETAL QUESTIONS

The broader reality, of course, is that a well-motivated individual can only do so much. Inevitably, innovation occurs in a social context shaped by the behaviors of institutions and governments that have substantial effects on the choices of the entrepreneur. Even so, such shapers of the entrepreneur's societal context mostly share a common belief in the general benefit to society from fostering enterprise and multiplying the value of innovation. This widely shared social value thus invites the question of how a society can hit the jackpot by aligning the behaviors of key institutions to grow the numbers of innovative enterprises.

This fundamental interaction between society and entrepreneurial culture is fundamental to the health and vigor of modern capitalist societies. It requires us to examine and evaluate the broad policies that enable enterprise to prosper and grow, stimulating the economic health of nations across decades of evolving technological innovation. Free markets, the contemporary mechanism that generates wealth in modern nations, should offer a recognizable structure within which managers of technical innovation can freely navigate. The stance of government shapes the market for new technology not only by setting rules but also by seeding the creation of technologies from which markets draw their power. The stewards of such powers can be scored for the quality of rulemaking and public expenditures that finance the technical infrastructure supporting innovative enterprises. One simple question needs to be clear in everyone's mind. How much of a role does government need to play in fostering innovative markets? To what extent must society call upon government to manage public investment and promote common benefits from general enterprise? Construed as interference, this set of concerns sometimes stirs a lion's roar inside political discourse. Yet all government and institutional actors, including the military, play key roles in the overall integration of a healthy economy.

- Jackpot questions: How to structure rules of competitors, roles of military and government, to get most out of societal potential.

A. Boils down to simple question: How active do we want government (subsumes military) to be in shaping markets?

Mainstream view: historical success of United States due to little intervention by government in markets.

But more theology than ideology—constantly have to make decisions about even minimal functions that governments need to dispense vis-à-vis markets.

1. For example, do we want to use antitrust laws to restrict Intel's dominance of microprocessor market? Or [should we] have done [the] same to Ford in the Model T era?

2. Seems preposterous in hindsight, but this is what we did to RCA in 1950s when it was a far less dominant TV producer that widely licensed its technology to potential competitors and had a much smaller net share than Intel.

   - Waged criminal as well as civil suits against RCA that eventually forced it to give up revenues from licensing of color TV patents to domestic rivals.

   - Few economists today would consider this wholly legitimate form of compensation to be a vehicle of RCA's market domination, as it was held to be at the time in U.S. courts. At the time, the firm held much less sway over the market for television than Intel possesses today in the market for semiconductors. It's not clear that government policy would have sought to change RCA's licensing practices toward Japanese producers, which effectively licensed RCA's—and the U.S. industry's—most significant future competitors. Yet it might have slowed the pace of Japanese takeover of the television market (LaFrance [1985]).

   - The court system's mistreatment of RCA may seem like an isolated case, but it turned out to be more like the first in a sequence of federal actions. The government also hounded other dominant firms that were leading innovators. Both IBM and Xerox are examples, and both I think signed consent decrees after their CEOs became preoccupied with the antitrust cases against them and perhaps got diverted from leading their organizations to innovate further. The same could be said for RCA's CEO getting diverted.

Theory of industry lifecycle/shakeouts in chapter 2 suggests [that we may] want to leave dominant firms alone—dominance occurs naturally, brings great innovations like RCA color TV, IBM system 360 and then 370—systems of mainframes for every use, Intel range of microprocessors, including ones to drive PCs.

B. Another big question about activist government—how activist do we want government to be in protecting a firm's (intellectual) property?

Intellectual property stands apart from traditional property in being an immaterial class of property that can be used simultaneously in multiple locations.

Legislated protection of intellectual property stands alongside even more encompassing protection of trade secrets, which enjoy a separate layer of law shielding innovative companies from theft of intangible assets.

1. But laws protecting trade secrets inevitably don't cover much private IP that is not constituted as a clear secret owned by firm—e.g., silicon-gate technology in *Intel v. Fairchild*.

   • Much lesser examples of how to address unique challenges such as building a market for a new technology like integrated circuits by keeping down the price and relentless innovating:
   • Hard to enforce this as a broad trade secret.
   • One "remedy" to this problem [that would] allow almost blanket enforcement of IP is non-compete covenants. Explain what these are.[12]

2. As Matt Marx and Lee Fleming[13] argue, the ubiquity of non-compete clauses—people agree to such covenants well before they have any real concepts of what they are signing away—creates a very conspicuous injustice.

3. Do they prove to be binding?

   • Marx et al. provide egregious examples.
   • Marx et al. difference-in-difference study with Michigan and California.

4. State policy: California as quirk of legal precedent, forbids enforcement of non-competes.

   • Does the variation in enforcement affect startups?—Stuart and Sorensen present a clever way to study such effects, which seems to suggest the answer is yes.[14]
   • California's reluctance to enforce these covenants is an element in the vibrancy of the Silicon Valley as an entrepreneurial region where

mobility allows the workforce to develop in a rich climate of opportunity for creating innovative technology. Even as the semiconductor cluster declined, others emerged to regenerate growth. In part because of other technologies related to semiconductors, like computers, but also this is where Stanford and secondarily Berkeley have played a role. Downplay their role in semiconductors, citing Moore for backup and my analysis of source of patent generators. But definitely seem important in preserving Silicon Valley. Also capitalized on being a place of entrepreneurship, which galvanized the venture capital industry there, which no doubt has encouraged indigenous activity in the Valley and also attracted activity from elsewhere, like Facebook.

- Vibrancy of Silicon Valley as region of entrepreneurship/mobility—how is this affected overall by more startups. Also, mobility versus potential inhibiting effect on intellectual property rights protection in the first place.

Continued vibrancy of region—Zhang;[15] paper on science parks[16] and statistics on vibrancy of Silicon Valley as a region.

Note [that Silicon Valley] is the only cluster that survived one industry giving rise to the cluster.

Note [the] importance of mobility and entrepreneurship (Saxenian about mobility;[17] also cite Kenney and Burg work here[18]).

- Seems like a no-brainer that the potential benefit of banning non-competes far exceeds potential harm.[19]

Discuss how these themes transcend the United States and semiconductor industry: develop Bangladesh story: the power of tacit knowledge to seed a gigantic, vibrant industry that greatly contributes to the growth of a country.[20] Trick in Bangladesh is to get a successor to cotton garments. For this, need government à la Taiwan and semiconductors. Note how "together" the government was in this case to make this work. Bangladesh lacks the government infrastructure to even think about something like this. Can see why countries can seldom mount the kinds of initiatives they need to get the tacit knowledge to break into new (to them) industries where they might have a comparative advantage.

Further support for critical nature of spinoffs comes from Israel and *Startup Nation*[21] and forthcoming Stanford book.[22] This is an important lesson for other countries—want to create environment, socially as well as legally, that facilitates if not encourages the formation of spinoffs.

VI. QUESTIONS SO FAR BEAR ON HOW MUCH GOVERNMENT SHOULD PLAY TRADITIONAL ROLE OF ENFORCING COMPETITION AND OWNERSHIP OF PRIVATE (INTELLECTUAL) [PROPERTY]. BUT REALLY BIG QUESTIONS CONCERN NOT MARKET-SUPPORTING ROLE OF GOVERNMENT BUT HOW ACTIVIST [IT] SHOULD BECOME

The nation derives distinct benefits from the stable functioning of high-tech markets. For such returns, government needs to fund and encourage the development and commercialization of innovative technologies. Along with a necessary mix of soft and hard investment in education and training, this type of investment pays off. We see the payoffs in the Silicon Valley and other U.S. centers of technological innovation and in other countries as well. Proactive support from government agencies has sustained impressive growth among high-tech industries in Israel and Taiwan. Both nations' policies reap enormous social payback from government support for high-tech industries, building economies around a healthy array of diverse industrial markets.

A. In 1960s–90s, crescendo of pleas/proposals for U.S. government to be far more involved in the economy based on success of our Asian competitors, especially the Japanese.

Develop a series of quotes from Hounshell book by influential thinkers, policy makers like Robert Reich.[23]

B. In the same period, a countervailing crescendo resisted these ideas, which flew in face of long-standing beliefs about sources of U.S. success in the high-tech sector.

Develop series of quotes/responses in Hounshell book.

C. This crescendo has certainly subsided with the long-term decline of Japan especially—perhaps relate figures on Japanese GDP.

Proponents of laissez-faire largely won battle.
True at federal level—limited amount done to counter Japan, etc. with the exception of trade policy.
Absence of industrial policy hardly dooms a country's success. Witness success of United States in autos, a European product, and tires, largely a European product as well at its inception. Obviously linked, and United

States had by far the biggest market, which aided the development of both industries by facilitating cost spreading.

But at the state and local levels, long followed suggestions for activist government.

1. Resonates with beliefs about clusters—*ubiquitous* reason to proactively promote regional activity.

    • Policies regarding clusters need to be rethought. Pick up on Josh Lerner book, *Boulevard of Broken Dreams*,[24] and failure of initiatives to build up clusters via promoting regional industry concentrations—widespread. Concentration of producers does not unleash self-reinforcing forces without spinoffs being prevalent, as TV receivers demonstrates. Ultimate question for all regions and particularly countries without major presence in an industry is whether government can grow innovative organizations at the technology frontier and then sponsor the formation of spinoffs from the innovative organizations to prime the spinoff process. Present Josh Lerner findings, paper on science parks[25] to argue that local efforts largely not effective beyond tax incentives to bring firms to a region.

2. And not clear [if these local efforts are not] even a zero-sum activity at the level of the whole country when losers as well as winners are considered. (Michael Greenstone work and findings).[26]

    • Resonates with findings on clusters.

D. But have we given up the fight at the federal level prematurely?

The Obama administration has not, as it has remained committed to priming economic pump via efforts on manufacturing, clean-energy, high-speed trains, and healthcare, including of course the change sought in the Affordable Care Act.

1. The National Academy of Sciences examines the authentic value of these initiatives while the Obama administration typically seeks to involve industry, universities, and defense interests in these initiatives.

    • There is ample precedent in the 4–6 industries studied here to support the potential benefit of support by defense establishment when technologies/industries are young. Can see this with penicillin. Germany dominated the world in chemicals and pharma for long time. United States not going anywhere on its own, and Florey's visit to U.S. companies did not do much. Government policy was key. Looking back, that was a model for sensible industrial policy, though not perceived that way. Military demand and involvement in penicillin was important (first user on a large scale, which is why the federal government got involved), compellingly important in semiconductors and lasers, and oddly important in radios leading to TVs. Provide rationale for why dedicated industry support at the start of new industries can be so helpful.

2. We can readily see this beyond the four examined industries:

- Computers, disk drives fundamentally supported by government.
- Aircraft and engines (jet) fundamentally part of military mission that nationally spilled over to civilian sector (Ed Constant book,[27] Dick Nelson on aircraft[28]).

   Guided missiles; radar; rocket engines also part of the defense/ space sphere; nuclear power.

- Discuss the Department of Defense's DARPA initiatives:

   Basic research related to procurement of weapons systems.

   But goes further—support for IT broadly and artificial intelligence allegedly had tremendous IT civilian ramifications—cite prior NAS study that my NAS study cited.[29]

   Discuss modern decline of DARPA's role in stimulating new civilian industries. Perhaps biotech article on early support by military. An agency in charge of buying has tools at its disposal to support private firms without investing in them, as in energy firms today. Note that recently announced program by President Obama is going to be executed/overseen by the executive branch, which is a political animal. Already the intention is to spread the proposed centers around the country. This is a political choice that does not make sense—the centers need to be located where the relevant expertise is concerning producers and universities.

   Signs suggest that passing of WWII and waning of Cold War had led to waning commitment. Note this kind of pump priming—figures on private vs. public U.S. R&D spending, comparison to rest of world—check out Hounshell book, publicly available data—could be separate box on this.

- Some useful themes about nature of past successes:

   a. Defense procurement key element of success. DARPA's emphasis on basic research to foster advanced military systems drew many universities into this work, stimulating visionary work in many technologies that stand astride the modern economy and global marketplace. We see this effect in semiconductors, lasers, and penicillin.[30]

b. DARPA's emphasis on basic research to foster advanced military systems drew many universities into this work, stimulating visionary work in many technologies.

- We see this effect in semiconductors, lasers, and penicillin.
- Book on Stanford and MIT during Cold War—Leslie.[31]

c. Short stints of top people de facto rotated back into the civilian sector key to success—certainly prevented regulatory capture.

VII. OTHER END OF SPECTRUM ABOUT ACTIVIST ROLE OF GOVERNMENT IS WHAT TO DO ABOUT OLD, WITHERING INDUSTRIES

A. Traditional manufacturing plants are also the target of activist government. Perhaps biggest challenge to policy pertains to old industries after they have gone through prolonged shakeouts and few firms left as gatekeepers of technological change in their industries. Powerful interests arise within companies that can thwart imitating leaders from other countries that introduce major innovations, contributing to sharp decline and even the demise of once very successful industries. Tremendously challenging to deal with. Long-standing observation that board of directors is not a potent force, and need to develop policies to make boards stronger.

Possible proactive steps to take:

1. Break up leaders.
2. Restrict salaries of top executives.
3. Engineer family control with banks.
4. Strengthen and require more independence of board. If have potential to fire top executives that do not take bold steps in the face of major challenges leading to steady decline in market shares, might avert worse cases like GM and Chrysler and possibly RCA.
5. Another possibility is to strengthen the ability of outsiders to gain control of sluggish innovators to install new management committed to righting the ship. Ford's experience in 1980s indicates that ship can be righted, but takes full focus of top management. Might want to make it

more difficult for incumbent management to resist hostile takeovers—also long-standing proposal.

- These proposals seem especially important regarding old industries with old leading firms.
- My own breakout—limitations on activist policies, but bad outcomes not inevitable and area deserves attention as important area of policy makers—try to provide some concrete suggestions

•   •   •

POTENTIAL MATERIAL FOR END OF CHAPTER 7

Sources of U.S. advantages in high-tech competition. One is that the United States is the largest national market, particularly important earlier when trade smaller.[32] Gave companies largest incentives to innovate over time—had larger levels of output over which to apply their innovations. Favors market integration à la Europe, free trade pacts that expand markets for firms. In four of the industries, U.S. government and military support helped industries get head start over foreign competition too—led United States to be pioneer in antibiotics, semiconductors, and lasers and to be potent competitor in radio and TV receivers. Given advantages of early entry, provided sizeable advantage to leading U.S. producers in these industries. Some other countries seem to have recognized the need for proactive government policies to compete with established U.S. firms in new industries—Japan and Taiwan in semiconductors, Japan in computers, Israeli policies regarding R&D and venture capital. Also sometimes need to invoke infant industry argument to protect fledgling domestic firms from more advanced foreign competitors—Japan and automobiles and TV receivers after World War II, for example.

Another advantage of United States stems from spinoffs, which are critical to moving industries forward and in the formation of clusters. In industries studied, few restrictions on employees leaving to start own firms, and United States blessed with formation of spinoffs in autos, semiconductors, lasers, and tires that helped propel these industries forward. Part of motivation in tolerating spinoffs is ability to attract labor that values option of starting own firm. Is quite different from Europe and Japan. Note that the spinoff model is not the only one for success—Japan has done well with large established firms pioneering disk drives and semiconductors, although it is not well understood if this works when an industry is catching up versus having to pioneer (though I think it pioneered in disk drives). *Startup Nation* suggests there is a cultural dimension to spinoffs, but historically Israel was plagued by low startups before Byrd and the like, and this was pointed out as a problem. Also, culture has a way of being reified when it emerges spontaneously in response to a need, which is my interpretation of high job hopping and its worship in Silicon Valley, which emerged because of the high rate of spinoffs there (which it also reinforced). Similarly, lifetime employment was viewed as highly virtuous when rotating top workers across different functions, made possible by lifetime employment, seemed a key strength of Japanese firms, but now lifetime employment has ebbed.

Maybe the most important theme is that talented people are always slated to have less influence on industry in parent than own spinoff. In the parent, they are subordinate. Not charged with coming up with novel strategic ideas that may be resisted by the parent, both because hard to evaluate novel ideas and natural reluctance to gamble with a successful firm in a new, risky area. Common view of spinoffs is that they were formed to bet the company on a new area, but judging from autos and semiconductors, a lot of spinoffs related to strategic disagreements over the best course for the company about production, compensation, direction of company following new ownership. Spinoffs stretched their industries via innovative ideas and product variants, leading to the growth of their industries. Further support for the critical nature of spinoffs comes from Israel and *Startup Nation*. This is an important lesson for other countries—you want to create an environment, socially as well as legally, that facilitates if not encourages the formation of spinoffs.

Lessons for the United States if to be successful in future. One is [the perils of] widespread support for employee non-compete covenants. Non-competes have been used to block movements. Discuss gratuitous social harm, which we can't readily tally because it involves contemplating the counterfactual. Imagine magnifying many times over in other industries and states. Now imagine other countries where culture is even more stifling about employees leaving to found firms in their own industry. On balance, judging from Silicon Valley, [non-competes] seems like bad policy. Trade secret law could be structured to allow for spinoffs while protecting intellectual property of incumbents.

Another lesson is recognizing that the United States has had a de facto industrial policy, but in all four products studied, this policy emanated from World War II efforts. Other government World War II efforts, like radar and synthetic rubber, also proved to be commercially important. But government and military support for R&D has long been waning. Need to revisit—including how government dispenses support for new industries—support of fundamental research versus individual firms via massive loans, like in the energy domain.

Various government-organized research missions might work to focus government research support so that it was well leveraged commercially. One mission would be on energy, which could include: (1) more efficient and safe methods of extracting all kinds of fuels, including fossil fuels, such as oil under the ocean and other waterways, shale in the ground like Marcellus shale, etc.; (2) development of all kinds of alternatives to fossil fuels, including nuclear, solar, wind, ethanol; (3) more efficient use of energy, including the development of an electric automobile industry and electric batteries for cars; (4) research on how to clean up the environment and reduce noxious emissions from processing fossil fuels and other energy sources, such as by harnessing bacteria for this purpose; (5) research on conserving energy via things such as more energy-efficient appliances, etc.

Another mission area would be education at all levels. Little productivity growth has occurred historically in this sector, which is causing the prices of schooling at all levels to skyrocket. This is not surprising considering how fragmented the industry is because of local control of schooling. Research could be sponsored on learning, computer-based tutoring, monitoring, diagnosing, etc. It could also be concentrated on the delivery of education and the effects of competition.

CONCLUSION

I want to emphasize the key ideas of nanoeconomics and present evidence and leading case studies to buttress my conclusions.[33] I hope that we can now see both the challenges and the way forward in a number of dimensions.

Nonetheless, there are no panaceas and no silver bullets. We still have much to learn. The concept of the submarket really stands out as an important area for study. It comes up repeatedly yet we still need to define it better, think it through more carefully, and encompass it in an economic model. On these tasks, we are standing at the starting line. We are beginning to get our heads around the main concepts, but broad theory is still lacking. We often invoke evolutionary analogies but study of the individual does not equal an evolutionary theory of the operations of the industrial world. This model also does not produce unique dividends from thinking like Darwin.

Perhaps the causality goes the other way. Perhaps the way forward will be to infuse the issue with what we learn from nanoeconomics. Evolutionary geography seems promising as a way to think about Silicon Valley and clusters—see my paper with Golman.[34] The intellectual challenges are great, yet we have the fortune of influencing an era when there is an extraordinary amount of data at our electronic fingertips, and we can hope to draw much faster progress from it.

I hope this book will galvanize the continued effort to seek the Holy Grail of how societies can best tap their full creative, innovative potential to generate growth and prosperity for the greatest good for the greatest number.

APPENDIX TO CHAPTER 7

These notes, taken by Joseph Plummer, provide more detail about how these ideas were to be developed.

Revolutionary products enjoy long lives. Yet the industries that create them enjoy mixed fates. Their fates belong also to regions where the revolutionary products of such innovators gain a foothold first. Detroit highlights the risks for an industrial region that fails to sustain its production after its leading industries create its place in a global market. In contrast, the Silicon Valley illustrates a much different experience where innovation defines a business culture and provides a common tool for making products that lead markets.

The industries of the Silicon Valley have sustained the output of civilization's most successful generator of new firms and products for more than a half-century. Meanwhile, the region has thus far avoided the extravagant risk of regional decline that stalks places where entrepreneurial energy concentrates within fewer and fewer firms. This is not to say that firm failure and shifts in market share do not haunt the Silicon Valley. Leaders among the myriad of companies formed there have had some stupendous falls over the decades of Silicon Valley's worldwide dominance of digital enterprise. Yet the region has sustained expansions and contractions without traumatic ruptures in its underlying growth. The enterprising ferment of the valley's creative force has grown larger with each cycle of the world economy, while the character of its business world grows smarter and more diverse in its ties to the global market.

Polar contrasts today, these regions' respective industries nonetheless faced very similar challenges in managing their leading firms' revolutionary innovations.

First, we have the example of the automobile and tire industries; inventors and purveyors of revolutionary technology providing individualized transportation to millions of people. The story is often told through the eyes of Henry Ford, who receives most of the credit for mass production of automobiles. In fact, he had an idea that others largely brought to life. The effects were huge and widespread. To serve auto owners, subsidiary industries grew across the nation, and their wealth spread across the Midwest as other major industries formed around myriad submarkets arising directly and indirectly from the technology of the automobile.

We learn early in school how Henry Ford showed the world how to create a revolutionary expansion of virtually every consumer market through the efficient organization of assembly lines. Less often do we learn early enough how Ford fell from the heaven he created and landed in the limbo of second place, even for a time descending into third place in the market. Perhaps that is a reason why the latter story has since been repeated many times in other industries. The autocratic industrial genius defies all advice and thus drives away those associates most able to correct the founder's vision. Soon the departed innovators carry the founder's original insight elsewhere and elevate it even higher inside a new and ultimately more successful firm than the one where they started. The value of talent walking out the door sometimes proves to be very large.

At the height of his accomplishment, Ford lost touch as a manager, resisted others' ideas, and in so doing drove away talented managers. His was a peculiar, perhaps pathologic resistance to the changing character of a market. Yet in it he spread common maladies of innovation management throughout Ford Motor Co. In his mind, he knew better than his customers what they wanted in a car, owing to his creation of the most successful automobile ever sold anywhere. He was also indifferent to every one of his advisors, autocratic in forcing the firm to continue in a direction he dictated. At this critical moment in Ford Motor's history, Henry Ford's son Edsel, attempting to move the brand forward, presided over the firm, while his father shared power only as a director. Those others were also paying attention to customers and wanting new model vehicles and then giving in to Ford's belligerence, ridicule, and resistance. Thus, he paralyzed the firm at the moment when it needed to pivot to a new market.

William Knudsen, one of Ford's top executives, moved to General Motors, first as president of Chevrolet and then of General Motors, in disgust with the state of leadership at Ford. With his new authority in a clear-minded firm, he stole the lead in auto markets for General Motors while Ford Motor Co. watched its share of market shrivel.

Ford Motor Co.'s game-changing fumble offers a dramatic example of a somewhat common experience. Under pressure to maintain market leadership, firms become stymied by their own success and fall back upon incremental innovation to refurbish fading brands. In the beginning, the actual steps of creating a novel product, building a firm to finance and protect the investment, and having income return from the product's sales in the market is often a rocky venture, full of lessons learned as innovative technology evolves into a marketable, perhaps revolutionary product. And so it was that Henry Ford's notions of a simpler, lower cost vehicle that everyone could afford required two initial ventures to develop before Ford Motor Co. created an automobile market with tens of millions of customers. The Model-T's production also effectively allowed Ford Motor Co. to own the North American market for automobiles and outpace competitors' sales by orders of magnitude. Meanwhile, new innovators take the lead. Before long, former pioneers are swept from their positions. For high-tech innovators, these histories illuminate the decades-long challenge of creating new industries and markets.

Building on innovation in style conceived by Ransom Olds and fashioned into Oldsmobile, alongside dramatic improvements in ignition and accessory functions engineered for the Cadillac by Charles Kettering, General Motors moved into a market extending well beyond Ford Motor's reach, extending upscale to consumers willing to pay more for power, comfort, and function. From the 1920s onward, GM committed itself to innovations that sustained its brand and boosted its leadership of the industry through the 1970s. Ford eventually regained momentum in the market it had nearly forsaken. Nonetheless, it never recovered from second place while in some years dropping into third. It had reversed its enormous initial decade of success and moved with its losses very close to bankruptcy. Unfortunately, neither firm controlled nor stood well positioned in relation to the global innovation that Japan began to bring into the North American automobile market in the 1960s. By then the sway of innovation had ceased to influence the direction of the industry. In Ford first and the entire industry eventually, the scenario of submarket insurgents toppling the original titan took vivid form.

Today the hollowed out region around Detroit, once thriving cities built around the plants of GM, Ford, Chrysler, and Dodge, offer a grim testament to the challenges to an industrial leader's long-term sustainability. It ascends the plateaus of global success on the strength of spectacularly successful innovations. At the same time, it creates new industries and seeds enterprises that will challenge its dominance with innovations that bring better applications of technology to the product lines that the industry leader has created.

For the firm, its industry, region, and nation, the economic and social effects of that oft-repeated market process create the vitality of a business climate that either suffers from the operation of firms that pay too little attention to innovation, the case of Detroit, or prosper with the successes of firms that manage innovation as an embedded part of manufacturing for markets, the case thus far of the Silicon Valley. And of course, both scenarios can play side by side among firms in an industry or industries in a region.

Why does the Silicon Valley follow a path of industrial development that appears after many decades to be more robust than the futures that played out in the unraveling of American industrial powers in the Rust Belt bordering the Great Lakes? Market challenges of similar magnitude buffet the industries of Silicon Valley. Yet its fortunes have never consolidated around a decisively dominant cluster of enterprises. Instead, its business ethos fostered innovation that brought new organizations to the forefront to exploit new evolutions of technology. Its entrepreneurs sought new opportunities in submarkets unforeseen in the creation of the original technology.

Silicon Valley had another factor of great leverage in creating such a commanding hub for global innovation, much more than the happy accident of the semiconductor industry's cranky grandfather William Shockley deciding he wanted to raise his family in what was then a sleepy hummock of West Coast civilization. It possessed a university of growing reputation and generally unpopulated agricultural landscape stretching south from San Francisco with a string of intermittent towns, including Palo Alto, running down the middle of the peninsula dedicated to some of the most productive agriculture in the United States. There he settled in after inventing the transistor with two colleagues at Bell Labs in New Jersey. Forming a company to design marketable electronic products based on the transistor, he recruited a dream team of scientists and the dynamic process of technical enterprise and innovation in the Silicon Valley got under way with a momentum that has not flagged after more than half a century.

A couple of lessons emerge from the comparison. The first is that Shockley's choice of Palo Alto for a home almost certainly was a happy accident for the location of the future Silicon Valley. Yet the same can be said for Dearborn and the Detroit region, which grew from Ford's selection of a familiar place to learn the crafts of a mechanic and probe the potential of the internal combustion engine for low-cost vehicles. However, as to process cause and economic effect, one ought to pay more heed to the long-term forces founders can set loose in firms with their style of absorbing market information and managing change. Those forces are a constant factor in market innovation and often long-lasting in shaping an industry's future course. In other words, an industry's success doesn't come from the water of the region where it is located. Rather, it comes from the commercial genius of a technologist who is a skillful innovator.

Another lesson emerges here that individuals shaping careers in innovative industries should note. General Motors stole the march into the larger market that Henry Ford blocked his firm from entering. And overall, in decades that followed, GM enjoyed the leadership of innovators of global stature, including the genius of industrial organization, Alfred P. Sloan, and his inventive deputy, Charles S. Kettering, who designed the electrical systems and other accessories that revolutionized the utility and comfort of the automobile.

Kettering created the revolutionary technology that enabled General Motors to steal the lead in the automobile market that Henry Ford let slip away. Kettering held 186 patents during his lifetime. He made his first fortune as co-inventor of the self-starter and founder of the Dayton Engineering Laboratories Co., better known as Delco. He then sold Delco to General Motors as the renamed General Motors Research Corporation. Substantially remunerated, he also retained command of the company he had sold when named GM vice president for research as part of the deal. With the impact of his inventive genius thus greatly magnified, he spearheaded innovation for GM and pioneered its scientific practice as an ardent apostle of technical education.

Yet hard lessons follow success under even the most inventive regimes. Kettering stumbled upon this humbling prospect by attempting to introduce a completely novel product, the 1923 Series M Copper-cooled Chevrolet. Yet the product was a costly failure. One thing it disclosed was the need for a system of product evaluation extending far beyond the inventor's pride in an innovative design.

Choosing copper as the more efficient metal for dissipating heat from an internal combustion engine, Kettering placed the air-foil dissipater atop a reengineered motor that pooled oil from leaks in the design and sometimes held so much heat that it burst into flame. Kettering's champion in the race to cool auto engines, boost horsepower, and give drivers and passengers a more comfortable ride was a worse performer than its predecessor and a costly failure. However, before disaster became catastrophe, Chevrolet killed production as the Series M reached the market and recalled and destroyed those few hundred that made their way into parking places, driveways, and garages of new car owners. The lesson for innovators is, don't stand around working on fixes for failures. Go back to the drawing board, which Chevrolet and Kettering did quickly.

Notes

CHAPTER 1: INNOVATION AND THE MARKET

1. As mentioned in the preface, we will provide equivalents in 2015 dollars using the "inflation calculator" provided by the U.S. Bureau of Labor Statistics (available online at http://www.bls.gov/data/inflation_calculator.htm). The earliest base year in this source is 1913, but given negligible inflation prior to this time, we treat all dollar values in years preceding 1913 as having the same value as in 1913.

CHAPTER 2: ONCE UPON A TIME

1. Klepper is alluding to the independent inventor Philo T. Farnsworth, whose patents on an electronic video camera that he called an "image dissector" led to interference proceedings with RCA's television system patents, as well as protracted court cases that eventually resulted in RCA's paying royalties to Farnsworth. Klepper was well aware of Farnsworth's work and had examined several biographies of Farnsworth that interpret him as a heroic genius independent inventor pitted against the giant, powerful RCA and draconian leader, David Sarnoff. (See, e.g., Daniel Stashower, 2002, *The Boy Genius and the Mogul: The Untold Story of Television*. New York: Broadway Books.) Without gainsaying the value of Farnsworth's work, Klepper followed the best, balanced scholarly accounts of the invention, development, and innovation of all-electronic black-and-white television in the United States, including the 2001 Carnegie Mellon University dissertation by Jennifer Bannister, "From Laboratory to Living Room: The Development of Television in the United States, 1920–1960," which is based on extensive research in RCA's corporate records and especially its R&D laboratory reports and researchers' notebooks. Bannister details the extensive "system development" investments that RCA had to make in order to introduce a robust, functional, and expansive all-electronic television system by the opening of the 1939 New York World's Fair.

CHAPTER 7: THE BEST OF TIMES, THE WORST OF TIMES

1. "Present cost spreading argument [the argument (see Cohen and Klepper, 1996) that larger firm size allows the spreading of returns to R&D investments over larger output, making it inherently more profitable for larger firms to increase their advantage over smaller firms in R&D-intensive, innovative industries], how

it resonates with data for four products on time of entry and domination of patenting by a small number of firms. Note how [the same argument] also came up in discussion of foreign firms displacing US incumbents in TV receivers, tires—once US firms fell behind in size, it was difficult for them to compete. Discuss how this does not rule out complementary factors like scale economies. Note dominant design idea."

"Discuss how same idea was used by Sutton to explain why R&D intensive industries often end up quite concentrated independent of their size—larger size only provides more incentive to spend on R&D, benefiting leaders rather than accommodating more firms. Illustrates power of cost amortization in explaining R&D escalations in notable industries in response to the development of major tech opportunities. These too result in a sharp increase in concentration. So it appears that rich opportunities for technological change can lead to high concentration, shakeout first if present from the start of industries."

2. "[S]ubmarkets . . . have been a powerful force in lasers—discuss all different lasers, then what triggered a shakeout. Sutton makes a similar distinction in trying to understand high-tech industries that don't become highly concentrated. Uses idea of technological change that opens up new submarkets rather than improving existing ones. Provide example of flow meters as extreme and any others he posits."

"Interesting feature of lasers is latent substitutability, which meant ultimately did go through shakeout and has potential to become more concentrated—is richer depiction than in Sutton. . . . Discuss dominant submarket, how related—need in order to have a large enough output to induce R&D effects. . . . Indeed, when opportunity for latent substitutability [opens up], range of potential dynamics gets richer, especially if new submarkets get improved sufficiently relative to mainstream ones that they unexpectedly eat into the demand for the mainstream. If the new submarkets are pursued first by new firms, such as spinoffs of incumbents reluctant to pursue them, [this] can lead to turnover in leaders and success of later entrants."

3. "Submarkets and submarket dynamics [are] not heavily studied in economics [because it] raises awkward issues about why firms' expertise/foresight [is] limited and tends to specialize by submarket. But [it] appears to be a rich concept to help understand evolution of industries. Can accommodate array of patterns that deviate from traditional shakeout dominated by early entrants. Discuss camera case of how a single market can also fragment, leading to a renewal of entry. But stress how the tendency is to develop innovations with broad appeal, which will augur toward a shakeout."

4. "The findings are less clear at economy level—discuss à la *Management Science* paper (Elfenbein et al. 2010) [Elfenbein, Daniel, Bart Hamilton, and Todd Zenger, "The Small Firm Effect and the Entrepreneurial Spawning of Scientists and Engineers," *Management Science* 2010, 4, 659–681—see below for more]. Why might this be true—large firms [are found] in old industries and so don't provide the training individuals need or frontier experiences that are so valuable for spinoffs. So [better people occurring at better firms is] especially [a] feature of evolving industries. My explanation—better people and better training at leading

firms. Fairchild University as an example. [Fairchild Semiconductor providing "unintended training" to almost all early Silicon Valley firms—see chapter 3.]

"Why spinoffs occur at these better firms? Lots of theories. But surprising how often top decision makers at firms [are] not able to recognize opportunities that arise, or lose confidence of employees, leading to departures. Findings about the source of leaders are quite modern, that is consistent across industries. Makes sense that [a prospective entrepreneur] needs to know a lot about challenges of managing in the industry a firm enters. [H]ow better to gain this knowledge than via high-level experience within incumbents, especially leading incumbents. [It] is an odd kind of breeding process in which incumbents unwittingly breed their competitors, who inevitably use what they learn at the incumbents without compensating them. Certainly opposing incentives . . . between incumbents and spinoffs, and [if the situation is] left to own devices not clear [that the spinoff process] will occur optimally. Will come back to." [See below about how letting spinoffs form freely does, in the end, lead to the socially optimal outcome.]

5. "[Klepper's heritage story] does not rule out conventional forces, but they [i.e., the conventional views of clusters] don't address spinoffs at all and why they should show up consistently as a driving force in early clustering. Questions idea of externalities and whether beneficial to locate in clusters."

6. "Indeed, clusters don't seem efficient if buyers spread out. [Clusters] go through a life cycle of their own. Certainly true of autos, tires, semiconductors less so. Can also result in land prices being bid up, necessitating higher wages—Silicon Valley seems [like a] prototype. In autos and tires, unions pushed up wages. All reasons that as leading firms expand, start building plants elsewhere to functions that least need specialized labor that leaders possess—export less sophisticated operations to low wage areas to save on [costs]. Certainly operated early on in the semiconductor industry—moved labor-intensive assembly offshore. Similar developments in disk drives. In older industries of autos and tires, did not move out of country, but moved assembly in autos around the country to save on transport costs and opened branch plants in non-unionized, lower wage areas. So clustering of base locations may persist, but natural for this to become less important for the clustered region as more of assembly and production located elsewhere. So clusters destined to decline, consistent with no real advantage of being in a cluster and potential disadvantage of higher costs. Happened in Detroit, sharply in Akron, and in the semiconductor industry—and disk drives. Also happened in a related way in [TV receivers]—in response to foreign competition from low-wage Japan, moved assembly operations to Mexico and Taiwan. Perhaps would have happened anyway in time."

7. "Evaluating one's work heritage plays an important role in the innovator's transformation into the creator of a robust commercial submarket. An entrepreneur needs to clarify the reasons for creating a startup and separate them from frustrations that force the innovator onto an independent path. The new path calls for a pivot from the motivation of escape from the stultifying employer left behind. Early in the startup, it's important to unleash the potential for a revolutionary product. The enterprising innovator draws upon a heritage that prepared her to build a new market and manage the enterprise far more capably than the

managerial structure that motivated a departure. Throwing off restraints, it's no longer necessary to curse them."

8. Monica C. Higgins, 2005, *Career Imprints. Creating Leaders Across an Industry*. San Francisco: Jossey-Bass.

9. Daniel Elfenbein, Bart Hamilton, and Todd Zenger, "The Small Firm Effect and the Entrepreneurial Spawning of Scientists and Engineers," *Management Science* 2010, 4, 659–681.

10. The data in Elfenbein et al. (2010) come from the restricted-use Scientists and Engineers Statistical Data System (SESTAT) (http://sestat.nsf.gov/). The National Science Foundation administered national surveys of individuals with (at least) a U.S. bachelor's degree in science or engineering to gather employment, education, and demographic information. The surveys distinguish between workers and business owners. The latter include individuals who answered in the affirmative the question whether their principal employment was in their own (incorporated or not) business, professional practice, or farm. Employment in not-own businesses is distinguished by the employer size, in particular.

11. The most likely reference here is Jeffrey R. Campbell and Mariachristina De Nardi, "A Conversation with 590 Nascent Entrepreneurs," *Annals of Finance* 2009, 5: 313–340.

12. A non-compete clause, or covenant not to compete, is a term used in contract law under which one party (usually an employee) agrees not to enter into or start a similar profession or trade in competition against another party (usually the employer): en.wikipedia.rg/wiki/Non-compete_clause. For a scholarly, historical treatment of non-compete contracts, see Catherine L. Fisk, 2009, *Working Knowledge: Employee Innovation and the Rise of Corporate Intellectual Property, 1800–1930*. Chapel Hill: University of North Carolina Press.

13. Matt Marx, Deborah Strumsky, and Lee Fleming, 2009, "Mobility, Skills, and the Michigan Non-Compete Experiment," *Management Science* 55 (6): 875–889.

14. Toby E. Stuart and Olav Sorenson, 2003, "The Geography of Opportunity: Spatial Heterogeneity in Founding Rates of the Performance of Biotechnology Firms," *Research Policy* 32: 229–253; Toby E. Stuart and Olav Sorenson, 2003, "Liquidity Events and the Geographical Distribution of Entrepreneurial Activity," *Administrative Science Quarterly* 48: 175–201.

15. Junfu Zhang, 2003, *High-Tech Startups and Industry Dynamics in Silicon Valley*. San Francisco: Public Policy Institute of California.

16. The most likely reference here is Scott Wallsten, 2001, "The Role of Government in Regional Technology Development: The Effects of Public Venture Capital and Science Parks," Stanford Institute for Economic Policy Research Discussion Paper No. 00-39.

17. AnnaLee Saxenian, 1996, *Regional Advantage: Culture and Competition in Silicon Valley and Route 128*. Cambridge, MA: Harvard University Press.

18. Kenney, Martin and Urs Von Burg, 2000, "Institutions and Economies: Creating Silicon Valley," in Martin Kenney, ed., *Understanding Silicon Valley: The Anatomy of an Entrepreneurial Region*. Stanford, CA: Stanford University Press.

19. "It is challenging to isolate examples of government policy that incorporates direct support for innovation as a primary component of its plan for pro-

moting industry. Nonetheless, through this work, I've found myself increasingly persuaded to the value of California's bias against enforcement of so-called non-compete clauses in employment contracts. I believe that policy, essentially a non-action by the state of California, serves as a relevant example of public policy that costs very little yet produces an economic benefit spread throughout California, as exemplified in the Silicon Valley. This prudential exercise of state government has the beneficial effect of promoting a workforce whose mobility among employers is recognized as a unique strength of Silicon Valley and prominent success factor for new industries forming there."

"California's approach makes an enterprising employee's move between firms less vulnerable to later arbitrary property claims a spurned employer may otherwise wish to press upon a former employee's new firm. A firm is not left unprotected when such prior restraints on an employee's future options are not enforced in state courts. "Non-compete" clauses often go well beyond criminal and civil laws that already protect a firm's trade secrets. Such contracts can place unacceptable financial and moral burdens on innovators who have a promising idea for a product that a current employer won't develop. Collaterally, such contracts imposed on labor encumber an industry's capacity to multiply its markets and diversify its technology inside submarkets. California chooses instead to maximize the opportunity for innovation to flourish by protecting paths to new business formation and neutralizing a weapon that incumbent firms could otherwise use to limit formation of enterprises that threaten the balance of competitors in their markets."

20. See Romel Mostafa and Steven Klepper, 2011, "Industrial Development Through Tacit Knowledge Seeding: Evidence from the Bangladesh Garment Industry," Working Paper, Carnegie Mellon University.

21. Dan Senor and Saul Singer, 2009, *Start-up Nation: The Story of Israel's Economic Miracle*. New York: Twelve Hachette Book Corporation.

22. Reference is unclear. Possibly, Martin Kenney, and David C. Mowery, 2014, *Public Universities and Regional Growth: Insights from the University of California*. Stanford, CA: Stanford University Press.

23. David A. Hounshell, 1984, *From the American System to Mass Production, 1800–1932: The Development of Manufacturing Technology in the United States*. Baltimore, MD: Johns Hopkins University Press. Here Steven Klepper alludes to the extended, intense "technology policy" debate in American politics that unfolded during the period in which American manufacturing was perceived to be under assault from Japanese manufacturers and, as convention went, "Japan, Inc.," roughly from the late 1970s well into the 1990s. For a contemporary history of this debate, see Otis L. Graham, 1992, *Losing Time: The Industrial Policy Debate*. Cambridge, MA: Twentieth Century Fund Books, Harvard University Press.

24. Josh Lerner, 2009, *Boulevard of Broken Dreams: Why Public Effort to Boost Entrepreneurship and Venture Capital Have Failed—and What to Do About It*. Princeton, NJ: Princeton University Press.

25. Scott Wallsten, 2001. "The Role of Government in Regional Technology Development: The Effects of Public Venture Capital and Science Parks," Stanford Institute for Economic Policy Research Discussion Paper No. 00-39.

26. Michael Greenstone, Richard Hornbeck, and Enrico Moretti, 2010, "Identifying Agglomeration Spillovers: Evidence from Winners and Losers of Large Plant Openings," *Journal of Political Economy* 118 (3): 536–598; see especially the discussion on pp. 591–592.

27. Edward W. Constant II, 1980, *The Origins of Turbojet Revolution (John Hopkins Studies in the History of Technology)*. Baltimore, MD: Johns Hopkins University Press.

28. Klepper may be referring here to Nathan Rosenberg and Richard R. Nelson, 1994, "American Universities and Technical Advance in Industry," *Research Policy* 23: 323–348.

29. "Prior NAS study" apparently refers to *Enhancing Productivity Growth in the Information Age: Measuring and Sustaining the New Economy*. Washington, DC: National Academies Press, 2007. "My NAS Study" refers to *Assessing the Impacts of Changes in the Information Technology R&D Ecosystem: Retaining Leadership in an Increasingly Global Environment*. Washington, DC: National Academies Press, 2009.

30. "Very involved government people [were important to success]: the role of military, and in penicillin the role of patriotically motivated civilians. Unusually not self-interested in the sense of being captured, corrupt, etc. Also supervised—had a mission and people to report to who were overseeing the government's efforts. But probably most important was that the mission was important to the sponsor, especially in the military projects. Will contrast with much government policy. Also, the military and even the penicillin program to a lesser degree were involved in the "long run." This was especially so for semiconductors and lasers. The support by the military extended for upwards of 20 years. The support for penicillin extended mostly for 3–4 years. The navy's support for RCA extended for some time also, if included is recruiting AT&T and Westinghouse to the deal. So ordinary programs that are not very long run won't work."

31. Stuart W. Leslie, 1993, *The Cold War and American Science: The Military-Industrial-Academic Complex at MIT and Stanford*. New York: Columbia University Press.

32. This section, probably written as a summation, is presented here in its original form.

33. These are the concluding paragraphs in Joseph Plummer's notes, which correspond to the last section of Steven's handwritten outline.

34. Russell Golman and Steven Klepper, 2013, "Spinoffs and Clustering," Working Paper, Carnegie Mellon University.

Afterword

The estate of Steven Klepper would like to express its deepest appreciation to all of Steven's colleagues and especially to Serguey Braguinsky, David A. Hounshell, and John H. Miller for their immeasurable help in editing the book in a manner that honors Steven's authenticity, legacy, and scholarship.

References

Achilladelis, Basil. "The Dynamics of Technological Innovation: The Sector of Antibacterial Medicines," *Research Policy* 22 (1993), pp. 279–308.

Agarwal, Rajshree, Raj Echambadi, April M. Franco, and M. B. Sarkar. "Knowledge Transfer Through Inheritance: Spin–out Generation, Development, and Survival," Academy *of Management Journal* 47, no. 4 (2004), pp. 501–522.

Aitken, Hugh G. J. *The Continuous Wave: Technology and American Radio, 1900–1932*, 1985, Princeton, NJ: Princeton University Press.

Andersson, Martin and Steven Klepper. "Characteristics and Performance of New Firms and Spinoffs in Sweden," Industrial and Corporate Change 22, no. 1 (2013), pp. 245–280.

Arnold, Horace Lucien and Fay Leone Faurote. *Ford Methods and the Ford Shops*, 1919, New York: Engineering Magazine Company (Elbion Classics Replica Edition, 2005).

Aspray, William. "The Intel 4004 Microprocessor: What Constituted Invention?," *IEEE Annals of the History of Computing* 19 (1997), pp. 4–15.

Bailey, L. Scott. *The American Car Since 1775*, 1971, New York: Automobile Quarterly.

Baldry, P. E. *The Battle Against Bacteria*, 1965, Cambridge, MA: Cambridge University Press.

Bannister, Jennifer Burton. *From Laboratory to Living Room: The Development of Television in the United States, 1920–1960*, 2001, doctoral dissertation, Carnegie Mellon University.

Baptista, Rui, Murat Karaöz, and Joana Mendonca. "Entrepreneurial Backgrounds, Human Capital and Start-up Success," Jena Economic Research Papers 2007–045, 2007. Friedrich Schiller University–Jena, Max Planck Institute of Economics.

Barnard, Harry. *Independent Man: The Life of Senator James Couzens*, 1958, New York: Charles Scribner's Sons.

Bassett, Ross Knox. *To the Digital Age*, 2002, Baltimore, MD: Johns Hopkins University Press.

Baxter, 3rd, J. P. *Scientists Against Time*, 1946, Boston: Little Brown & Co.

Berlin, Leslie. *The Man Behind the Microchip*, 2005, Oxford: Oxford University Press.

Bhaskarabhatla, Ajay and Steven Klepper. "Latent Submarket Dynamics and Industry Evolution: Lessons from the U.S. Laser Industry," *Industrial and Corporate Change* 23, 6 (2014), 1381–1415.

Bilby, Kenneth. *The General*, 1986, New York: Harper and Row.

Biting, Jr., Robert C. *Creating an Industry*, 1963, masters thesis, MIT.

Blackford, Mansel G. and K. Austin Kerr. *BFGoodrich*, 1996, Columbus: Ohio State University Press.

Boschma, Ron, A. and Rik Wenting. "The Spatial Evolution of the British Automobile Industry: Does Location Matter?" *Industrial and Corporate Change* 16, no. 2 (2007), pp. 213–238.

Braun, Ernst and Stuart MacDonald. *Revolution in Miniature*, 1978, Cambridge, UK: Cambridge University Press.

Bresnahan, Timothy and Franco Malerba. "Industrial Dynamics and the Evolution of Firms and Nations Competitive Capabilities in the World Computer Industry," in *The Sources of Industrial Leadership*, 1999, D. Mowery and R. Nelson, eds., Cambridge, MA: Cambridge University Press.

Breznitz, Dan. "The Israeli Software Industry," in *From Underdogs to Tigers*, 2005, Ashish Arora and Alfonso Gambardella, eds., Oxford: Oxford University Press, pp. 72–98.

Brinkley, Douglas. *Wheels for the World*, 2003, New York: Penguin Books.

Brockman, Maxwell and Albert Lawrence Elder, eds. *The History of Penicillin Production*, 1970, New York: American Institute of Chemical Engineers.

Bromberg, Joan Lisa. *The Laser in America, 1950–1970*, 1991. Cambridge, MA: MIT Press.

Brown, George H. *and part of which I was*, 1979, Princeton, NJ: Angus Cupar Publishers.

Bruderi, Robert. *The Machine that Changed the World*, 1996, New York: Simon & Schuster.

Bud, Robert. *Penicillin: Triumph and Tragedy*, 2007, Oxford: Oxford University Press.

Buenstorf, Guido. "Evolution on the Shoulders of Giants: Entrepreneurship and Firm Survival in the German Laser Industry," *Review of Industrial Organization* 30, no. 3 (2007), pp. 179–202.

Buenstorf, Guido and Steven Klepper. "Heritage and Agglomeration: The Akron Tyre Cluster Revisited," *Economic Journal* 119 (2009), pp. 705–733.

Buenstorf, Guido and Steven Klepper. "Why Does Entry Cluster Geographically? Evidence from the U.S. Tire Industry," *Journal of Urban Economics* 68 (2010), pp. 103–113.

Bylinsky, Gene. "Here Comes the Second Computer Revolution," *Fortune*, November 1975, pp. 135–138, 182, 184.

Byte Staff. "Micro, Micro: Who Made the Micro?," *Byte Magazine*, January 1991, pp. 305–312.

Cantner, U., K. Dressler, and J. J. Krüger. "Firm Survival in the German Automobile Industry," *Empirica* 33 (2006), pp. 49–60.

Carbonara, Corey P. *A Historical Perspective of Management, Technology, and Innovation in the American Television Industry*, 1989, doctoral dissertation, University of Texas at Austin.

Casey, Robert. *The Model T: A Centennial History*, 2008, Baltimore, MD: Johns Hopkins University Press.

Chain, Sir Ernst. "A Short History of the Penicillin Discovery From Fleming's Early Observations in 1929 to the Present Time," in *The History of Antibiotics A Symposium*, 1980, John Parascandola, ed., Madison, WI: American Institute of the History of Pharmacy, pp. 15–29.

Chatterji, Aaron. "Spawned with a Silver Spoon? Entrepreneurial Performance and Innovation in the Medical Device Industry," *Strategic Management Journal* 30, no. 2 (2009), pp. 185–206.

Chesbrough, Henry. "The Governance and Performance of Xerox's Technology Spin-Off Companies," *Research Policy* 82 (2003), pp. 403–421.

Chesbrough, Henry and Richard S. Rosenbloom. "The Role of the Business Model in Capturing Value from Innovation: Evidence from Xerox's Technology Spin-Off Companies," *Industrial and Corporate Change* 11 (2002), pp. 529–555.

Cheyre, Cristobal, Steven Klepper, and Francisco Veloso. "Spinoffs and the Mobility of the U.S. Merchant Semiconductor Inventors," *Management Science* 61, no. 3 (2015), pp. 487–506.

Christensen, Clayton M. "The Rigid Disk Drive Industry: A History of Commercial and Technological Turbulence," *Business History Review* 67 (1993), pp. 531–588.

Christensen, Clayton M. *The Innovator's Dilemma*, 1997, Cambridge, MA: Harvard Business School Press.

Chrysler, Walter P. *Life of an American Workman*, 1950, New York: Dodd, Mead & Company.

Cohen, W. M., and S. Klepper, "A Reprise of Size and R&D," *The Economic Journal*, July, 1996, 925-951.

Combes, Pierre-Philippe and Gilles Duranton. "Labour Pooling, Labour Poaching, and Spatial Clustering," *Regional Science and Urban Economics* 26 (2006), pp. 1–28.

Commission of the European Communities. "Communication from the Commission to the Council, The European Parliament, The European Economic and Social Committee and the Committee of the Regions," (2008), http://eur–lex.europa.eu/LexUriServ/LexUriServ.do?uri=COM:2008:0652:REV1:EN:PDF.

Cringley, Robert X. *Accidental Empires*, 1993, New York: Harper Collins.

Dahl, Michael S. and Toke Reichstein. "Are You Experienced? Prior Experience and the Survival of New Organizations," *Industry and Innovation* 14, no. 5 (2007), pp. 497–511.

Datta, Yudhishter. *Competitive Strategy and Performance of Firms in the US Television Set Industry: 1950–60*, 1971, doctoral dissertation, State University of New York at Buffalo.

Denoual, Daniel-Guy. *The Diffusion of Innovations: An Institutional Approach*, 1980, doctoral dissertation, Harvard Business School.

Doolittle, James R. *The Romance of the Automobile Industry*, 1916, New York: Klebold Press.

Dreher, Carl. *Sarnoff: An American Success*, 1977, New York: Quadrangle/New York Times Book Company.

Dumais, Guy, Glenn Ellison, and Edward L. Glaeser. "Geographic Concentration as a Dynamic Process," *Review of Economics and Statistics* 84 (2002), pp. 193–204.

Dunham, Terry B. and Lawrence R. Gustin, *The Buick: A Complete History*, 1992, Kutztown, PA: Automobile Quarterly.

Duranton, Gilles and Diego Puga. "From Sectoral to Functional Urban Specialization," *Journal of Urban Economics* 57, no. 2 (2005), pp. 343–370.

Elder, Albert L. "The Role of the Government in the Penicillin Program," in *The History of Penicillin Production*, 1970, Maxwell C. Brockman and Albert L. Elder, eds., New York: American Institute of Chemical Engineers, pp. 3–11.

Ellison, Glenn and Edward L. Glaeser. "Geographic Concentration in U.S. Manufacturing Industries: A Dartboard Approach," *Journal of Political Economy* 105 (1997), pp. 889–927.

Ellison, Glenn, Edward L. Glaeser, and William R. Kerr. "What Causes Industry Agglomeration? Evidence from Coagglomeration Patterns," *American Economic Review* 100 (2010), 1195–1213.

Eriksson, Tor Viking and Johan Moritz Kuhn. "Firm Spin-Offs in Denmark 1981–2000—Patterns of Entry and Exit," *International Journal of Industrial Organization* 24, no. 5 (2006), pp. 1021–1040.

Faggin, Frederico. "The Birth of the Microprocessor," *Byte*, March 1992, pp. 45–150.

Federal Trade Commission. *Report on the Motor Vehicle Industry*, 1939, Washington, DC: U.S. Government Printing Office.

Federal Trade Commission. *Economic Report on Antibiotics Manufacture*, 1958, Washington, DC: U.S. Government Printing Office.

Federal Trade Commission. *Staff Report on the Semiconductor Industry: A Survey of Structure, Conduct, and Performance*, 1977, Washington, DC: Government Printing Office.

Flamm, Kenneth. *Creating the Computer: Government, Industry, and High Technology*, 1988, Washington, DC: Brookings Institute Press.

Fleming, Alexander. "On the Antibacterial Action of Cultures of a Penicillium, with Special Reference to Their Use in the Isolation of *B. Influenzae*," *British Journal of Experimental Pathology* 10 (1929), pp. 226–236.

Franco, April M. and Darren Filson. "Spin–outs: Knowledge Diffusion through Employee Mobility," *Rand Journal of Economics* 37, no. 4 (2006), pp. 841–860.

French, Michael J. *The U.S. Tire Industry: A History*, 1991, Boston: Twayne Publishers.

Gage, Deborah. "Why Dmitry Medvedev wants a Russian Silicon Valley," 2010, http://www.smartplanet.com/blog/thinking–tech/why–dmitry–medvedev–wants–a–russian–silicon–valley/4531.

Gertner, John. *The Idea Factory*, 2012, New York: Penguin Press.

Goldmark, Peter C. *Maverick Inventor*, 1973, New York: Saturday Review Press/E. P. Dutton & Co.

Goldstein, Andrew. "Jack Avins, The Essence of Engineering," in *Facets: New Perspectives on the History of Semiconductors*, 1997, Andrew Goldstein and William Aspray, eds., New Brunswick: IEEE Center for the History of Electrical Engineering, pp. 133–214.

Graham, Margaret B. W. *The Business of Research RCA and the VideoDisc*, 1986, Cambridge, UK: Cambridge University Press.

Gort, Michael and Steven Klepper. "Time Paths in the Diffusion of Product Innovations," *Economic Journal* 92 (1982), pp. 630–653.

Greene, Allan J. and Andrew J. Schmitz, Jr., "Meeting the Objective," in *The History of Penicillin Production*, 1970, Maxwell C. Brockman and Albert L. Elder, eds., New York: American Institute of Chemical Engineers, pp. 80–88.

Gustin, Lawrence R. *Billy Durant*, 1973, Grand Rapids, MI: William B. Eerdmans Publishing.

Halberstam, David. *The Reckoning*, 1986, New York: Avon Books.

Hecht, Jeff. *Beam: The Race to Make the Laser*, 2005, New York: Oxford University Press.

Helfand, W. H., H. B. Woodruff, K.M.H. Coleman, and D. L. Cowen, " Wartime Industrial Development of Penicillin in the United States," in *The History of Antibiotics: A Symposium*, 1980, John Parascandola, ed., Madison, WI: American Institute of the History of Pharmacy, pp. 31–56.

Herold, Edward W. "History and Development of the Color Picture Tube," *Proceedings of the S.I.D.* 15 (1974), pp. 141–149.

Hobby, Gladys L. *Penicillin Meeting the Challenge*, 1985, New Haven, CT: Yale University Press.

Holbrook, Daniel U. *Technical Diversity and Technological Change in the American Semiconductor Industry*, 1999, doctoral dissertation, Carnegie Mellon University.

Holbrook, Daniel, Wesley Cohen, David Hounshell, and Steven Klepper, "The Nature, Sources, and Consequences of Firm Differences in the Early History of the Semiconductor Industry," *Strategic Management Journal* 21, 10/11, Special Issue: The Evolution of Firm Capabilities (Oct.–Nov. 2000), pp. 1017–1041.

Hounshell, David A. *From the American System to Mass Production, 1800–1932*, 1984, Baltimore, MD: Johns Hopkins University Press.

Hounshell, David A. "Why Corporations Don't Learn Continuously: Waves of Innovation and Desperation at Ford Motor Company, 1903–2003," 2003, mimeo.

Hvide, Hans K. "The Quality of Entrepreneurs," *Economic Journal* 119 (2009), pp. 1010–1035.

Hyde, Charles K. *The Dodge Brothers*, 2005, Detroit, MI: Wayne State University Press.

IC Insights. *The McLean Report, 2000 Edition*, 2000, IC Insights, Inc., Scottsdale, AZ.

Ingrassia, Paul. *Crash Course*, 2010, New York: Random House.

Integrated Circuit Engineering. *Status 1988*, 1988, Scottsdale, AZ: Integrated Circuit Engineering Corp.

Jackson, Tim. *Inside Intel*, 1997, New York: Plume.

Jacobs, Jane. *The Economy of Cities*, 1969, New York: Random House.

Jacobson, Sava. "CBS and Color Television, 1949–1951," 2001, David Sarnoff Library, http: www.davidsarnoff.org/jac–maintext.html, accessed 5/16/2010.

Jovanovic, Boyan and Glenn M. MacDonald. "The Life Cycle of a Competitive Industry," *Journal of Political Economy* 102 (1994), pp. 332–347.

Katz, Harold. *The Decline of Competition in the Automobile Industry, 1920–1940*, 1977, New York: Arno Press.

Keller, Maryann. *Rude Awakening*, 1989, New York: William Morrow and Company.

Kenney, Martin and Urs von Burg. "Technology, Entrepreneurship and Path Dependence: Industrial Clustering in Silicon Valley and Route 128," *Industrial and Corporate Change* 8 (1999), pp. 67–103.

Kimes, Beverly R. *Standard Catalog of American Cars, 1890–1942*, 3rd edition, 1996, Iola, WI: Krause Publications.

Kimes, Beverly R. and Robert C. Ackerman. *Chevrolet, A History from 1911*, 1986, Iola, WI: Krause Publications.

Klepper, Steven. "Firm Survival and the Evolution of Oligopoly," *RAND Journal of Economics* 33 (2002), pp. 37–61.

Klepper, Steven. "Disagreements, Spinoffs, and the Evolution of Detroit as the Capital of the U.S. Automobile Industry," *Management Science* 53 (2007), pp. 616–631.

Klepper, Steven. "The Origin and Growth of Industry Clusters: The Making of Silicon Valley and Detroit," *Journal of Urban Economics* 67 (2010), pp. 15–32.

Klepper, Steven and Elizabeth Graddy. "The Evolution of New Industries and the Determinants of Market Structure," *Rand Journal of Economics* 21, no. 1 (1990), pp. 27–44.

Klepper, Steven, John Kowalski, and Francisco Veloso. Technological Spillovers and the Agglomeration of the Semiconductor Industry in Silicon Valley. Working Paper, Carnegie Mellon University, 2011.

Klepper, Steven and Kenneth L. Simons. "Technological Extinctions of Industrial Firms: An Inquiry into Their Nature and Causes," *Industrial and Corporate Change* 6 (1997), pp. 379–460.

Klepper, Steven and Sally Sleeper. "Entry by Spinoffs," *Management Science* 51 (2005), pp. 1291–1306.

Kollins, Michael J. *Pioneers of the U.S. Automobile Industry, Vol. 1*, 2002a, Warrendale, PA: Society of Automotive Engineers.

Kollins, Michael J. *Pioneers of the U.S. Automobile Industry, Vol. 3*, 2002b, Warrendale, PA: Society of Automotive Engineers.

Kowalski, John. *Industry Location Shift through Technological Change—A Study of the US Semiconductor Industry (1947–1987)*, 2012. Unpublished PhD dissertation, Carnegie Mellon University.

LaFrance, Vincent A. *The United States Television Receiver Industry: United States Versus Japan, 1960–1980*, 1985, doctoral dissertation, Pennsylvania State University.

Law, Harold B. "The Shadow Mask Color Picture Tube: How It Began—An Eyewitness Account of Its Early History," *IEEE Transactions on Electron Devices* ED–23 (1976), pp. 752–759.

Lécuyer, Christopher. "Fairchild Semiconductor and Its Influence," in *The Silicon Valley Edge*, 2000, Chong-Moon Lee, William F. Miller, Marguerite Gong Hancock, and Henry S. Rowen, eds., Stanford, CA: Stanford University Press, pp. 158–183.

Lécuyer, Christopher. *Making Silicon Valley*, 2006, Cambridge, MA: MIT Press.

Lécuyer, Christopher and David C. Brock. *Makers of the Microchip. A Documentary History of Fairchild Semiconductor*, 2010, Cambridge, MA: MIT Press.

Levy, Jonathan D. *Diffusion of Technology and Patterns of International Trade: The Case of Television Receivers*, 1981, doctoral dissertation, Yale University.

Lindgren, Nilo. "The Splintering of the Solid State Industry," in *Dealing with Technological Change*, 1971. Princeton, NJ: Auerbach Publishers, pp. 36–51.

Lyons, Eugene. *David Sarnoff: A Biography*, 1966, New York: Harper and Row.

MacFarlane, Gwyn. *Howard Florey: The Making of a Great Scientist*, 1979, Oxford: Oxford University Press.

MacLaurin, W. Rupert. *Invention & Innovation in the Radio Industry*, 1949, New York: MacMillan.

Magaziner, Ira and Robert Reich. *Minding America's Business: The Decline and Rise of American Economy*, 1982. New York: Harcourt Brace Jovanovich.

Malone, Michael. *The Microprocessor: A Biography*, 1995, New York: Springer Verlag.

Marshall, Alfred. *Principles of Economics*, 8th edition, 1948, New York: MacMillan.

Mathews, John A. and Dong-Sung Cho. *Tiger Technology*, 2000, Cambridge, UK: Cambridge University Press.

May, George S. *R. E. Olds*, 1977, Grand Rapids, MI: William B. Eerdmans Publishing.

Mazor, Stanley. "Moore's Law, Microcomputers, and Me," *IEEE Solid–State Circuits Magazine*, Winter 2009, pp. 29–38.

McGuire, J. M. "Antibiotics—Past, Present, and Future," *Proceedings of the Indiana Academy of Science* 71 (1961), pp. 248–257.

McKendrick, David G., Richard F. Doner, and Stephan Haggard. *From Silicon Valley to Singapore*, 2000. Stanford, CA: Stanford University Press.

McPherson, Thomas A. *The Dodge Story*, 1992. Sarasota, FL: MBI Publishing.

Mines, Samuel. *Pfizer . . . An Informal History*, 1978, New York: Pfizer.

Misa, Thomas J. "Military Needs, Commercial Realities, and the Development of the Transistor, 1958–1968," in *Military Enterprise and Technological Change*, 1985, Merritt Roe Smith, ed., Cambridge, MA: MIT Press, pp. 253–287.

Mitton, Donald G. "Bring On the Clones: A Longitudinal Study of the Proliferation, Development, and Growth of the Biotech Industry in San Diego," in *Frontiers of Entrepreneurship*, 1990, N. Churchill, W. Bygrave, J. Hornday, D. Muzyka, K. Vesper, and W. Wetzel Jr., eds., Babson Park, MA: Babson College.

Moore, Gordon. "The Role of Fairchild in Silicon Technology in the Early Days of Silicon Valley," *Proceedings of the IEEE* 86 (1998), pp. 23–30.

Moore, Gordon. "The Accidental Entrepreneur," *Engineering & Science*, Summer 1994, pp. 23–30.

Moore, Gordon and Kevin Davis. "Learning the Silicon Valley Way," in *Building High-tech Clusters: Silicon Valley and Beyond*, 2004, Timothy Bresnahan and Alfonso Gambardella, eds., Cambridge: Cambridge University Press, pp. 7–39.

Muendler, Marc, James E. Rauch, and Oana Tocoian. "Employee Spinoffs and Other Entrants: Stylized Facts from Brazil," *International Journal of Industrial Organization* 30, no. 5 (2012), pp. 447–458.

Nebeker, Frederik. *Sparks of Genius: Portraits of Engineering Excellence*, 1994, Piscataway, NJ: IEEE Press.

Neushul, Peter. *Science, Technology and the Arsenal of Democracy: Production Research and Development During World War II*, 1993, doctoral dissertation, University of California at Santa Barbara.

Nevins, Allan, with Frank Ernest Hill. *Ford: The Times, The Man, The Company*, 1954, New York: Charles Scribner's Sons.

Noyce, Robert N. and Marcian E. Hoff, Jr. "A History of Microprocessor Development at Intel," *IEEE Micro* 1 (1981), pp. 8–21.

Paley, William S. *As It Happened*, 1979, Garden City, NY: Doubleday.

Parascandola, John. "Industrial Research Comes of Age: The American Pharmaceutical Industry, 1920–1940," *Pharmacy in History* 27, no. 1 (1985), pp. 12–21.

Pelfrey, William. *Billy, Alfred, and General Motors*, 2006, New York: American Management Association.

Perry, Tekla S. "The Longest Survivor Loses Its Grip," *IEEE Spectrum*, August 1988, pp. 16–20.

Petersen, Donald E. and John Hillkirk. *A Better Idea*. 1991, Boston: Houghton Mifflin.

Phillips, Damon J. "A Genealogical Approach to Organizational Life Chances: The Parent-Progeny Transfer," *Administrative Sciences Quarterly* 47, no. 3 (2002), pp. 474–506.

Pirtle III, Caleb. *Engineering the World*, 2005, Dallas: Southern Methodist University Press.

Porter, Michael. *The Competitive Advantage of Nations*, 1990, New York: Free Press.

Powell, Walter W., Kelley Packalen, and Kjersten Whittington. "Organizational and Institutional Genesis: The Emergence of High-Tech Clusters in the Life Sciences," in *The Emergence of Organization and Markets*, 2012, John Padgett and Walter Powell, eds., chapter 14, Princeton, NJ: Princeton University Press.

Pursell, Carroll. "Science Agencies in World War II: The OSRD and Its Challengers," in *The Sciences in the American Context: New Perspectives*, 1979, Nathan Reingold, ed., Washington, DC: Smithsonian Institute Press.

Rajan, Raghuram, Paolo Volpin, and Luigi Zingales. "The Eclipse of the U.S. Tire Industry," in *Mergers and Productivity*, 2000, Steven Kaplan, ed., Chicago: University of Chicago Press, pp. 51–86.

Raper, Kenneth B. "Research in the Development of Penicillin," in *Advances in Military Medicine, Volume II*, 1948, E. C. Andrus, D. W. Bronk, G. A. Carden, Jr., C. S. Keefer, J. S. Lockwood, and J. T. Wearn, eds., Boston: Little Brown, pp. 723–745.

Reid, Thomas R. *How Two Americans Invented the Microchip and Launched a Revolution*, 1986, New York: Simon & Schuster.

Renner, Gail Kenneth. *The Hudson Years: A History of an American Automobile Manufacturer*, 1973, doctoral dissertation, University of Missouri–Columbia.

Riordan, Michael. "The Silicon Dioxide Solution," *IEEE Spectrum*, December 2007.

Riordan, Michael and Lillian Hoddeson. *Crystal Fire*, 1997, New York: W.W. Norton.

Roberts, Peter W., Steven Klepper, and Scott Hayward. "Founder Backgrounds and the Evolution of Firm Size," *Industrial and Corporate Change* 20, no. 6 (2011), pp. 1515–1538.

Romanelli, Elaine and Maryann Feldman. "The Anatomy of Cluster Development: The Case of U.S. Biotherapeutics, 1976–2003." *Cluster Genesi*, 27 (2006), pp. 87–113.

Rosenbloom, Richard S., Don Sull, and Richard S. Tedlow. "Technological Discontinuity in the U.S. Tire Industry: The Radial Age," 1996, mimeo.

Rosenthal, Stuart S. and William C. Strange. "Evidence on the Nature and Sources of Agglomeration Economies," in *Handbook of Urban and Regional Economics, Volume 4*, 2004, J. Vernon Henderson and Jacques Francois Thisse, eds., Amsterdam: North Holland, pp. 2119–2171.

Saxenian, AnnaLee. *Regional Advantage*, 1996, Cambridge, MA: Harvard University Press.

Schaller, Robert R. *Technological Innovation in the Semiconductor Industry: A Case Study of the International Technology Roadmap for Semiconductors (ITRS)*, 2004, doctoral dissertation, George Mason University.

Schwartzman, David. *Innovation in the Pharmaceutical Industry*, 1976, Baltimore, MD: Johns Hopkins University Press.

Sciberras, Edmond. "International Competitiveness and Technical Change: A Study of the US Consumer Electronics Industry," 1979, Science Policy Research Unit, University of Sussex.

Sheehan, John. *The Enchanted Ring*, 1982, Cambridge, MA: Cambridge University Press.

Shurkin, Joel N. *Broken Genius. The Rise and Fall of William Shockley, Creator of the Electronic Age*, 2006. New York: Macmillan.

Smith, Douglas K. and Robert C. Alexander, *Fumbling the Future: How Xerox Invented, then Ignored, the First Personal Computer*, 1988, New York: William Morrow & Co.

Smith, Philip H. *Wheels within Wheels*, 1968, New York: Funk and Wagnalls.

Smith, Thomas Herman. *A Description and Analysis of the Early Diffusion of Color Television in the United States*, 1970, doctoral dissertation, Ohio State University.

Sobel, Robert. *RCA*, 1986, New York: Stein and Day.

Sørensen, Jesper B. "Bureaucracy and Entrepreneurship: Workplace Effects on Entrepreneurial Entry," *Administrative Science Quarterly* 52 (2007), pp. 387–412.

Sørensen, Jesper B. and Damon J. Phillips. "Competence and Commitment: Employer Size and Entrepreneurial Endurance," *Industrial and Corporate Change* 20, no. 5 (2011), pp. 1277–1304.

Sorensen, Charles E. with Samuel T. Williamson. *My Forty Years with Ford*, 1962, New York: Collier Books.

Spencer, L. V. "Metamorphosis of the Motor Car," *Motor Age* 9 (1916), pp. 5–11.

Sporck, Charles E. *Spinoff*, 2001, Saranac Lake, NY: Saranac Publishing.

Stelzer, Lawrence H. *A Financial History of the American Automobile Industry*, 1928, Boston: Houghton Mifflin.

Stewart, Irvin. *Organizing Scientific Research for War*, 1948, Boston: Little Brown and Company.

Stuart, Toby E. and Olav Sorenson. "Liquidity Events and the Geographic Distribution of Entrepreneurial Activity," *Administrative Science Quarterly* 48 (2003), pp. 175–201.

Sull, Donald N., Richard S. Tedlow, and Richard S. Rosenbloom. "Managerial Commitments and Technological Change in the US Tire Industry," *Industrial and Corporate Change* 6 (1997), pp. 461–501.

Sutton, John. *Technology and Market Structure. Theory and History*, 1998. Cambridge, MA: MIT Press.

Swann, John P. *Academic Scientists and the Pharmaceutical Industry*, 1988, Baltimore, MD: Johns Hopkins University Press.

Szudarek, Robert G. *How Detroit Became the Automotive Capital*, 1996, Detroit, MI: Typocraft Company.

Teal, Gordon K. "Single Crystals of Germanium and Silicon—Basic to the Transistor and Integrated Circuit," *IEEE Transactions on Electron Devices* ED-23, no. 7 (1976), pp. 621–639.

Tilton, John E. *International Diffusion of Technology: The Case of Semiconductors*, 1971, Washington, DC: Brookings Institution.

Utterback, James M. and Fernando F. Suárez. "Innovation, Competition, and Industry Structure," *Research Policy* 22 (1993), pp. 1–21.

von Rein, Kristina. "Heritage and Firm Survival—An Analysis of German Automobile Spinoffs 1886–1939," *Economics Bulletin* 12 (2008), pp. 1–8.

Walker, Rob. *Silicon Destiny*, 1992, Milpitas, CA: C.M.C. Publications.

Warner, Stanley L. *Innovation and Research in the Automobile Tire and Tire-Supporting Industries*, 1966, doctoral dissertation, Harvard University.

Wells, Percy A. "Some Aspects of the Early History of Penicillin in the United States," *Journal of the Washington Academy of Sciences* 65, no. 3 (1975), pp. 96–101.

Wenting, Rik. "Spinoff Dynamics and the Spatial Formation of the Fashion Design Industry, 1858–2005," *Journal of Economic Geography* 8 (2008), pp. 593–614.

White, Lawrence J. *The Automobile Industry since 1945*, 1971, Cambridge, MA: Harvard University Press.

Wolfe, Tom. "The Tinkerings of Robert Noyce," *Esquire Magazine*, December 1983, 346–374.

Womack, James T., Daniel T. Jones, and Daniel Roos. *The Machine that Changed the World*, 1991, New York: HarperCollins.

Wooster, James Howard. *Industrial Policy and International Competitiveness: A Case Study of US–Japanese Competition in the Television Receiver Manufacturing Industry*, 1986, doctoral dissertation, University of Massachusetts.

Yanik, Anthony J. *Maxwell Motor*, 2009, Detroit, MI: Wayne State University Press.

Index

Note: Page numbers in *italics* indicate illustrations; those with a *t* indicate tables.